S0-BZT-001

Winning with money:
A guide for your future

Winning with money:
A guide for your future

Beryl W. Sprinkel

Robert J. Genetski

Dow Jones-Irwin
Homewood, Illinois   60430

© DOW JONES-IRWIN, 1977

All rights reserved. No part of this publication may be
reproduced, stored in a retrieval system, or transmitted,
in any form or by any means, electronic, mechanical,
photocopying, recording, or otherwise, without the prior
written permission of the publisher.

This publication is designed to provide accurate and
authoritative information in regard to the subject matter
covered. It is sold with the understanding that the
publisher is not engaged in rendering legal, accounting, or
other professional service. If legal advice or other expert
assistance is required, the services of a competent
professional person should be sought.

*From a Declaration of Principles jointly adopted by a Committee
of the American Bar Association and a Committee of Publishers.*

First Printing, May 1977

ISBN 0-87094-135-6
Library of Congress Catalog Card No. 76-47751

Printed in the United States of America

To our wives,
Barbara and Maureen,
for their loving contributions.

Preface

This book is written for people who want to understand economic policies and the implications they can have for both the nation and the individual. We have attempted to eliminate most of the economic jargon, mathematics, and references to statistical techniques that make a good deal of the current economic literature comprehensible only to other economists. Our aim is to provide a basic understanding of major economic trends and the impact that these can have on the individual's pocketbook. The causes of inflation, unemployment, and economic instability are discussed, and strategies are developed to put you on the winning side of whatever policies are adopted. Our hope is that this book will be understandable to those with little or no formal background in economics. Only the reader can judge whether we have succeeded in our objective.

We are grateful to numerous individuals who have helped to make this book possible. Our largest intellectual debt is owed to Professor Milton Friedman, who through lectures and writings has taught and inspired us in many of our endeavors. Maureen Doherty and Nanci Rogers have our gratitude for their thoughtful, persistent, and conscientious assistance in producing this book. Grazina Juodelis has our appreciation for her assistance in providing research materials; and Pat Sawczak has our grateful thanks for typing many drafts of this manuscript.

April 1977   **Beryl W. Sprinkel**
                                                Robert J. Genetski

Contents

What's so bad about inflation?
  Benefits?
  Costs
  Who wins and who loses?

Monitoring inflation

Forecasting inflation trends

Price controls—Can we declare inflation illegal?

The investment decision

A long-term perspective
  The performance of financial assets
  The performance of real assets
  A comparison

How money affects investment values
  Why should money affect investments?
  Does money really work this way?—The evidence

Inflation and investment returns
  Short-term fixed-income securities
  Bond yields
  The evidence—Inflation and interest rates
  Stocks
  Inflation, profits, stock prices—The evidence

The inflationary environment and financial assets
  Deflation
  Price stability and moderate inflation
  Rapid inflation

The inflationary environment and real assets

Timing and investment returns

Summing up—What the evidence suggests for the future

Money, business activity, inflation—The evidence for
foreign economies
  Money and total spending
  Money per unit of output, and prices
  Money and inflation

List of charts

List of tables

1

Money—It's the name of the game

> With old inflation riding the headlines, I have read till I am bleary-eyed, and I can't get head from tails of the whole thing. We are living in an age of explanations, and plenty of them, too, but no two things that's been done to us has been explained twice the same way—by even the same man.
>
> *Will Rogers, 1934*

Today, as yesterday, an overabundance of explanations and advice is doled out to individuals on how to survive and prosper in the midst of economic uncertainty. Unfortunately, not all explanations are of the same quality, and it's often difficult to distinguish good advice from bad. An advisor's popularity, recent track record, or credentials do not necessarily provide an indication of the quality of his recommendations, and by the time the advisee discovers this it's often too late.

In general, periods of rapid inflation and economic upheaval tend to bring forth all sorts of homespun advice that may be ideal for surviving the crisis which has already passed. The advice often makes the advisor rich, but only at the expense of the advisee.

If an advisor's popularity, recent track record, or credentials do not necessarily provide an indication of the quality of his advice, what can an individual do to protect and increase the value of his assets in the future? He should acquire a good understanding of major economic developments and how they influence investments.

1

The objectives of this book are twofold. The first objective is to discuss the causes of recessions and inflation and how they can be avoided. Although we conclude that economic instability is man-made and can therefore be avoided, this doesn't mean that it will be. History has shown us time and again that stable economic performance is the exception rather than the rule. As a result, knowing what policies will ensure economic stability is not sufficient. The individual must also know the implications of alternative policies, and how they will influence his net worth. Even though instability is costly for the nation as a whole, there are inevitably winners and losers. The second objective of this book is to present an investment strategy designed to place an individual on the winning side of whatever economic policies develop in future years.

Much of the investment advice given during periods of inflation or economic turmoil assumes that such developments are unique and that unique explanations are therefore needed to understand them. Nothing could be further from the truth. Neither rapid inflation nor economic turmoil is unusual. In the United States, rapid rates of inflation have characterized a fifth of the period since the start of the century. Falling business activity has been only slightly less frequent, characterizing on average a sixth of the period since the mid-1800s.

The very fact that these events have occurred provides us with a substantial amount of history and experience that could prove invaluable in the future. Although history never repeats itself precisely, numerous economic factors have shown consistent patterns for centuries. One purpose of this book is to indicate what those patterns have been, why they have occurred and reoccurred, and what implications they hold for the future. It is our contention that the first step toward economic survival in the future is to understand business activity and investment performance in the past.

RISK AND RETURNS—LOOK BEFORE YOU LEAP

Whether we realize it or not, virtually everyone has to make decisions concerning investments—to buy a home or to rent one, to take out a life insurance policy or to maximize current income, to purchase stock or to place funds in a savings account. An important consideration in making investment decisions is to recognize that different risks are associated with different investments. Generally, the larger the risk or potential loss, the greater the potential return. Moreover, the risks associated with any investment are continually changing in response to economic conditions and to the length of time an investment is likely to be held. How can we evaluate the risks and returns from alternative investments? While there is no surefire plan, there are some useful guidelines.

An individual should have some confidence that he understands the factors which will influence the value of his investment and the events which will cause those factors to change. If the individual doesn't have such confidence, then his perceptions of the risks involved are likely to be heavily influenced by daily newspaper headlines and other highly subjective and short-sighted analyses. As a result, he is more likely to follow the crowd and jump into and out of different investments at precisely the wrong times.

For individuals who are uncomfortable with volatile investments, and for those who don't have confidence in their understanding of such things as government policies, business activity, inflation, and international factors, the risks of holding volatile assets are even greater than would otherwise be the case. Such investors are more likely to compound the inherent risks of buying high and selling low.

In late 1974, when economies all over the world appeared to be coming apart at the seams and stock prices were plunging rapidly, fears of an economic collapse led many investors to cash in their chips and get out of the stock market and into the "safety" of gold or fixed-income securities. A number of investment managers were told by their overseers to sell all stocks under their control. One investment director was actually told not to consider reinvesting in stocks until the Dow Jones Average reached 1,000, as it did a little more than a year later!

This book is designed to provide individuals with an understanding of the major factors influencing the values of their investments. That objective takes us deeply into the field of economics for an understanding of the money supply, business cycles, inflation, economic growth, and other relevant topics.

Since no single explanation of economic phenomena applies

precisely at all times, historical evidence is consistently presented to show the extent to which the explanations we present have worked in the past. Our hope is to give the investor some idea of the degree of confidence he can place in our explanations. While understanding how the economy influences the value of various key assets is important, an investor's success will depend primarily on how this information is used to anticipate future developments, a subject that we will also consider.

In addition to understanding the risks involved in various investments, the individual should have a reasonable idea of the returns he can expect. Hence, we provide guidelines to help the individual evaluate the risks and returns from different investments under alternative economic conditions.

MONEY PLAYS THE LEAD ROLE

Understanding economics can often be more baffling than solving a mystery which provides only a scattering of clues in the first chapter. There is no reason why this should be true, so unlike the writers of mystery novels, we intend to reveal the plot and the villain in this initial chapter. In our story, the villain or hero, depending on your persuasion, is the nation's money supply. Although money goes under a host of aliases, the significance of which we will discuss in the next chapter, it is usually considered to consist of currency (dollar bills and coins) held by the public and of checking account deposits in commercial banks.

The main thesis of this book is that changes in the nation's money supply represent the primary culprit influencing business conditions, inflation, short-term swings in investment values, and international crises. The money supply is by no means the only thing which influences these phenomena, and on occasion it is not even the most important influence, but the extent to which money has a bearing on each of these items is presented so that the reader can judge for himself the importance it deserves.

Since in our view money is so important, we devote two chapters (Chapters 2 and 3) to discussing it. While all of us know (or should know) where the money in our pockets came from, there is a great deal of confusion about where the total amount of money in our economy comes from and what causes that amount to change. The conclusion of Chapter 2 is that, as the old saying puts it, money does not grow on trees, but rather that it is manufactured by the government, with a modest influence from banks and the public. Chapter 3 describes the influence of various factors on the behavior of the money supply and suggests ways in which the investor can monitor such factors in the future.

Before anyone would be willing to devote time and effort to following monetary developments, there would have to be good reasons. Chapters 4 through 7 provide the reasons. Chapter 4 deals with the relationship between the nation's money supply and the pace of business activity. It begins by discussing what the money supply can and can't do. Money does a poor job at making a dent in an economy's long-term development and efficiency, but on a year-to-year basis, it can do a magnificent job of changing interest rates, sales patterns, and employment levels, and creating general havoc.

Chapter 5 is devoted to inflation. Its key point is that although the federal government can be accurately charged with inefficiency in any number of areas, it has been a model of efficiency when it comes to manufacturing money. The government has often manufactured more money as its solution to a crying need for additional governmental spending, such as occurs during military wars, wars on poverty, and wars on unemployment. Initially this action will normally win major battles in whichever war is being fought, since the creation of more money is usually followed by more sales, higher incomes, and a demand for more workers. However, inflation develops if too much money is manufactured, so that from an economic point of view the war is lost. The primary cause of inflation is simply the creation of too much money! Chapter 5 discusses why this is true, just how bad inflation is, and who wins and who loses from inflation. It also contains a section on monitoring inflationary developments and some guides for forecasting inflationary trends.

Having completed the groundwork on money, business activity, and inflation, in Chapter 6 we deal with the impact of these forces on investments. Stocks, bonds, short-term fixed-income securities, and real assets are discussed, with an emphasis on the types of risks and returns that the investor might expect from these various assets. The chapter also explains how risks and returns change in different economic settings. In general, past experience suggests that over the long haul stocks have been the most attractive investment, producing an average yearly return of about 8 percent over the past 104 years. Since inflation averaged only 1½ percent per year during this period, an investment in stocks returned about 6 percent per year in terms of real buying power. Stocks, however, are not for the nervous investor. The total value of assets held in the form of stocks was down on average one year out of every three over this period, with declines ranging from a negligible 1 percent to as much as 42 percent! Moreover, many of the declines continued for several years before the downward trend was reversed. Also, stocks have performed erratically during periods of rapid inflation—sometimes they have performed well, while at other times they have represented a poor investment.

In contrast to stocks, returns to corporate bonds and short-term fixed-income securities have not been particularly rewarding over an extended period of time. Bonds have performed somewhat better than short-term securities during periods of price stability, but they have done consistently worse than most financial assets during inflationary periods. Commercial paper, a short-term security which earns a fixed rate of interest, produced an average yearly return of approximately 4 percent over the 104-year period considered, a return similar to that produced from investing in corporate bonds.

Investments in property or real estate performed consistently well during inflationary periods. The returns on housing have been good not only during inflationary periods but over the long haul as well. In contrast, investments in precious metals, such as silver and gold, or in other real assets have not done well over the long haul, and are likely to be attractive only to investors who are able to anticipate accurately an explosive rise in inflation and its eventual slowdown.

In addition to presenting the historical returns to various investments over an extended period of time, Chapter 6 considers the returns to various assets in alternative inflationary environments in an attempt to provide some guidelines toward expected returns from various investments in future years.

The increased importance of multinational companies, the oil cartel, grain deals, and international money markets has added a new dimension to investors' concerns. Chapter 7 discusses the impact of international factors on money and inflation in the United States. In the process, it analyzes the relationship between money and business activity, and between money and inflation, in major foreign countries. The general impact of money in many foreign countries is shown to be similar to its impact in the United States. The chapter also takes up the problems of international monetary systems, and considers the importance these systems can have for the investor.

The final chapters present the implications of the preceding chapters for winning the money game. Chapter 8 presents rules by which we can win the money game as a nation, and Chapter 9 presents rules by which you can win the money game on your own.

2

Everything you ever wanted to know about money ...and then some

That money talks,
I won't deny;
I heard it once,
It said "Goodbye."
Richard Armour

By reputation, money is an esoteric subject, understandable only to the practitioners of high finance. That, of course, is wrong. Even many practitioners of high finance don't understand it. It is indeed true that the details of monetary theory and practice can be perplexing and difficult, but the essence of the forces that bring about rapid or slow expansion in the money supply are important to investors and can be understood.

This chapter is devoted to the mechanics of money—what it is, where it comes from, the forces that cause it to change, and other related issues. In our opinion it's the most difficult chapter in the book, but it's also critically important to an understanding of money.

MONEY-WHAT IS IT?

Money can be and has been defined in a host of different ways, but in essence it is any item that can be used as a general means of exchange for other items. Money may be valuable in its own right, as when gold or silver are used in exchange for other items, or it may be a piece of paper which has value only because people generally accept it in return for goods and services.

Getting a handle on money—Alternative measures

Any number of items may be included among the measures of a nation's money supply. The most common measure of money, often referred to as M_1, consists of currency held by the public and checking account or demand deposits at commercial banks. Other measures add certain savings or time deposits at commercial banks—M_2; still others add savings deposits at savings and loans and other thrift institutions—M_3; and so on up to higher M's which add government securities, savings bonds, and other assets that can be readily converted to a means of exchange. With so many possible measures of money to choose from, which should we pay attention to?

Will the true money supply please stand up?

There is no single correct measure of the nation's money supply. The measure that should be used depends on the purpose at hand. For our purposes, which include determining the impact of changes in the money supply on business activity and inflation, it is necessary to determine which definition of money is the most reliable indicator.

As Chart 2–1 indicates, changes in alternative measures of the money supply often show similar patterns. The reason for this is that people tend to hold a certain proportion of their money assets in different forms—so much in currency, so much in checking account balances, so much in savings accounts, and so much in various other forms. The proportion held in each form depends on convenience, the interest rate structure, and a host of other factors. So long as these factors are not changing, there is no apparent reason for the public to arbitrarily shift money assets from one form to another, and therefore no reason for the various measures of money to perform differently. However, when banking regulations or other factors serve to make one money asset relatively more attractive than it had been previously, the public will tend to

Chart 2-1
Alternative measures of monetary growth

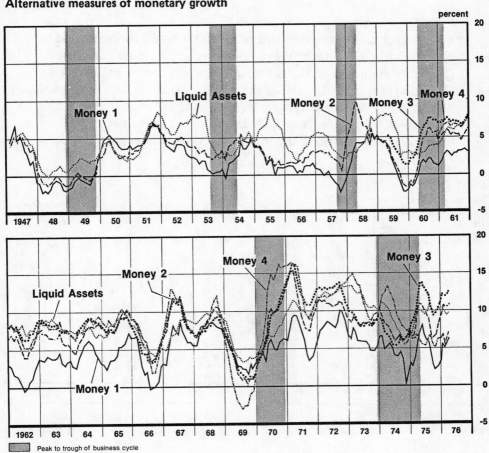

Peak to trough of business cycle
Money 1: Demand deposits plus currency
Money 2: Money 1 plus time deposits at commercial banks other than large certificates of deposit
Money 3: Money 2 plus deposits at nonbank thrift institutions
Money 4: Money 2 plus large certificates of deposit
Liquid asset holdings of private domestic nonfinancial investors
Data are 6-month seasonally adjusted annual rates of change plotted at the midpoint of the interval.

Source: Board of Governors of the Federal Reserve System

increase the proportion of money held in that form, and the patterns of the alternative money measures will differ.

This occurred, for example, in 1969, when free-market interest rates rose above the rates that banks were permitted to pay. Individuals therefore reduced their holdings of savings deposits, preferring to hold market instruments that yielded more attractive

12

returns. This pattern was even more pronounced for large negotiable certificates of deposit—CDs. These are bank deposits of $100,000 or more which banks issue to attract funds. When market interest rates exceeded the rates that banks were permitted to pay for large CDs, there was a sharp reduction in the amount of CDs outstanding, and the measure of money which includes CDs (M_4) fell sharply. In 1970 the combination of lower market interest rates on short-term securities and the elimination of maximum rates on certain large CDs led to an explosive rise in M_4 (see Chart 2-1). Similarly, in the mid-1970s various changes in banking

Chart 2-2
Money$_1$ and money$_2$

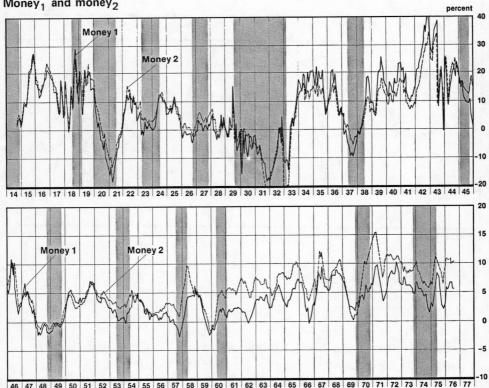

Shaded areas: Peak to trough of business cycle.
Money$_1$: Demand deposits plus currency.
Money$_2$: Money$_1$ plus time deposits at commercial banks other than large certificates of deposit.
Data are six-month seasonally adjusted annual rates of change plotted at the midpoint of the interval.
Source: Board of Governors of the Federal Reserve System; National Bureau of Economic Research.

regulations served to increase the attractiveness of savings accounts. As a result, money measures which exclude savings deposits tended to grow less rapidly as the public switched a greater proportion of its money assets into savings accounts.

Which measure of money should we use? Normally, it doesn't make any difference. When banl 'ng regulations change the attractiveness of holding money assets in a particular form, it is desirable to use a money supply measure that is least influenced by changes in regulations and that has a long record of reliably foreshadowing business activity. In our judgment, the measures M_1 and M_2 best meet these objectives. Their historical performance is shown on Chart 2-2, where the shaded areas represent recessions or periods of declining business activity. Both measures tend to show slower expansion rates prior to recessions and faster expansion rates prior to business upturns. But the relation of money to the economy is the subject of Chapter 4; at this point our main concern is money itself. Having discussed what it is, we now consider where it comes from.

THE MONETARY PROCESS—WHO'S INVOLVED?

The monetary process is really very simple. Three groups can influence the amount of money in the economy—the monetary authorities, commercial banks, and the public. The monetary authorities, which in the United States consist primarily of the Federal Reserve System and to a lesser extent the U.S. Treasury, control the basic ingredients of money. These ingredients are often referred to as "base money," "high-powered money," or the "monetary base." The banks and the public take the ingredients and turn them into the more conventional forms of money.

Actually, if we simplify the situation for a moment by considering the money supply to include currency plus all deposits at commercial banks, only two factors will cause the growth in money to differ from that of the monetary base. One is a change in the public's preference for holding money in the form of currency versus bank deposits, and the other is a change in banks' preference as to the proportion of their deposits that they hold as excess reserves. Banks are required by law to hold a certain amount of non-income-earning assets as "reserves" or backing for their deposits. Any cash assets over and above the legal requirement are termed excess reserves. If the public is happy with its holdings of bank deposits relative to its holdings of currency, and if banks are satisfied with the amount of excess reserves they hold relative to their deposits, then there is a fixed relationship between the monetary base and the money supply. Under such conditions a change in the monetary base by the monetary authorities would lead to a predetermined change in the money supply. By the same token, if the monetary authorities leave the base unchanged, there can be no change in the money supply. By understanding only these three key factors—the monetary base, the role of the banking system, and the role of the public—and what influences them, the reader will gain an understanding of the mechanics of money. Since these three factors are so crucial, it is important to look at each more closely.

Monetary authorities—The Fed and the Treasury

One of the most frequently asked questions concerning money is, Where does it come from? While a complete answer would include a discussion of the role of the banking system and the nonbank public, the heart of the answer is that money originates as a liability or debt on the balance sheets of the monetary authorities. In essence, money is a financial liability of the authorities which issued it.

The Federal Reserve System (Fed), which has primary responsibility for monetary policy, holds a substantial amount of securities (Treasury bills, notes, bonds, and so on) in its portfolio. In acquiring these assets, the Fed creates offsetting liabilities which take the form of either Federal Reserve Notes (dollar bills) or member bank deposits (deposits of banks that are members of the Federal Reserve System). Most of the reserves of commercial banks which are members of the Federal Reserve System are held in the form of deposits with the Federal Reserve. Thus, both member bank deposits and currency are liabilities of the Federal Reserve, and together they comprise the monetary base. In order to increase the base, the Fed simply adds to its financial assets. The most common way of doing this is for the Federal Reserve to purchase outstanding government debt in the form of government securities.

The Fed pays for this increase in assets by writing a check on its own account; the amount of the check offsets the increase in assets with an equal increase in liabilities. Once the check is presented for payment by a commercial bank which is a member of the Federal Reserve System, the Fed credits the amount to that bank's account with the Federal Reserve.

The monetary base—Origin of our money. In essence, the bulk of the liabilities of the monetary authorities to the private sector represent the basic ingredients of the money supply. From a practical standpoint, there is no effective limit on the amount of base money that the monetary authorities are capable of creating. Every time they purchase a financial asset and create a corresponding liability to the public, the monetary base increases. By selling assets, the monetary authorities reduce their liabilities and thus reduce the amount of base money. This, in brief, describes the nature of the monetary base and how its quantity is usually changed. However, as will be explained shortly, each increase of base money tends to be accompanied by a multiple increase in ordinary money.

Since the monetary base is the basic ingredient controlling the money supply, it is useful to look somewhat deeper into its make-up. Unfortunately, such a discussion becomes somewhat technical, and since it is not entirely essential to an understanding of the nature of money, those readers who wish to skip the next section can do so without losing any continuity.

A closer look at the monetary base. Actions by both the Federal Reserve and the U.S. Treasury can influence the monetary base. Consequently, it is useful to combine their financial activities for purposes of analyzing the impact of those activities on the monetary process. Table 2–1 shows the combined balance sheet of the monetary authorities. It is organized so as to show the major sources and uses of the monetary base. The sources are primarily items that supply funds for the base, while the major items that absorb those funds are termed uses.

The primary sources are Federal Reserve credit, the gold stock of the United States, and assorted other items. The major uses of the monetary base are member bank deposits with the Federal Reserve and currency in circulation. These two factors are directly related to the money supply. Several fairly minor uses of the

Table 2-1

Factors influencing the monetary base (sign indicates effect on the monetary base) (millions of dollars)

Sources			Uses	
U.S. government securities	$92,962		Member bank reserves§	$ 38,104
Loans	129			
Float plus other Federal Reserve assets	6,599		Currency held by public	75,000
Federal Reserve credit		$ 99,690		
Treasury deposits with Federal Reserve		−3,955		
Gold stock plus other items†		17,369		
Reserve adjustment‡		9,002	Reserve adjustment‡	9,002
Monetary base		$122,106		$122,106

Monthly averages of daily figures, December 1975, not seasonally adjusted.

*Includes acceptances of $722 million in December 1974 and $853 million in December 1975.

†Includes SDRs held by Federal Reserve banks, Treasury currency outstanding, Treasury cash holdings, deposits with the Federal Reserve other than Treasury deposits and member bank reserves, and other Federal Reserve liabilities and capital accounts.

‡Adjustment for reserve requirement ratio changes and shifts in the same type of deposits between banks where different reserve requirement ratios apply. Reserve adjustment computed by the Federal Reserve Bank of St. Louis.

§Includes member bank deposits at Federal Reserve and vault cash of all commercial banks.

Source: Federal Reserve Bank of St. Louis, "Monetary Trends," January 1976.

monetary base act to drain money from the system, and these items are listed as negative sources. Although they may take on importance on a weekly or monthly basis, over time they tend to have little influence on the monetary process.[1]

By far the most important source of the monetary base is Federal Reserve credit. It is the most important in terms of total dollars, and it is usually the most important in terms of changes. It is not surprising, therefore, that changes in Federal Reserve credit have been the major source of changes in the monetary base.

An increase in Federal Reserve credit may come about, first, through an increase in the holdings of securities by the Federal

---

[1] For an excellent detailed discussion of the monetary process see Robert E. Weintraub, *Introduction to Monetary Economics* (New York: Ronald Press Co., 1970), pp. 91–181.

Reserve, usually U.S. government securities, and very probably Treasury bills. When the Federal Reserve places an order to buy Treasury securities with a government bond dealer, it makes payment by issuing a check payable to the government bond dealer. The bond dealer, in turn, places that check on deposit with his commercial bank. When his bank presents the check to the Federal Reserve for payment, the Fed credits the bank's account with the Federal Reserve, thus increasing that member bank's deposits at the Federal Reserve.

Second, the Federal Reserve may increase the amount of Federal Reserve credit outstanding by loaning or advancing funds to banks or businesses, usually banks. If the Fed makes a loan to a bank, payment is made by crediting that bank's reserve account with the Federal Reserve, and again, the member bank's reserves go up. Finally, an increase in Federal Reserve credit may come about as a result of an increase in "float." "Float" occurs when a bank depositing a check received from another bank is credited by the Fed with reserves before the other bank has its reserves reduced—that is, the same reserves are counted twice. Although the float that a check creates will be eliminated once the check is cleared, new deposits are continually being made so that some float is always present.

By far the most important change in Federal Reserve credit is a result of Federal Reserve purchases and sales of U.S. government securities, usually Treasury bills. An increase in holdings of those securities increases the reserves of the banking system and adds to the monetary base. Conversely, the sale of securities by the Federal Reserve decreases bank reserves and reduces the monetary base.

Changes in the U.S. gold stock can also bring about similar changes in the monetary base. At present our country has no obligation to buy or sell gold at a fixed price, and changes in the gold stock are therefore nominal and quite infrequent. In the days when the Treasury had an obligation to back its currency with gold, it made gold purchases by issuing Treasury notes. In principle, the process was similar to present-day purchases of government securities, except that the limitations in the supply of gold limited the potential expansion of the monetary base. In the mid-1960s the Treasury was still obligated to exchange gold at a price of $35 an ounce for dollars held by foreigners. Since the rest of the world believed that gold was worth more than $35 an ounce, foreign purchases reduced the U.S. gold stock. In order to prevent such purchases from reducing the monetary base, the Federal Reserve stepped up its purchases of government securities to neutralize the impact of the gold drain. Since the Federal Reserve has the power and the obligation to offset any minor changes which do occur in this item, the gold stock is of minimal importance in present-day monetary actions. Purchases of foreign currencies are also of minimal importance for the United States, though tremendously important for many foreign countries. To the extent that the Federal Reserve or any other central bank buys foreign currencies it increases its liabilities, and hence the monetary base, just as it does when it purchases gold or government securities.

Treasury currency outstanding is the next larges contributor to the monetary base. Technically, it corresponds to the Treasury's coin and currency in circulation. It consists of the tangible assets (silver, copper, and so on) incorporated in or used to back the Treasury's coin and currency, as well as the intangible (fiat) asset which makes coin and currency legal tender. As with gold, changes in this factor do occur, but they are typically of minor proportions and can be offset by changes in Federal Reserve purchases of government securities. Other minor technical factors may also influence the monetary base, but their influence can also be offset by Federal Reserve actions.

The final item in Table 2-1 is an adjustment for reserves that incorporates most of the influence of reserve requirements in the monetary process. As was noted previously, banks are legally required to hold a certain amount of non-income-earning assets in the form of either deposits with the Fed or cash in their vaults. The amounts of such reserves held against a bank's deposits differ for different types of banks. The various reserve requirements complicate the relation between base money and the money supply, since with other factors unchanged, the lower the average reserve requirements, the larger the amount of money that can be supported by a given amount of base money. Since the Federal Reserve controls changes in reserve requirements, it is useful to adjust the monetary base to incorporate such changes. As with the technical factors mentioned above, changes in this category, which result from changes in reserve requirements and shifting deposits among banks with different reserve requirements, can be offset by Federal Reserve purchases and sales of government securities. A more desirable method of minimizing the influence of such adjustments would be to establish uniform reserve requirements among banks.

Try not to be confused by these various technical factors. The

Chart 2–3
Money and the monetary base

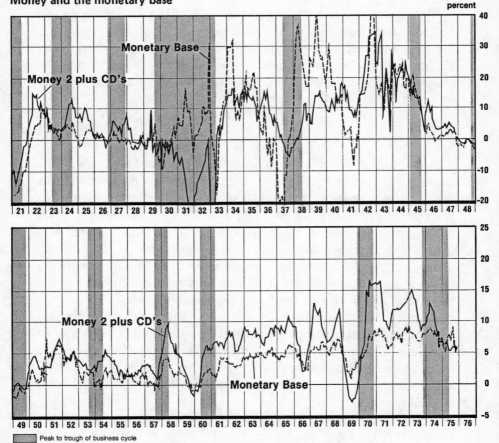

Peak to trough of business cycle

Money 2 plus CD's consists of currency, demand and time deposits at commercial banks including large certificates of deposit.
Monetary base consists of member bank reserves at Federal Reserve Banks and currency, adjusted for reserve requirement changes.
Data are 6-month seasonally adjusted annual rates of change plotted at the midpoint of the interval.

Source: Board of Governors of the Federal Reserve System; National Bureau of Economic Research; Federal Reserve Bank of St. Louis

important thing to remember is that the Federal Reserve System has the ability and the responsibility to control the monetary base. Its main tool for this purpose is the purchase or sale of securities to the public. Such actions can be undertaken either to initiate a change in the monetary base or to offset a change brought about by one or more of the items shown in the left-hand column of Table 2–1.

Our reason for discussing the monetary base is that it represents the foundation for the money supply. As shown in Chart 2–3, movements in the money supply are often closely related to movements in the monetary base. The linkage between them is provided by the banking system. Owing to the banking function of accepting deposits and lending or investing some portion of those deposits, the actual money supply is much greater than the monetary base. Understanding how changes in the monetary base affect the money supply involves an understanding of the banking process, our next topic.

Commercial banks and the money supply

We noted above that member banks of the Federal Reserve System are required by law to maintain reserves on deposit with the regional Federal Reserve Bank. An important principle to keep in mind is that only when the banking system possesses excess reserves, that is, reserves over and above the legal requirement, is it possible to increase the money supply. The critical question, therefore, is what methods exist for bringing about an increase in excess reserves. The most common method is for the monetary authorities to increase the monetary base.

Going back to our earlier example, let's assume that the Federal Reserve places an order with a private government bond dealer to buy $1 million in Treasury securities. The Federal Reserve makes its payment by issuing a check payable to the government bond dealer, who, in turn, places that check on deposit with his commercial bank. Initially there is an increase of $1 million in the monetary base and an increase of $1 million in the conventional money supply, since the money supply includes demand deposits at commercial banks as well as cash in the hands of the public. Although the government bond dealer has a credit for $1 million in his account, which he may soon write a check against, the bank is required to send money over to the local Federal Reserve Bank to fulfill its reserve requirement, which amounts to some percentage of the new deposit. If, for example, the reserve requirement against demand deposits is 20 percent, the bank must make a $200,000 interest-free deposit with the regional Federal Reserve Bank. The bank will send the newly acquired checks to the Federal Reserve Bank for credit to its account, so that it will have deposited $1 million with the Fed, of which $200,000 is required. Therefore, it has $800,000 in excess reserves which are not earning interest. As a practical matter, these excess reserves will be loaned or invested almost immediately.

If the bank chooses to make a loan to a business for that amount, it would usually make the money available by crediting the checking account of that business with $800,000. The business would then have the right to write up to $800,000 in checks against its checking account, and these would, of course, later clear through the Federal Reserve Bank and back to the local bank. The instant the loan for $800,000 was made, there was a net increase of that amount in the money supply. At this point, the $1 million increase in the monetary base has led to a $1.8 million increase in the money supply through the operations of our fractional reserve banking system. And the process of money creation is not over, because the next bank receiving the $800,000 deposit will now find itself with excess reserves of $640,000 or 80 percent of its new deposits.

By this time the bewildered reader may be crying out—"Stop!" What happens when the government bond dealer cashes his check for $1 million, as he is sure to do before very long? Won't the first bank be prevented from loaning out the excess reserves if it's about to lose the dealer's deposit. The answer is that it probably would if it believed that the check written by the dealer would be cashed at another bank. But the key to the banking system's ability to create money is that the initial $1 million demand deposit stays in the system. If the bond dealer writes a check which is credited to an account at another bank, then the second bank, and not the first, will have the excess reserves, and it will be able to make an additional loan. Alternatively, the first bank could borrow $800,000 from the second bank in order to service the loan. The point is that the initial demand deposit produced by an increase in high-powered money stays in the banking system, giving the banking system as a whole $800,000 in excess reserves to lend. Even after the $800,000 is loaned out, $640,000 of excess reserves will remain in the system.

Several points about the monetary process are worth noting at this time. First, when excess reserves exist, bankers can make loans and thereby increase the money supply, but your banker could also increase the money supply by buying some U.S. Treasury bills, a highly liquid short-term liability of the U.S. Treasury. In fact, he would buy those bills from a U.S. government bond dealer, and would make payment to the dealer by writing a check. The government bond dealer, in turn, would deposit the check in his bank, and the money supply would then go up in the same way that it would if a loan had been made. It therefore follows that the banker can increase the money supply either by making an additional loan to the extent of the excess reserves or by purchasing some form of investment, including U.S. Treasury bills. Unfortunately, most textbook writers discuss the first possibility and not the second; that is, they suggest that the money supply can increase only when borrowers are willing to borrow money. In periods of recession, borrowers frequently pay off their debts, and loan demand is generally weak. But as debts are paid off, excess reserves are created in the banking system, and the banker, who prefers to make some money on his excess funds, would then make an investment. If he maintains his excess reserves with the Federal Reserve System he will receive zero interest, whereas if he invests the funds in securities, this will yield a return and, of course, will also increase the money supply.

A second point is the commonly heard notion that banks can lend more than they have in the form of excess reserves, that they can increase their profitability by a multiple expansion of their loans and investments. For any one bank this statement is incorrect. An individual bank dare not lend or invest more than the amount of its excess reserves, because if it does so, once the checks resulting from the creation of deposits clear, the bank will lose reserves and be in a deficit position, thereby forcing a reduction in its loans and investments. However, it is true that for the banking system as a whole more deposits may be created than exist in the form of reserves or deposits with the Federal Reserve

Bank. To put it somewhat differently, in December 1975, when member bank reserves amounted to $38 billion, the demand deposits outstanding at commercial banks amounted to $228 billion, and a highly liquid but less readily spendable form of bank deposits—savings deposits—amounted to $448 billion. Therefore, on the basis of $38 billion in reserves, the total deposits held by the commercial banking system amounted to $676 billion. The banking system had turned $38 billion of base money in the form of bank reserves into many times that amount of money assets.

A given $1 million purchase of U.S. Treasury bills by the Federal Reserve System makes possible an increase in the money supply in excess of the amount of purchase because the excess reserves created work their way through the banking system, leading to a multiple expansion in loans and investments, and hence to a multiple expansion in the money supply. In recent years a $1 million purchase of Treasury bills has led on average to a $2½ million increase in the money supply defined as M_1. That's why the liabilities or base money created by such purchases is sometimes referred to as "high-powered money." Through its ability to buy and sell securities in the open market, the Federal Reserve has the power to bring about a multiple expansion or contraction in the money supply. It is indeed "high powered."

Sometimes you hear it argued that attempts by the Federal Reserve to increase the reserves of the banking system through its various devices are like "pushing on a string"—that the banking system does not respond, and hence there is no increase in the money supply. Clearly, this argument is indefensible for the simple reason that banks receive zero return on their excess reserves with the Federal Reserve. If they invest those reserves or loan out those reserves they will, of course, receive some positive return. In ordinary circumstances, the only assumption that one must make concerning the relation between Federal Reserve action and the money supply is that bankers prefer more to less. We have known many bankers and have yet to meet one who prefers less to more. Excess reserves fluctuate very little and remain at a nominal level under almost all circumstances. Hence, it is very clear that the Federal Reserve can indeed expand the money supply provided that it increases Federal Reserve credit, which leads to an increase in excess reserves, and then, of course, provided that the banks either lend or invest those funds. Regardless of whether the excess

24

reserves are utilized by expanding loans or by expanding investments, the money supply goes up. From this point of view, monetary policy is not like "pushing on a string"—it's like "pushing on
a ramrod," because you can depend on those bankers to lend or
invest the excess funds.

To summarize. The main function of the banking system in the
monetary process is to transform the monetary base into bank
deposits. Through its ability to lend or invest a portion of its
deposits, the banking system expands the monetary base by some
multiple. The only way the banks can alter this multiplier effect,

Chart 2-4
Commercial bank and public influences on the money supply

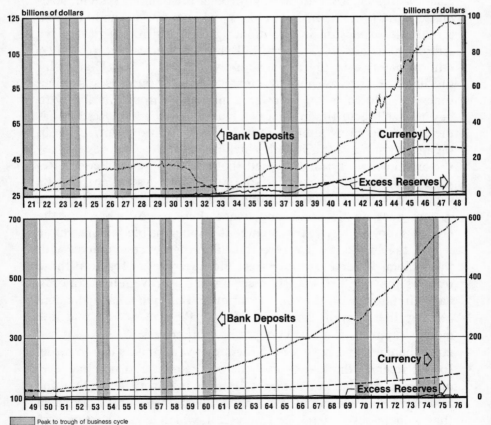

Peak to trough of business cycle
Bank deposits consist of demand and time deposits at commercial banks including large certificates of deposit.
Excess reserves are defined as total reserves minus required reserves.
All data are seasonally adjusted except excess reserves.

Source: Board of Governors of the Federal Reserve System; National Bureau of Economic Research

and therefore affect the total money supply, is to hold more re-serves relative to their deposits. Since banks are legally required to hold a certain amount of reserves, their only real discretion is to decide how much in excess reserves to hold relative to deposits. The greater the amount of the excess reserves banks hold relative to deposits, the lower the multiplier between base money and actual money will be. However, since excess reserves earn no interest, banks tend to keep them at a minimum. Hence, the bank-ing system might alter the normal multiplier between the mone-tary base and ordinary money during periods of great uncertainty, when excess reserves might be needed to fulfill depositors' requests for currency, or during periods when interest rates are so low that the income lost by not investing excess reserves is not worth the effort required to invest them. Needless to say, such circum-stances have not been a normal characteristic of the U.S. economy. As shown in Chart 2-4, excess reserves have normally been an extremely small percentage of bank deposits except during the 1930s and early 1940s, when the fear of bank runs led to an actual increase in excess reserves. In the early 1930s, as bank failures became widespread, excess reserves actually increased while bank deposits declined sharply. As a result, the proportion of excess re-serves to bank deposits rose dramatically and this served to reduce the amount of actual money created from a given amount of base money (see Chart 2-3). Aside from periods of great financial uncer-tainty, excess reserves have been kept to a minimum, and for all practical purposes banks have had little discretion in influencing the relationship between the monetary base and the money supply.

The public and the monetary process

The public can influence the monetary process by its desire to hold more or less of its money in the form of currency as opposed to bank deposits. The more the public decides to hold more currency relative to bank deposits, the less money there will be for a given amount of base money. This is because the substitution of currency for deposits reduces excess reserves for a given mone-tary base. However, like increases in excess reserves, increases in the public's holdings of currency as opposed to bank deposits are highly unusual. As shown in Chart 2-4, such an increase occurred during the early 1930s, when the public became concerned over the safety of its bank deposits. At that time, currency holdings increased moderately in the face of a sharp decline in bank deposits. Since the establishment of federal insurance of bank deposits in 1934, the public's faith in the safety of bank deposits has increased, and it has become highly unusual for the public to erratically change its preference for holding more currency relative to bank deposits.

The public can influence the money supply in one other way and this applies only if the money supply is narrowly defined as currency plus checking account or demand deposits, M_1. If the public switched its bank deposits from checking account balances to savings deposits, the narrowly defined money supply would tend to rise less rapidly. However, this would have little effect on the relation between the monetary base and the more broadly defined money supply, M_2, which includes savings or time deposits.[2] Since, as indicated in Chart 2-2, changes in the rate of growth of either M_1 or M_2 tend to follow the same pattern, the influence of this factor is usually minor.

Hence, under normal circumstances the monetary authorities should be able to control the money supply through control of the monetary base. In the event of widespread uncertainty about the banking system, when banks hold a greater proportion of excess reserves to deposits and the public demands more currency relative to bank deposits, the multiplier between base money and ordinary money would be lowered. This is what happened during the early 1930s. However, even under such adverse circumstances, the monetary authorities could offset the decline in the amount of money produced from a given increase in the monetary base by further increasing the base. Therefore, the monetary authorities should be able to retain control over the money supply except for very short periods, during which some erratic move by the banking system or the public might influence the relationship between money and the base.

The only rational argument that can be used to suggest that the monetary authorities do not control the money supply, would be

---

[2] There is an additional technical factor which enables the public to bring about minor changes in different measures of money. Since there are different reserve requirements for different classifications of bank deposits, the public can affect a change in *average* reserve requirements by shifting to different deposit categories. Although the influence of this factor is minor, it could be eliminated by establishing uniform reserve requirements among various deposit categories.

to argue that somehow changes in the monetary base have a direct effect on the amount of excess reserves to deposits held by banks or on the amount of currency to deposits held by the public. Such an argument would require banks to desire additional reserves to deposits *because of* an increase in the monetary base, or alternatively, would require the public to desire more currency to deposits *because of* an increase in base money. Neither possibility appears reasonable.

MONEY MECHANICS AND FEDERAL RESERVE ACTIONS

In recent years, as the understanding of and belief in the importance of money have increased, there has been a growing disenchantment with Federal Reserve monetary policy. The essential reason for this disenchantment can be noted by referring back to Chart 2-2, which indicates that monetary policy has been more volatile in the late 1960s and early 1970s than in the period between the early 1950s and the mid-1960s. Moreover, on average it has become increasingly expansionary during the past decade. As a result, many have argued that the volatile changes in monetary growth have promoted volatile economic changes, with recurring rapid increases in spending followed by slow increases. Since the volatile trend in monetary growth has been upward, these policies have on average resulted in too much spending, thereby bringing on serious inflation. But why has this been the case?

Since 1970, Federal Reserve officials have placed more emphasis on the importance of the money supply. In fact, in recent years the Federal Open Market Committee, the major policy arm of the Federal Reserve System, has explicitly stated its objectives in the form of a particular growth in the money supply. Meetings of this committee are held at least monthly, and on each occasion either old money supply objectives are confirmed or new ones established. A careful perusal of the committee's minutes indicates that the targets for monetary growth do not indicate massive changes in the Federal Open Market Committee's objectives, yet volatile performance has occurred. The real problem is that the Federal Open Market Committee establishes not only monetary growth targets but also provides for interest rates, specifically an interest rate known as the Fed funds rate. The Fed funds rate is the rate charged by banks when they lend money to other banks for overnight use. Movements in the highly sensitive Fed funds rate reflect both the demand for and the supply of excess reserves as determined by monetary policy.

A typical objective might read as follows: In the month ahead the Federal Reserve Board wants to achieve an annual rate of increase in M_1 of 5 percent, and an annual rate of increase in M_2 of 8 percent, provided that the Fed funds rate is maintained at, say, 7 percent. The essential difficulty with this sort of objective is that it is frequently unachievable. There is no consistent relationship between the interest rate target and the monetary growth target. In a period of rising credit demands, with corporations attempting to accumulate inventories and borrowers finding it unattractive to sell bonds, the demand for bank loans often rises. But this also tends to be a period when upward pressure is being exerted on interest rates. If the Fed funds rate goes above the 7 percent target, the manager of the Open Market desk at the Federal Reserve Bank may attempt to prevent this from occurring. How can this be achieved? Certainly not by waving a magic wand or resorting to an "open mouth" policy. He must take specific action by purchasing government securities, usually Treasury bills. This raises the price, lowers the yield, and tends to ease short-term interest rates. However, it also increases the monetary base and excess reserves of the banking system, and hence creates an automatic incentive for the commercial banks to expand loans and/or investments, thereby increasing the money supply. At the end of the month, when the members of the Federal Reserve Board look back to see whether or not their objectives were achieved, they frequently find that during a period of rising credit demands they have hit their interest rate target on the nose while overshooting their target for money supply growth. Consequently, in a period of serious inflation, when there tends to be a rather consistent upward pressure on interest rates, the Federal Reserve tends to resist the interest rate rise by providing more reserves to the system. This, of course, leads to even more growth in the money supply and ultimately to even greater inflation.

In contrast, during a period in which the demand for credit is weak, such as occurred in late 1974 and early 1975, business borrowers tend to liquidate inventories and pay off loans at their banks, while consumers pay off their debts. Some borrowers find it attractive to sell bonds in the open market and to use their receipts from the bond sales to pay off short-term bank debt. In such an environment there is a consistent tendency for interest rates, especially short-term interest rates, to decline. Now, suppose that the Federal Reserve has the same objective as before, but that instead of being faced with rising credit demands and upward pressure on short-term interest rates, it is faced with declining credit demands and downward pressure on short-term interest rates. For example, suppose that the Fed funds rate begins to drop below the targeted 7 percent rate. On the basis of recent history and, in fact, on the basis of the long-term history of the Federal Reserve, what might we expect the reaction of the money market desk to be? The manager of the desk knows very well how to rig or set short-term rates. This is what he does, but unfortunately it leads to great problems. To avoid a decline in the Fed funds rate below the 7 percent target, the manager attempts to tighten up the money market by selling U.S. Treasury bills in the open market, thereby depressing the price of Treasury bills and also increasing their yield. This action tends to raise the rates on other short-term instruments, and the Fed funds rate moves up to the 7 percent target. But what has happened in the meantime? By selling government securities, the Federal Reserve tends to reduce the monetary base and excess reserves of the banking system, creating an incentive for banks to liquidate loans and/or investments and thereby bring down the money supply. The lower monetary growth then tends to reinforce the developing weakness in business activity. To put it differently, a Fed funds target that is too high at a time when the demand for credit is weak, will inevitably lead to a monetary shortfall.

The perceptive reader might be wondering how this could happen. Surely, if the economy were in a recession, the Federal Reserve should be attempting to increase the money supply, not contract it. Not so! Let us look at the data, for example, from the middle of 1974 until January 1975. During that period it became increasingly clear that the economy was in a very serious recession. Short-term interest rates were declining, not because of an increase in the money supply or because of an easy Federal Reserve policy, but essentially because the demand for credit was weakening at a very rapid pace. The Open Market Committee minutes of the Federal Reserve Board over those months show that in almost all months the Federal Reserve succeeded in achieving its Fed funds target, but that in almost all of those same months it had a severe shortfall in terms of its monetary growth target! Now, doesn't this mean that the Federal Reserve found it impossible to increase the money supply? Not at all. What it does mean is that if the Fed insists on achieving a Fed funds target which is artifically set too high, then it cannot achieve sufficient monetary growth. To put it differently, in recent years, even when the Federal Reserve established monetary targets it continued to place primary emphasis on short-term interest rate targets. In the short run, the Federal Reserve has the power either to fix short-term interest rates or to achieve a given increase in the money supply—it often does not have the power to do both. Changes in the demand for credit during the course of the business cycle have resulted in severe fluctuations in monetary growth because of the Federal Reserve's proclivity for zeroing in on short-term interest rates instead of on a given growth rate in the money supply.

Consequently, many critics have argued that the Federal Reserve should change its method of executing policy. There has, in fact, been very little disagreement with the monetary targets set by the Federal Reserve in its Open Market Committee meetings. The criticism has arisen because the monetary targets have not been achieved since the Federal Reserve frequently sets a Fed funds rate which is inconsistent with the monetary objective. During periods of heavy credit demands, the Fed funds target is frequently too low, leading to excessive monetary growth; conversely, during periods of weak credit demands the Fed funds target is too high, leading to a smaller increase in the money supply than that desired by the Federal Reserve.

A policy improvement—Federal Reserve targets

How should the Federal Reserve avoid this dilemma? The easiest method would be for it to estimate what change in the monetary base is needed to bring about the desired increase in the money supply and to permit market forces to set interest rates. Some observers suggest that this procedure might lead to extreme volatility in interest rates. Indeed, in the short run there would probably be greater volatility than exists under the Fed's present methods. However, in the longer run, interest rates would almost certainly be less volatile for the simple reason that economic activity would be stabilized. This would eliminate the existing cycle of recurring inflations, followed by recessions, followed by over-stimulation, leading to ever higher rates of inflation. To a large extent, interest rates reflect expectations in the marketplace about what is going to happen to the real value of money. Hence, volatile monetary policy certainly promotes volatility in interest rates. Therefore, it seems reasonable to expect that once the system becomes adjusted to a stable growth rate in the money supply, there would be much less fluctuation in interest rates than occurs when the Fed misses its monetary targets while attempting to rig interest rates.

Summing up money mechanics

The monetary process is fairly straightforward. Changes in the money supply are brought about by changes in the monetary base and bank reserves. When excess reserves go up, incentives are created for banks to either lend or invest the excess reserves because otherwise they receive zero return on them. Hence the money supply expands. Conversely, a contraction in bank reserves tends to reduce excess reserves and to promote a liquidation in loans and/or investments; hence, a reduction in the money supply. The major factor bringing about a change in the monetary base, and therefore in the banking system's reserves, is a change in Federal Reserve credit. By far the most important technique available to the Fed for bringing about a change in Federal Reserve credit is the purchase and sale of U.S. government securities. By lending or investing its excess reserves, the banking system expands the amount of deposits supported by bank reserves. Hence we find that at any given time the existing money supply is substantially greater than the reserves maintained by commercial banks with the Federal Reserve.

Although the banks and the public can influence the relationship between the monetary base and money, this influence is normally minor. In order to change the relationship between the monetary base and money, banks have to change their desired proportion of excess reserves to deposits, while the public has to alter its desire for currency relative to deposits. Even during the unusual periods in which such changes occur, the monetary authorities are capable of offsetting the influence of such changes in the preferences of the banks or the public by engineering a faster or slower change in the monetary base. As a result, monetary policy is not like "pushing on a string." If the Federal Reserve increases excess reserves, those reserves will be utilized, since the profit motive leads to an increase in either investments or loans, and in turn, to an increase in the money supply. Furthermore, it makes little difference which measure of the money supply—M_1, M_2, and so on—is investigated. All measures tend to move up and down together and reflect to a great extent changes brought about in the monetary base by Federal Reserve purchases and sales of government securities. We have also noted that, despite an increasing emphasis on the importance of money, the conduct of monetary policy deteriorated in the early 1970s. Monetary policy became more volatile, thereby inducing volatile performance in the economy, and from a longer-term perspective, monetary policy was much too expansive, thereby constituting a major cause of serious inflation. This volatility results, not from an attempt by the Federal Reserve to promote volatile monetary growth, but rather from the mechanism that the Fed uses to execute its policy objectives. Unfortunately, the Federal Reserve seeks to achieve dual objectives: monetary growth targets and Fed funds or interest rate targets. Frequently the objectives are inconsistent with each other. When the Federal Reserve sets an interest rate target that is too low to achieve its monetary growth target, this inevitably leads to monetary overshoot because the Federal Reserve then constantly attempts to reduce the Federal funds rate by increasing its holdings of government securities and thus increasing the reserves of the banking system. Conversely, when the Fed places its interest rate target too high, the opposite pattern occurs.

We suggested that the Federal Reserve could avoid this problem by concentrating its attention on the monetary base, and attempting to estimate the amount of change in the monetary base that would bring about its targeted changes in the money supply. In the process, the Federal Reserve should permit the marketplace to determine interest rates. In a few years, a policy promoting a stable growth pattern in the money supply would lead to less volatility in interest rates than we experienced in the early 1970s.

3

Political influences—Is money a Democrat or Republican?

It is no accident that in our subject the term "principles" is so often used in the titles of general treatises. Especially so far as economic policy is concerned, principles are practically all that we have to contribute.

Von Hayek, 1962

Understanding what causes money to change involves more than simply understanding the mechanics of money. Of equal importance is an understanding of the politics of money. This chapter deals with the relationship of money to federal budget deficits, the political dilemma associated with monetary policy, and some recent political developments which could have a significant influence on the behavior of money in future years. The chapter also provides some guidelines for monitoring the monetary process so that investors can keep tabs on developments and avoid being caught off guard by subsequent changes in policies.

RELATION OF MONETARY TO FISCAL POLICY

While monetary policy is concerned with actions by the Federal Reserve Board which influence the cost of credit and the rate of growth in various monetary aggregates, fiscal policy is concerned with spending and taxing decisions carried out by the federal government.

Money and credit markets

When the federal government runs a deficit by spending more than it takes in from tax receipts, it must sell bonds or other government securities to support or finance its deficit. The federal government's deficits can be financed in two ways. The government, like any private debtor, can compete for the private savings supplied by consumers and businesses or the deficit can be financed with newly created money.

Competing for savings. Savings represent the portion of income which is not spent for consumption items. Since the supply of savings is limited, funds acquired by the federal government to finance its deficits reduce the savings available to other debtors. This important point is worth pursuing a little further. The total amount of savings which various creditors provide to the economy and the total amount of funds which are borrowed must by definition be equal. A dollar cannot be borrowed unless someone provides it by refraining from consumption and saving it.

The credit markets, that is, the markets for savings and investment, are balanced by interest rates. If debtors want more funds than savers wish to provide, they can offer higher interest rates for the use of funds. Higher interest rates tempt consumers to put off their purchases and provide more funds to debtors, but they also cause some debtors to reevaluate their borrowing needs. As rates move higher, more private borrowers tend to cancel their plans for debt. This does not apply to the federal government. Once Congress approves a particular level of expenditures, the government will either pay for those expenditures with tax receipts or borrow to cover any shortfall. Regardless of the interest rate, the federal government will always get the proportion of available savings that it needs. In the process, however, it often outbids other potential borrowers, such as home builders, businesses seeking to expand their facilities, and state and local governments.

Creating new money. The federal government can also finance its deficits in an alternative way, which initially does not involve crowding other potential borrowers out of the market. When the Federal Reserve purchases government securities with newly created money, private borrowers may continue to tap the available savings pool, and for the moment everyone appears to have benefited. Unfortunately, for society as a whole there is no such thing as a free lunch!

As was noted previously, purchases of government securities by the Federal Reserve lead to an increase in the monetary base and, in turn, to an increase in the money supply. In effect, when the Federal Reserve purchases new government debt, it pays for the government deficit by printing money. When too much debt is purchased, the money supply grows too rapidly, and eventually serious inflation results. When this happens, the federal debt is paid for by the inflation, which can be viewed as a tax on money — a tax which reduces the value of everyone's money holdings. Unfortunately, since the inflation tax is not immediately evident, and since it is not explicitly voted by Congress, there are enormous pressures to finance federal deficits through Federal Reserve purchases of newly issued government securities. For this reason, the size of the federal debt frequently has a direct bearing on the amount of new money created.

Federal budget deficits

Let's take a quick look at the recent history of federal budget deficits and money creation. From fiscal 1955 through fiscal 1965, federal budget deficits totaled $31.0 billion, of which the Federal Reserve System purchased 50 percent, or $15.5 billion, creating new money to pay for its purchases. Newly created money tends to be deposited in banks, creating excess reserves. Banks then lend or invest those reserves, thereby creating more money. When the multiple expansion process is completed, additions to the monetary base lead to a multiple increase in the money supply. In the period from 1955 to 1965, when the deficits were small and the Federal Reserve purchased $15.5 billion of the newly created debt, the annual rate of growth in the money supply was a quite moderate 2.2 percent, amounting to about $32 billion. During this period the consumer price increase averaged 1.7 percent yearly, and long-term interest rates for high-grade corporate bonds averaged only 4.1 percent. But let us turn to the next ten years. New federal debt between 1965 and 1975 totaled $141 billion; the Federal Reserve purchased a third of that debt, or $45.5 billion; and the money supply grew by $123.5 billion.

This amounted to an annual monetary growth rate of approximately 5.5 percent. Inflation rose to an average of 5.4 percent, and long-term interest rates averaged 6.9 percent. Although there is not necessarily a consistent relation between the size of the federal deficit and the rate of increase in the money supply, the pressure to finance new government expenditures with newly created money has frequently linked large deficits to large increases in the money supply.[1]

It should be emphasized in passing that large government deficits do not necessarily have to be paid for with newly created money. This was the case in fiscal 1976, when about 10 percent of a $66 billion government deficit was purchased by the Federal Reserve. Although monetary growth can proceed rapidly or slowly regardless of the size of the government deficit, the Federal Reserve has often felt obligated to purchase enough Treasury debt to keep private borrowers from being crowded out of credit markets. Hence, large deficits create pressure on the monetary authorities to manufacture more money.

The political pressures to pay for federal deficits by increasing the money supply, and the relation between the size of those deficits and the amount of monetary growth, are strong indications that if we are to have stable and moderate growth in the money supply, it is important to limit the size of federal deficits.

THE POLITICAL DILEMMA—LAGS AND ELECTIONS

The lags between a stimulative economic policy and its ultimate impact on business activity cause a serious political dilemma. These lags complicate the process of achieving a stable economic policy. As noted earlier, the initial effect of a policy designed to increase monetary growth is to provide downward pressure on short-term interest rates. Shortly after monetary growth has begun to rise, the pace of total spending picks up, and this stimulates business activity. As will be shown in Chapter 5, it is often about two years before higher monetary growth leads to higher inflation. In other words, an increase in the money supply tends to bring the good news first and the bad news later! Similarly, slower

---

[1] Beryl W. Sprinkel, *Formulating Monetary Policy: The Challenge Ahead,* testimony before the Senate Committee on Banking, Housing, and Urban Affairs, April 29, 1975.

monetary growth initially creates pressure for higher short-term interest rates, and before too long, a reduced rate of spending and a slowdown in business activity. Unless the money supply drops sharply and a major recession develops, it often takes two years or so before good news in the form of lower inflation is evident.

There are strong political pressures which favor economic policies that produce favorable results in the immediate future rather than two or three years down the road. Representatives are elected every two years, as are a third of the senators. Presidential elections are, of course, held every four years. As a result, there is frequently a temptation to stimulate the economy so that the good news in the form of improved production, employment, and profits will come first, while the serious costs in terms of higher inflation are borne at a later date.

An excellent example of this type of action began in the middle of 1971. The 1970 recession, which had been brought on primarily to get inflation under control, was successful. By August 1971 the inflation rate had declined from a peak of approximately 6½ percent to about 4 percent. In addition, monetary growth had begun to accelerate during the latter part of the recession, and in the early phase of the recovery economic activity was indeed expanding. Nonetheless, the unemployment rate, which tends to be a slow mover, was an uncomfortably high 6 percent. With a presidential election coming up in the fall of 1972, there were great incentives to undertake actions which would bring good news prior to the fall of 1972, despite the bad news which would come later. Unfortunately, such actions were taken. Wage and price controls were adopted in August 1971, and there was a speedup in monetary growth. In the short run the results were all good. Unemployment did decrease, and for a while prices did not show a serious tendency to go up, especially under the blanket of wage and price controls.

However, by 1973 and 1974 the damage brought about by the massive stimulus to economic activity was clearly evident. The artificially low prices, due to price controls, had encouraged sales and discouraged production, thereby creating shortages in numerous areas. By 1974 the jig was clearly up, and in an effort to encourage production and eliminate shortages, price controls were abolished. Even before the controls were abolished, prices rose very sharply, reflecting the growing pressure from the prior years of monetary stimulus. The rapid increase in prices encouraged businessmen to accumulate inventories before prices went even higher, and the entire process exerted a major destabilizing force on the economy which contributed to subsequent sharp declines in output.

In the summer of 1975, with the unemployment rate at about 9 percent, there was again a great temptation to stimulate the economy. In many ways the situation was similar to that of 1970, except that both inflation and unemployment were worse. Again, many argued that, owing to the substantial amount of excess capacity, it would be desirable and prudent to adopt a very high rate of monetary growth. Although the disadvantages of this kind of action had been demonstrated in the 1971-74 experience, there was a substantial threat that such action would be taken again. Fortunately, policymakers ignored calls for double-digit increases in monetary growth and resorted to a moderate increase instead. As a result, business activity advanced at a steady pace in the first year of recovery, and prospects for at least a temporary slowdown in inflation were enhanced.

Once an economy adjusts to a higher rate of monetary growth, it is very difficult to slow that growth to a rate consistent with the economy's long-term output, nominal inflation, and relatively low interest rates. Going from higher rates of monetary growth to lower and sustainable rates inevitably induces a slowdown in economic activity, and usually results in a serious recession, such as occurred in 1974.

To avoid such consequences, many economists, including the authors, contend that short-run policies should be consistent with longer-run objectives. Although it is desirable to encourage real growth, it is necessary to keep the rate of inflation under substantial restraint. This suggests that even though the economy is operating at less than full employment, it is prudent to avoid sizable expansion in monetary growth. If immediate stimulus in the form of double-digit monetary growth is pursued, the economy will expand vigorously, but in the process of returning to a sustainable monetary growth pattern, we would return again to the "go-stop" economic policies that caused so much havoc in our economy in the late 1960s and 1970s. Unfortunately, the policies that would bring about sustained economic benefits are the very policies that would incur the greatest political liabilities. As a result, the lags between instituting economic policies and realizing the final results of those policies make it very difficult to pursue reasonably stable economic policies, and in turn, to generate stable economic performance.

HOPE FOR THE FUTURE

Two recent legislative developments offer some hope that somewhat more stable economic policies will be pursued in the future despite the problems created by the lag between policy action and policy results.

The Budget Reform Act

In 1974, after considerable debate and much discussion, Congress adopted the Congressional Budget and Impoundment Control Act. In essence this act requires Congress to determine early in the year what size budget and deficit it desires, given the economic environment. Once the overall level of the budget has been determined by agreement between the House and the Senate, the various spending programs must be designed in such a way that the total of all spending items in the budget is in line with the overall budget constraint.

If this experiment is successful, it will be the first time in decades that individual spending decisions in Congress are made in the context of an overall budget constraint. Previously, each individual congressional committee considered the budget for its activity, and almost inevitably, when all the commitments had been added up, they equaled an amount well in excess of the estimated tax revenues. A provision in the Congressional Budget and Impoundment Control Act permits Congress to reconsider later in the year. If the total is too large, then some actions must be taken to raise taxes, to cut back individual spending components, or to permit the deficit to run larger than was previously estimated. Although it is far too soon to know whether or not this attempt at fiscal discipline will be successful, at least it is a step in the right direction. To the extent that this overall approach to budget-making is successful in containing increases in federal spending and in reducing the size of federal deficits, it will be of considerable aid in reducing the tendency for the money supply to grow too rapidly and therefore the tendency for inflation to become more serious. The first year's experience with the new federal budget procedures, in fiscal 1976, was encouraging. The new controls, combined with presidential vetoes and growing public skepticism toward government programs, slowed the growth in federal spending. Preliminary efforts on the fiscal 1977 budget suggest even greater benefits for the period ahead.

The Joint Monetary Resolution

As mentioned earlier, recent developments in the monetary policy area also have the potential for greatly improving the quality of monetary policy. Throughout the history of the Federal Reserve, and, in fact of many other central banks around the world, monetary policymaking has tended to take place in secret— the general public being unaware of its objectives—and with little attempt to coordinate monetary policy with fiscal policy. Whereas with budgets it has been traditional for the merits of the Administration's spending proposals and its recommended deficit or surplus to be discussed publicly, in the monetary policy arena no such attempts at a public discussion of appropriate policies have been made. There would probably have been no pressure for more open monetary policymaking in this country had we witnessed excellent monetary policies recently. But, as previously argued, monetary policy has been quite volatile, and much of the time it has been highly expansive, thereby contributing both to recessions and to very serious inflation. In the year 1975 an attempt was made to eliminate the imperfections in our monetary policymaking procedures. A resolution introduced in the Senate and the House laid down some ground rules relating to the Federal Reserve's formulation and execution of its monetary policy. As finally passed, the resolution was labeled H.R. Concurrent Resolution 133.

There are two major points in the resolution. First, Congress instructs the Federal Reserve to maintain long-run growth of the monetary and credit aggregates proportionate to the economy's long-run potential to increase production, so as to effectively promote the goals of maximum employment, stable prices, and moderate long-term interest rates. Second, the Federal Reserve Board is instructed to consult periodically with Congress about objectives and plans with respect to the growth ranges of monetary and credit aggregates in the upcoming 12 months and to present the Fed's own targets.

However, the latter part of the joint resolution provides that "nothing in this resolution shall be interpreted to require that such ranges of growth or diminution be achieved if the Board of Governors and the Federal Open Market Committee determine that they cannot or should not be achieved because of changing conditions. The Board of Governors shall report to the Congress the reasons for any such determination during the next hearings held pursuant to this resolution." In practice, the Federal Reserve chairman has reported to the Senate Banking and the House Banking committees in alternate quarters.

Both provisions of the congressional resolution could prove crucial to the development of future monetary policies. The first provision, that the growth in monetary and credit aggregates be proportionate to the economy's long-run potential to increase production, can be interpreted in various ways. To the authors, the provision clearly suggests that growth in the money supply should be approximately equal to the long-term real growth potential of the economy. In our judgment, the potential growth of the economy under present circumstances is in the range of 3 percent to 4 percent per year. Thus, the first provision of the resolution would suggest that the money supply, usually defined to include currency plus demand deposits, should grow 3 percent to 4 percent per year on average over a long period of time. That is about half the rate of growth experienced in recent years and, if actually accomplished, would lead to a considerable reduction in inflation.

The more important provision of the resolution may be the one specifying that at quarterly hearings with Congress the Federal Reserve Board detail its monetary growth plans for the year ahead. Never before has the Federal Reserve been forced to state its intentions to Congress and the general public. Hopefully, an objective exposed to public view will receive more careful attention than one that can be buried in the archives of the Federal Reserve.

The resolution certainly permits Congress to ask penetrating questions about the appropriateness of the targets established by the Federal Reserve, and it provides a forum for economists outside the Federal Reserve System to express their views on what appropriate policies might be and also to express their criticisms of what the Federal Reserve is actually doing.

There has been some concern that the new procedure could lead to even worse monetary policy performance than we have witnessed recently. Some have argued that it might encourage Congress to lean more heavily on the Federal Reserve to establish even more volatile and expansionary monetary policies than would otherwise be adopted.

Another reservation concerning the adequacy of the joint resolution relates to the fact that the Federal Reserve may state specific monetary aggregate targets and yet fail to achieve them. In 1974, and again in early 1975, we saw that quite reasonable monetary growth targets in the 5 percent to 7 percent range were not achieved. These failures occurred primarily because short-term interest rates were declining, and the Federal Reserve was unwilling to permit the Fed funds rate to decline sufficiently to allow the growth in the monetary base needed to achieve its monetary targets. This may happen again. However, there is now clearly an incentive for the Federal Reserve to try very hard to achieve its stated monetary growth targets. If the Federal Reserve policymakers shift from meeting interest rate objectives toward achieving stable growth in monetary aggregates, the resolution will certainly make a major contribution to achieving a more stable and moderate monetary policy in the years ahead. As with the new budget procedure, the first year's experience with the new monetary approach proved promising. In May 1975 Dr. Arthur F. Burns, chairman of the Board of Governors of the Federal Reserve System, established an annual target of 5 percent to 7½ percent growth in M_1 and 8½ percent to 10½ percent growth in M_2 for the 12 months ending in March 1976. At the end of that period, growth in M_1 was slightly below the original target, and M_2 was within the guidelines. In May 1976 Dr. Burns reduced the targeted growth for M_1 to 4.5 percent to 7 percent and indicated the Fed's intent to further reduce monetary growth in line with the long-term congressional targets. Although short-term volatility of monetary growth continued in 1975-76 due to contradictory money supply-interest rate targets, the new monetary approach appears to result in better Federal Reserve planning and execution.

It seems fair to conclude that both the Congressional Budget and Impoundment Control Act of 1974 and the Joint Monetary Resolution have created policymaking instruments which may result in a somewhat more stable monetary-fiscal input than we have witnessed in recent years. It is much too soon to conclude that the law and the resolution will in fact result in more stable economic growth and less inflation over the years, but clearly the potential is there. Certainly, private observers will have an input into the policymaking process. They will be able to state their agreement or disagreement with the various congressional budget committees and Federal Reserve policymakers. Until we see evidence to the contrary, we are inclined to believe that the law and resolution represent a significant plus for those who prefer less erratic economic policymaking. The first year's experience reinforced that view.

MONITORING THE PROCESS—HOW AND WHY

It is probably fair to say that less than 1 percent of our total population has any understanding of monetary policy or any desire to monitor what is happening at the Federal Reserve Board. These matters are considered too complicated—something that should be left to the experts. However, if monetary policy is as important as we have argued, then it is something much too crucial to be left to the experts alone. One function that will be performed by the House and Senate committees will be to improve the general public's understanding of monetary policy. Already financial editors and writers, and even TV commentators, are beginning to devote more attention to what's going on at the Fed. It is not true that monetary policy is of no interest or relevance to the general public. The general public has demonstrated an intense interest in what happens to financial markets, to real disposable income, to the rate of inflation, and to the availability of jobs. If the public is interested in these end results, then it certainly has an obligation to remain informed about what is happening to monetary policy, because that policy will have an important bearing on the public's future economic well-being.

How does the layman remain informed about the Federal Reserve's intentions and about its success in living up to its stated objectives? The new monetary approach requires a Federal Reserve Board representative to appear publicly each quarter before either the Senate or House Banking Committee. Hence, every three months the public will be updated on how the Federal Reserve views current economic circumstances and what it intends to do. The Fed may state its objectives in terms of a rate of growth for M_1, the narrow definition of the money supply, which includes currency and checking account deposits only, or the Fed may state its objectives from time to time in terms of broader money supply aggregates, such as M_2, which also includes most savings deposits at commercial banks. Therefore, the way to begin monitoring the Federal Reserve's intentions is to be alert to testimony presented by Federal Reserve officials to the Senate and House Banking committees. These officials are obligated to state in quantitative terms what they plan to do to monetary aggregates in the year ahead.

But having examined the Fed's statement of intent, how can one determine whether or not the Fed is achieving its stated objectives? The data are readily available, and very little effort is required to see whether or not the Federal Reserve is achieving its target. Each week, with an eight-day lag, the Federal Reserve Board publishes seasonally adjusted data on the M_1 and M_2 money supply. A private observer can get access to these data by writing to the Federal Reserve Board and asking to receive the weekly release. The difficulty with that approach is that the data must then be processed by the observer. The monetary data must be converted into rates of change before the observer can tell whether the changes that have occurred are in line with the Fed's stated objectives.

A much easier method is to write the Federal Reserve Bank of St. Louis and ask to be placed on the mailing list for its weekly publication U.S. Financial Data. In the authors' opinion, this publication is the single most useful source of data relating to what is happening in the monetary policy area. Currently the report publishes weekly data on the monetary base. As was discussed earlier, the monetary base, or "high-powered money," is a key factor influencing monetary growth. An addition of a billion dollars to the monetary base tends to lead to an expansion in the narrowly defined money supply—M_1—about 2½ times as large, that is, about $2½ billion. This relationship between the money supply and the monetary base is depicted in the money multiplier, a second series reported by the Federal Reserve Bank of St. Louis. The multiplier shows the extent to which factors other than the monetary base are influencing the money supply. Recently, the multiplier relating the monetary base to M_1 has been running near 2.5. Also reported are the growth rates in M_1 and M_2 over various time periods. These data provide the information needed to update some of the charts presented in this book. Other series in the report include yields on selected securities, short-term interest rates, and net time deposits of commercial banks. For many series, the rates of change between various beginning dates in the past and the present are also given.

In addition to being aware of what is said at the hearings before the Senate and House Banking committees and monitoring the data, it is certainly wise to pay some attention to what members of the Federal Reserve Board say from time to time in private speeches. Reading speeches is a time-consuming task, and for many laymen who have only a peripheral interest in monetary policy, it is probably not worth the effort. However, those who want to remain fully informed should write to the Federal Reserve Board and ask to be placed on the mailing list for speeches given by each of the seven members of the board. Knowing what individual board members are concerned about and what they think about monetary policy as it is evolving can provide important clues to possible future changes in Federal Reserve policy.

Finally, it might be useful to ask yourself: "If I were in the position of a Federal Reserve Board policymaker and had committed myself to a particular monetary aggregate objective at the last hearing, after witnessing what has been happening in the economy, how would I react? Would I be inclined to adopt a somewhat easier monetary policy, or would I be inclined to adopt a less expansive policy?" There is nothing in the joint resolution that prevents the Federal Reserve from changing its policy on an interim basis. Therefore, being alert to what is happening to financial markets, and being aware of the biases of all observers, including Federal Reserve Board members, will sometimes enable you to anticipate a change in monetary policy before it takes place.

WRAPPING IT UP

The main objective of the last two chapters was to discuss the nature of money, how it is created, and the factors which influence its movements. We analyzed the roles played by the Federal Reserve System, the banks, and the public in the monetary process, and by analyzing movements in the monetary base, we indicated the extent to which specific actions by the monetary authorities have influenced past monetary trends. We concluded that the Federal Reserve Board has both the ability and the responsibility to control the money supply. We also reviewed past policy objectives of the Federal Reserve, with particular emphasis on interest rate objectives versus monetary aggregate objectives. We suggested that much of the undesired volatility in the monetary aggregates stems from the Fed's preoccupation with interest rate objectives. In addition, we discussed the relationship between monetary and fiscal policy, pointing out that large federal deficits make it more difficult to follow a stable, moderate monetary path. We also discussed the political dilemma that inevitably results from the lag in the policymaking process—the tendency of policies directed at long-term economic benefits to have large short-term political costs. Hence, there are frequently political incentives to overstimulate the economy so that the good news will come before election time, while the bad news on the inflation front will come after the elections. We also considered recent developments in Congress—the Congressional Budget and Impoundment Control Act and the Joint Monetary Resolution. We concluded that these measures have improved our policymaking framework and have the potential for substantially improving the monetary and fiscal input into our economy. Finally, we reviewed briefly the possibility of monitoring monetary developments as they occur, pointing out that looking over the stated objectives of Federal Reserve Board members at quarterly congressional hearings and then following the data will keep you well informed about what is being attempted in the monetary policy field. If you do these things you will certainly be better informed about monetary matters than 99 percent of the American public, and we believe that the results will be well worth the time and effort.

4

When money talks, business listens

A feast is made for laughter, and wine maketh merry:
but money answereth all things.

Ecclesiastes 10:19

Market-oriented economies tend to be characterized by rapid increases in output, employment, and living standards. However, the basic upward long-term trend has frequently been interrupted by cyclical swings. Periods of hectic business activity—economic booms—followed by periods of declining output—recessions—have characterized the trend toward higher living standards. These cycles in business activity have long been a major economic problem.

In recent years, various groups have begun to view economic growth itself as another problem. Many environmentalists associate growth with increased pollution, depletion of resources, and other social or economic ills. The purpose of this chapter is to describe both economic growth and the business cycle, and to explain the role of money in each of these developments.

ECONOMIC GROWTH AND MONEY

In economics it is important to distinguish "nominal" or dollar developments from "real" developments. "Nominal" refers to something measured in current dollar terms, when both physical volume and price changes are included. "Real" refers only to actual physical volume, without considering price changes. This distinction is crucial to the concept of economic growth, which deals with increases in real output over an extended period of time. It makes little sense to view an economy as growing if sales and production are increasing only due to higher prices.

It should come as no surprise that the primary ingredients fostering "real" growth are "real" ingredients. These consist of changes in the number of workers, in the number of hours they work, and in their efficiency or productivity. Although each of these ingredients tends to rise and fall over the course of a business cycle, for longer time periods the ingredients have increased at a fairly stable rate. As an example, the number of workers available to an economy usually grows at a steady and predictable rate, changing only with changes in the decisions of various groups to enter the work force, in immigration trends, and in birth-rates. However the main ingredient for improving living standards in an economy is neither an increase in the work force nor an increase in the number of hours they work—it is worker productivity. The efficiency of an economy's work force determines the standard of living enjoyed by the economy's citizens and the extent to which living standards rise.

While measures of an economy's productivity often change abruptly from year to year in response to business conditions, over an extended period of time the rise in productivity normally proceeds at a fairly stable rate. A common measure of productivity is real output per hour worked. During the first 74 years of this century, output per hour worked in the private domestic nonfarm sector of the U.S. economy rose at an average rate of about 2 percent a year. By choosing periods of high employment so as not to be fooled by short-term cyclical movements, Table 4-1 helps us see the type of stability that has characterized long-term productivity changes.

Table 4-1
Output per hour worked in the private domestic nonfarm economy (annual rates of change)

1900-1929	1929-1950	1950-1973
2.1%	2.2%	2.1%

Source: National Bureau of Economic Research; U.S. Department of Labor, Bureau of Labor Statistics.

Productivity—The key to economic well-being

These steady long-term gains in productivity have made the U.S. economy the most efficient in the world. Table 4-2 shows the average output per worker in certain countries in 1974. Unfortunately, for many reasons the figures are not strictly comparable. Even so, some of the more striking differences in efficiency among countries are readily apparent. In 1974 the average U.S. worker produced 22 percent more than his or her counterpart in France, 78 percent more than the average worker in the United Kingdom, and more than 2½ times as much as his or her counterpart in the Soviet Union.

Table 4-2
Output per worker in different countries for 1974 (U.S. dollars)

United States	$16,370
France	13,430
Germany	12,150
Japan	9,540
Italy	9,360
United Kingdom	9,190
Soviet Union	6,290

Source: Irving B. Kravis et al., *A System of International Comparisons of Gross National Product and Purchasing Power*; Federal Reserve Bank of St. Louis; U.S. Department of Commerce, Bureau of Economic Analysis; U.S. Department of Labor, Bureau of Labor Statistics; Abram Bergson, Russian Research Center, Harvard University.

The absolute superiority of the U.S. economy in terms of efficiency is interesting, but from an investor's point of view improvement in productivity is of greater interest. When efficiency is increasing rapidly, a greater percentage of output is available for distribution among consumers, investors, and the government. In contrast, slow gains in productivity lead to small percentage gains in output, a situation that can create conflicts among different groups which feel that they are not getting the gains they deserve.

What causes changes in productivity?

Many ingredients contribute to the long-term productivity trend in a given economy. One of the most important factors is the share of a country's income that is devoted to the production of plant

Table 4-3
Investment and growth in selected countries,* 1960-1973

	Average output growth rate	Investment as a percentage of real output
Japan	10.8%	29.0%
West Germany	5.5	20.0
France	5.9	18.2
Canada	5.4	17.4
United Kingdom	2.9	15.2
Italy	5.2	14.4
United States	4.1	13.6

*Organization for Economic Cooperation and Development (OECD) concept of investment and national product. The OECD concept includes nondefense government outlays for machinery and equipment in the private investment total. This necessitated special adjustment in the U.S. national accounts for comparability. National output is defined here as "gross domestic product" to conform with OECD definitions.
†Investment expenditures in nonresidential fixed.
Data estimated for 1973.
Source: U.S. Department of the Treasury.

and equipment, or investment goods. As is shown in Table 4-3, those countries which devote the highest proportion of their yearly income to building factories and machines tend to experience the most impressive gains in productivity and therefore in real growth.

While increasing the amount of income devoted to investment pays dividends in terms of more output in future years, such increases are not always easy to accomplish. In order to increase the share of income devoted to investment, it is necessary to reduce spending in other areas, such as consumer goods. The choice is the very basic and crucial one of reducing the consumption of such items as autos, TV sets, clothing, and health services today so that an even greater amount can be produced at some time in the future. As we can see from Table 4-3, of the seven countries listed the United States devotes the smallest share of its income to investment and has one of the lowest growth rates. While a huge accumulation of factories and machines helped make the U.S. economy the most efficient in the world, in recent years the gains in efficiency in other countries have been far more impressive.

Factors other than the share of investment make important contributions to the growth of an economy's efficiency. One is the education or know-how of the average worker, and another is the business climate. While both of these factors are extremely difficult to measure, it should be apparent that an economy strapped by such obstacles as extensive government regulation, high tax rates which discourage incentives and innovation, and the protection of inefficient industries and jobs, will tend to suffer from low productivity. Under such conditions, it may be necessary to spend a very large share of income on investment goods just to grow at a relatively moderate rate. Historically, this is exactly what has happened in the Soviet Union, an economy which represents a model of inefficiency. Increases in productivity in the Soviet Union have trailed increases in the United States even though the Soviet Union devotes as much as 30 percent of its output to investment goods.[1]

Where does money fit in?

Up to now, the whole point of this section has been to indicate that the factors which influence economic growth are real factors—workers, the hours they work, and their efficiency. Moreover, these factors tend to change very slowly over an extended period of time. Changes in the key factor—productivity—depend on the growth in factories and machines, the know-how of workers, and the climate for business. So far we have not mentioned money. This is because there is little evidence that the growth of the money supply has any lasting impact on an economy's real growth.

In order to have a lasting impact, money would have to influence the long-term productivity trend, the size of the work force, or the number of hours worked. While large and erratic changes in a country's money supply can disrupt the business climate, and thereby adversely influence real growth, there is little indication that monetary growth has had any significant influence on real growth over extended time periods. The figures in Table 4–4 show that over time real growth has been fairly stable in the United States, regardless of the rate of monetary growth.

Although the speed at which the money supply increases has not had a major impact on real growth, it has had an impact on the rate of inflation. Periods of rapid monetary growth are often accompanied by more inflation, whereas periods of slow monetary

---

[1] G. Warren Nutter, *Growth of Industrial Production in the Soviet Union* (Princeton, N.J.: Princeton University Press, 1962), pp. 225-82.

Table 4-4
Money supply and real growth in the United States
(annual rates of change)

	Money supply*	Real growth†
1890-1900	5.2%	3.8%
1900-1920	8.8	3.3
1920-1929	3.3	4.0
1929-1950	7.2	2.5
1950-1965	2.6	3.7
1965-1974	5.8	3.0

*Prior to 1921, money supply is measured as currency plus demand and time deposits. Thereafter, time deposits are excluded.
†Prior to 1929, real growth is based on Kendrick's series of constant dollar GNP.
Source: National Bureau of Economic Research; Board of Governors of the Federal Reserve System; U.S. Department of Commerce, Bureau of Economic Analysis; U.S. Department of Labor, Bureau of Labor Statistics; U.S. Department of Commerce, Bureau of the Census.

growth tend to be associated with less inflation. As will be shown in the following chapters, this relationship holds true not only for the United States but for other countries as well. The lasting influence of monetary growth is not on an economy's real growth rate but rather on its rate of inflation. Although growth in money has not had a major influence on long-term economic growth, it has had a tremendous impact on business conditions over shorter time periods. Let us see what that impact has been.

THE BUSINESS CYCLE

The first step toward understanding the causes of changes in business conditions is to look into the nature of the business cycle and see what happens when business activity is expanding or contracting. Although history never repeats itself exactly and each cycle has certain unique characteristics, there are many broad similarities among business cycles. Consequently, it can be extremely useful to analyze the characteristics of past cycles of business activity. For the better part of this century, this task has been an ongoing objective of the prestigious research organization known as the National Bureau of Economic Research. Economists at the National Bureau have analyzed the performance of thousands of measures of business activity, and on the basis of their analyses, have dated the expansions and contractions in business activity in the United States, beginning in 1854. According to the National Bureau, there have been 27 contractions or recessions from 1854 to 1970—an average of one recession every four years. The average length of a recession has been approximately a year and a half. This tally excludes the downturn which ended in the spring of 1975 since the National Bureau has not as yet officially dated its beginning and end.

History repeats itself

Alternating periods of rapid expansion and contraction in business activity continue to plague the U.S. economy. Why has business activity been so volatile? Is there something in the nature of a market-oriented economy that breeds instability? The questions are important ones. To begin to find answers, it is useful to describe what happens during a typical business cycle.

Starting with the initial phase of a business expansion, sales usually increase more than businessmen expect. As a result, profits rise and inventories fall below the level that businessmen prefer. To replenish the inventories, new orders are placed for goods and materials. Initially, businessmen respond by lengthening the work-week or by having existing employees work overtime. Once there is some assurance that the increase in sales is likely to last, new workers are hired to gear up production. Lengthening the work-week or adding new workers causes total income to rise. The increased income provides fuel for an even larger increase in sales. More sales stimulate the need for more production and more employment, which in turn, means still higher income and even greater sales. Once under way, an expansion has a natural tendency to feed on itself—expansion breeds expansion.

There are many desirable features during the initial stages of a business expansion. Aside from the obvious benefits of reduced unemployment and rising incomes, productivity tends to show above-average increases. As unused capacity is put back to work, output rises more rapidly than employment. As a result, output per hour worked advances sharply. This cyclical rise in efficiency reduces the costs of production, thus increasing profits and reducing the pressure for businesses to charge higher prices. Once the expansion has been under way long enough to convince businessmen that it will continue, bank loans tend to increase as businesses attempt to build inventories. Finally, spending on plant and equipment begins to rise.

The potential for an end to the expansion is reached when bottlenecks develop. Costs begin to rise as labor and materials become scarce. Profits prove disappointing as costs rise and sales fail to maintain the types of increases that businessmen have come to expect. When this occurs, inventories pile up and profits turn sour. In an effort to reduce unwanted inventories, businessmen shorten the workweek or lay off workers. New orders for consumer goods and industrial materials begin to weaken, and the formation of new businesses begins to slow. Contracts and orders for plant and equipment become less plentiful, and new building permits decline. In the process, total incomes fall, and this in turn results in a further cutback in sales. Lower sales mean more unwanted inventories, higher production costs, more layoffs, and even lower incomes. Like expansion, contraction tends to feed on itself.

When business activity is declining, productivity also tends to decline, since output generally falls faster than the work force or the workweek. This in turn means that the costs of production tend to rise more rapidly during a recession than during a recovery. As a result, profits usually fall, and this makes for upward pressure on prices despite the weak demand for products. This does not mean that prices always rise or that they rise more rapidly during a recession. It only suggests that, owing to the rise in the average cost of production, the pressure to raise prices tends to be very great during a recession. For this reason the most significant reduction in inflation often occurs during the initial stages of a recovery rather than during a recession.

The potential for an end to the downturn occurs when inventories have been trimmed to a bare minimum, when less efficient businesses have closed shop, and when the ongoing long-term rise in demand for goods and services causes sales to exceed the expectations of the businesses that are still in operation. At this point, the potential for recovery has been established once again, and the entire process is ready to repeat itself.

A look at leading indicators

There are various measures of business activity which move in a fairly predictable manner. Some lead the cycle, others move with the cycle, and still others tend to lag the cycle. The National Bureau has attempted to categorize most economic series into either leading, coincident, or lagging indicators of business activity. The series that move with the cycle include production, employment, and sales, while such series as capital expenditures and loan demand tend to move after broad movements in the economy.

For forecasting purposes, the most important indicators are those which tend to move prior to the business cycle. These leading indicators of business activity include such series as the average workweek, the layoff rate, new orders for durable goods, net business formation, new building permits, and stock prices. Table 4–5 lists 12 of the most dependable leading indicators with their lead times. On average, these indicators tend to move down almost a year before overall activity declines and to move up several months prior to a business recovery.

Table 4-5
Performance of leading indicators of business activity (lead time prior to post-World War II business cycles*)

	Peaks	Troughs
Total index	12	3
Components:		
Average workweek, manufacturing	12	2
Layoff rate, manufacturing (inverted)	12	2
New orders, consumer goods and materials, 1967 dollars	10	3
Vendor performance	9	5
Net business formation	14	2
Contracts and orders, plant and equipment, 1967 dollars	9	3
New building permits, private housing units	16	6
Change in inventories on hand and on order, 1967 dollars	7	4
Stock price index, 500 common stocks	9	5
Percent change, price index for crude materials	12	6
Money supply, 1967 dollars	12	8
Percent change, liquid assets	8	8
Average of components	11	5

*Excludes 1974-1975 downturn.
Source: U.S. Department of Commerce, Bureau of Economic Analysis.

Although the leading indicators can be a helpful tool for analyzing and predicting changes in business conditions, their extreme volatility and, at times, relatively short advance warning often limit their usefulness. Leading indicators are more effectively used to complement other approaches to forecasting changes in business conditions.[2]

In summary, the U.S. economy has exhibited a long-term pattern of real growth which has led to higher income levels, increased employment, and higher living standards. However, this growth pattern has been characterized by frequent cycles in business activity that have involved alternating periods of expansion and contraction.

By the very nature of a market economy, there is a potential for expansion and contraction in business activity. Does this potential mean that volatile business conditions must exist? Put in more general terms, the question really refers to what causes business cycles. Why do some expansions end long before labor or capital goods become scarce, while others continue for many years? Why are some recessions short and relatively mild, while others are prolonged and severe?

EXPLAINING THE CYCLE

The answer to these questions is crucial if an investor is to have any confidence in a decision which depends on an evaluation of future business prospects. In economic literature, the answer to these questions falls under the forbidding classification "theories of aggregate demand." All that this pretentious label refers to are the various explanations of why the total demand for goods and services moves up and down, thus resulting in the business cycle. There have been many explanations of changes in total demand, but these explanations can be narrowed down to two categories: (1) the Keynesian explanation, alternatively referred to as the income-expenditure or fiscalist view, and (2) the monetarist explanation.

---

[2] Recently the leading indicators were revised in an effort to reduce some of the misleading signals which might appear in a highly inflationary economy. For an excellent insight into the nature of the leading indicators and the criteria used to determine them, see Victor Zarnowitz and Charlotte Boschan, "Cyclical Indicators: An Evaluation and New Leading Indexes," *Business Conditions Digest,* May 1975, pp. v-xxii.

Keynesian expectations—A question of sentiment

The Keynesian explanation starts with the belief that changes in expectations or sentiment on the part of consumers or businessmen are the major factors initiating changes in total demand. An underlying assumption of this explanation is that the economy is basically unstable, or at least that it does not tend to promote stable high employment growth. The Keynesian theory further suggests that changes in government spending and taxes have a strong, predictable influence on the economy. Hence, Keynesians tend to favor government action to adjust the total demand for an economy's output in a desired direction.

If sentiment turns down and a recession develops, Keynesian theory suggests that some combination of increased government spending and lower taxes should be adopted. The large government deficits that result from these actions are seen as contributing to a healthy economy since they are supposed to increase demand and stimulate employment. Furthermore, Keynesians suggest that monetary policy should be geared toward lowering interest rates so that businesses will find it less expensive and therefore more attractive to increase spending on factories and machines. If consumers and businessmen get euphoric, and business activity starts to boom, Keynesians argue that the above policies should be reversed—that government spending should be cut, taxes and interest rates increased, and budget surpluses encouraged.

Finally, Keynesians tend to relegate money to a minor role. They often view inflation as resulting from irresponsible wage demands, monopolistic power, or higher costs for particular items. Consequently, Keynesians often argue for government controls, guidelines, or other such measures to hold the line on inflation.

While countless equations have been solved and diagrams drawn to show how deficits and more spending by government can offset the effects of less spending by consumers and business, there has been little in the way of hard evidence to support the basic Keynesian assumptions. Although the information was not available in 1935 when Keynes laid out the justification for these views, it has since been established that surveys of consumer sentiment are an indicator which moves almost identically with the average worker's real earnings after taxes, while the investment expectations of business are a lagging indicator of business conditions. Neither indicator helps explain what has caused changes in total spending. Moreover, the policy prescriptions of a generation of economists weaned on Keynesian principles have been disastrous. In the United States, a preoccupation with more government spending, large deficits, low interest rates, and either price controls or price guidelines has been accompanied by rapid inflation and volatile economic performance. In the United Kingdom, where hyper-Keynesian policies have been carried to an extreme, crippling inflation and economic stagnation have developed.

Monetarist explanations—The monetary influence

Monetarists do not regard changes in expectations or sentiment as a major factor in business cycles. Rather, they assume that the economy tends to be basically stable or at least relatively stable. This is not to say that wars, strikes, droughts, natural disasters, expectations, and sentiment do not influence changes in total demand. They do. However, it is a major thesis of this book that changes in the money supply have been and continue to be the single most important factor influencing changes in total demand. Other factors, such as those mentioned above, tend to influence the time interval between changes in the money supply and changes in total demand. They may lead to a somewhat larger or smaller change in business activity than would be suggested by the behavior of money alone. In some instances, a factor such as sentiment may even be the dominant factor influencing changes in total demand, but it is our contention, and the contention of most monetarists, that this is the exception rather than the rule. For the most part, money is the dominant factor affecting changes in demand and hence the business cycle.

The view that money is a key factor influencing business activity is not new—it has a long history. For over a century and a half some economists have contended that the amount of money in an economic system is the important determinant of total spending. Although the monetarist theory was the conventional explanation prior to the Great Depression, for many years subsequent to 1935, the date of the publication of John Maynard Keynes' *The General Theory of Employment, Interest, and Money,* monetarism went into eclipse. Since the 1960s, with the emergence of worldwide inflation as an increasingly evident and important problem, there has been a revival of monetarist thinking. Undoubtedly the man most responsible for this renaissance is Professor Milton Friedman of the University of Chicago, who has done extensive research in the theory of money.

History is fine, but if an investor is going to place his faith (not to mention his money) on the line, he must know more about money and the economy. For beginners, the question is, Why should changes in money affect the demand for an economy's output? There are at least two explanations. The first, the equation of exchange, represents the original monetarist explanation, while the second, the portfolio adjustment, is a more recent development.

The money formula. The first detailed explanation of why changes in money influence total demand for the economy's output was presented by Irving Fisher at the turn of the century. He developed an equation to use as a framework for explaining the role of the money supply. The equation is:

$$MV = PT$$

which simply states that for any particular time period, money *(M)* times its velocity *(V)*, or the number of times it is spent for buying goods and services, is equal to the average price level *(P)* times the volume of goods and services purchased or transacted *(T)*. Since the price level multiplied by transactions *(PT)* is total sales, all the equation says is that for a given period the stock of money multiplied by the number of times it is used for purchases equals total sales. For example, if the total money supply averages $100 billion in a particular year and each dollar is used an average of five times during that year, then total sales for the year must be $500 billion.

Up to this point there is nothing very amazing or debatable about the equation. All it does is isolate the major categories that monetarists are concerned with—the money supply, its usage, the general price level, and the volume of business activity. Several refinements are needed to make the equation a meaningful tool. First, it is necessary to make certain assumptions concerning the dependence of the different items and to determine which item provides the motivating force for changing the others. Monetarists view money as the independent item in the equation, as the item which provides the initial force that changes the other items. They also assume that velocity, or money usage, moves in a fairly stable and predictable pattern. Given these suppositions, it is easy to see why monetarists argue that changes in the money supply tend to have a major influence on changes in total spending. Moreover, since potential real output or long-term growth is determined by such long-range factors of production as the amount of labor and capital available, as well as by the productivity of these factors, long-term growth is essentially independent of money, velocity, and prices. To the extent that the monetarist assumptions are valid, over the long run increasing the money supply will not result in more growth, but rather in higher prices.

Since the initial impact of faster monetary growth is on total spending, over short periods of time money might influence either real output or inflation, depending on the level of resource utilization. If unemployment is high and there is much excess capacity in the economy, an increase in total spending should lead mostly to increases in output, employment, and production. As resources become more fully utilized, less additional output can be produced, and further increases in total spending would result primarily in upward pressure on prices rather than an increase in real output.

Viewing the spending process from this perspective, a monetarist would predict that an increase in the money supply initially leads to an increase in total expenditures. This in turn would lead to increased output and, if continued to full-capacity levels, to an increase in prices. Conversely, a decline in the money supply would tend to put downward pressure on total expenditures. If prices do not respond immediately to a downturn in outlays, then the early effect of reduced spending would be reduced output, employment, and production rather than lower prices.

The key to this argument on the importance of money depends on the stability or predictability of velocity. Nonmonetarists contend that changes in velocity often offset changes in the money supply so that the effect on total spending is a washout! Who's right? The only way to answer this question is to observe the extent to which changes in total spending are related to changes in the money supply. But before we turn to the evidence, it should be noted that we have not really explained the process by which more money influences total spending. Precisely what happens when the monetary authorities change the money supply and thereby change total spending?

Portfolio adjustments. Although the equation of exchange provides a framework for viewing the relationship between money and economic activity, it does not explain the process by which a change in money brings about a change in total spending. The process becomes clearer if we view the adjustments of various asset portfolios to changes in money. This explanation is presented in detail in Chapter 6, where its implications for the prices of investments are discussed, but a brief discussion may be helpful here.

To begin with, it is important to recognize that all economic units hold various proportions of assets in their portfolios, such as money, short-term securities, bonds, stocks, and real assets. The amounts of each asset held depend on many factors, but of key importance are price and expected return. At any given time, individuals and businesses are attempting to bring about the best distribution of the assets in their portfolios for a given set of prices and returns. Changes in the money supply initiate changes in the whole range of asset prices that create incentives for increasing total spending. In essence, this is how it works.

When the Federal Reserve increases the money supply, its usual move is to purchase government securities. In effect, the Fed takes government securities from the public and exchanges these for money (usually in the form of new bank deposits). In order to persuade holders of government securities that they should sell, the Federal Reserve normally offers a higher price than had previously existed for the securities. As a result, two things happen:

1. Those who sold government securities to the Federal Reserve now have money instead of an income-earning asset.
2. Government securities now carry a higher price with respect to all other assets than they did before the sale.

These conditions make it economically attractive for those with newly acquired money assets to bid for other assets, such as stocks and bonds. As the prices of these other assets are bid up, an interesting thing happens. The new money that has been placed in the system stays there, since whoever sells such assets as bonds or stocks receives money in return. As the prices of bonds and stocks rise, real assets appear to be priced relatively low, and holders of the new money now find it attractive to purchase these items. The attempt to acquire more real assets leads to an increase in total demand or total spending. Hence, an increase in the money supply sets into motion strong economic forces which tend to increase total spending.

Similarly, a decrease in the money supply brings about pressures for a decline in total spending. Sales of Treasury bills by the Federal Reserve lower the prices on such bills and thereby raise the interest rate. In the process, the money supply declines, while prices of bonds, stocks, and real assets appear high relative to Treasury bills. Just as in the preceding example the public could not get rid of the excess money, in this example the public cannot replace the money which has been taken out of the economic system. However, attempts to do so lead to sales of bonds, stocks, and real assets, resulting in lower prices for these assets and a decline in total spending. In the process of adjusting, the public is not able to increase the amount of money, so it reduces the amount of spending to a level consistent with the money that does exist. The pressure to acquire more money by selling real assets leads to a decline in aggregate demand or total spending.

The portfolio adjustment process is essentially a short-term phenomenon. Once a certain increase in monetary growth accompanied by a corresponding increase in total spending has existed for a long enough period of time, relative prices and interest rates will tend to adjust to the new situation. At this point, it would take a further increase in monetary growth to stimulate the adjustment process described, and further increase the growth in total spending. Similarly, it would take a slower rate of monetary growth to reverse the process and bring about a slower growth in total spending.

We have now come full circle by suggesting that more money leads to an increase in spending, first on liquid assets and later on goods and services, whereas less money brings about a decrease in spending on liquid assets and eventually on goods and services. Thus, the monetarist theory argues that swings in monetary growth initiate the business cycle which has characterized modern capitalist economies.

The monetarist theory of business cycles is based on a well-reasoned set of economic principles, and it has a long historical tradition. Neither of these factors should lead one to place very much faith in the theory. Alternative theories can be equally well thought out, and long-held beliefs are not necessarily the correct ones. How can we determine the extent to which the monetarist theory represents an accurate and useful explanation of changes in business activity? The answer lies with historical experience.

MONEY AND DEMAND—THE EVIDENCE

Chart 4-1 shows changes in the money supply and in total spending over a period of about 60 years. As with most economic

Chart 4-1
Money and total spending

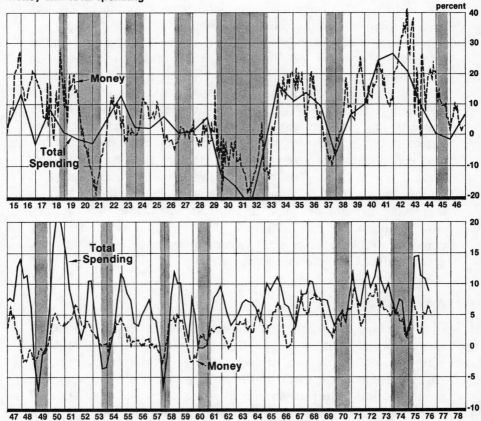

Peak to trough of business cycle

Money data, defined as currency plus demand deposits, are six-month seasonally adjusted annual rates of change.
Total spending, as measured by gross national product, are one-year rates of change prior to 1947, two-quarter annual rates of change thereafter.
All data are plotted at the midpoint of the interval.

Source: Board of Governors of the Federal Reserve System; National Bureau of Economic Research; U.S. Department of Commerce, Bureau of Economic Analysis

relationships, the relationship is not perfect. On some occasions after World War II and the outbreak of the Korean War, total spending rose very rapidly, while the money supply advanced at a moderate pace. Those were the times when changes in velocity had an important impact. However, such instances appear to be the exception rather than the rule. For the bulk of the 60-year period, changes in the money supply were closely related to changes in total spending. When the money supply rose moderately, as it did during the latter part of the 1920s, total spending also rose at a moderate rate. When the money supply fell sharply in the early 1930s, so did total spending. In spite of an economic collapse in the early 1930s, a rapid rise in money in the mid-1930s was accompanied by a rapid pickup in spending.

In the period after World War II, a combination of higher interest rates and regulations preventing interest payments on checking account deposits caused the public to shift its holdings of money assets from checking accounts to savings deposits. As a result, M_1, the money measure which does not include savings deposits, has since grown at a slower rate than either total spending or other measures of money. Even so, the basic relationship between changes in money and changes in total spending continued. In the late 1950s and early 1960s money increased at an average yearly rate of about 2 percent while spending increases averaged 5 percent per year. In contrast, in the late 1960s money rose at about a 6 percent rate while spending grew at about a 9 percent rate. As in prior years, a pickup in monetary growth was accompanied by a speedup in spending.

A matter of timing

It is readily apparent from the chart that in the past 60 years a slowdown in monetary growth preceded every recession; conversely, a speedup preceded every recovery. On average, over the past 50 years the growth of the money supply slowed about 12 months prior to the beginning of a recession and rose about 9 months prior to the start of a recovery. However, the timing has not been consistent. Monetary growth has begun to slow anywhere from 7 to 19 months prior to the onslaught of a recession, while monetary growth has begun to speed up from 2 to 13 months prior to business recoveries.

While the lag between a change in the money supply and the beginning of a recovery or recession has been on the order of 9 to 12 months, the lag between a change in the money supply and the first sign of a change in business activity has been even shorter. Normally, business activity will rise less rapidly before actually declining. In order to observe the timing between the first indication of a slowdown in the economy and a slowdown in monetary growth, changes in industrial production were compared to changes in monetary growth. Peaks and troughs in these series were compared to the established peaks and troughs in the business cycle. As Table 4-6 shows, a slowing in industrial production

Table 4-6
Relationship between monetary growth rate turning points and industrial production growth rate turning points

Monetary growth rate peaks	Industrial production growth rate peaks	Months money led industrial production
Lead before downturns		
September 1922	December 1922	3
August 1925	January 1926	5
January 1929	March 1929	2
July 1936	September 1936	2
June 1947	December 1947	6
December 1951	November 1952	11
January 1957	November 1956	−2*
January 1959	January 1959	0
October 1968	April 1969	6
October 1972	June 1972	−4*
Range		−4 to 11
Average		2.9

Monetary growth rate troughs	Industrial production growth rate troughs	Months money led industrial production
Lead before upturns		
August 1923	June 1924	10
November 1926	October 1927	11
February 1932	April 1932	2
November 1937	January 1938	2
February 1949	April 1949	2
January 1954	January 1954	0
December 1957	February 1958	2
February 1960	November 1960	9
November 1969	March 1970	4
February 1975	February 1975	0
Range		0 to 11
Average		4.2

Money is defined as currency plus demand deposits. All data are six-month annual rates of change placed at the midpoint of the interval. In order to make the data less volatile, a six-month moving average was used.
*Money lagged industrial production.
Source: National Bureau of Economic Research; Board of Governors of the Federal Reserve System.

has occurred on average three months after a similar slowing in monetary growth. Prior to a recovery, the decline in production eases some four months after a pickup in monetary growth.

On a few occasions, changes in money and production appear to peak and trough at the same time. There are even two instances—in late 1956 and in 1972—when business activity showed signs of slowing prior to a slowdown in monetary growth. These examples serve as a reminder that money isn't the only factor which may initiate changes in business conditions. Even so, the data support the view that seldom, if ever, has it been possible to experience a sustained pickup in total spending or business activity without a similar pickup in monetary growth, nor does it appear likely that a sustained slowdown in total spending or business has existed without a corresponding slowdown in monetary growth.

Real money—A misleading indicator

In recent years, as inflation has become more serious, many observers have suggested that the measures of money be adjusted to remove the impact of inflation. They argue that the resulting "real" money supply would offer a more reliable guide to the actual amount of improvement or lack of improvement in future business conditions. One argument for this adjustment is simply that changes in real money might provide a better guide to real changes in the economy than would the nominal money supply. Furthermore, some have argued that in order to promote real increases in business activity, the monetary authorities should always assure an adequate supply of real money, as opposed to nominal money. We do not consider these arguments valid. In fact, policy recommendations based on such arguments could easily lead to economic chaos.

Since on the surface the reasons for viewing the real money supply as a guide to business conditions sound so appealing, it is useful to begin by pointing out some of the obvious mistakes which might have been made if this procedure had been applied in the past. In the early 1930s, in the heart of the most severe recession on record, the real money supply rose for nine consecutive months, as prices declined faster than the decline in nominal money. Although real economic activity fell by about 30 percent during the entire recession, the real money supply was essentially unchanged. Had an investor used the real money supply as a guide to economic developments at that time, he would have completely misjudged the economic collapse that was developing. Furthermore, had policymakers used the real money supply as a guide, they might have engineered an even more drastic reduction in money than actually occurred, and the recession of the early 1930s might have been even worse than it was.

A second instance in which investors would have been misled by the real money supply occurred in 1950, at the outbreak of the Korean War. For 12 months, the rise in inflation associated with the outbreak of the war led to a decline in the real money supply, while production and stock prices continued to soar. Recently a similar phenomenon occurred. The real money supply declined not only during the recession of 1974–75, but also for a year after the recovery! Those investors who used real money as a guide to business activity completely missed the recovery in both the economy and the stock market in 1975–76. Although nine times out of ten it does not matter whether an observer uses changes in nominal or real money as a guide to business developments, the tenth time can be extremely important.

In order to understand why the real money supply does not necessarily provide a reasonable guide to real business activity, it is useful to consider the factors that determine the growth of nominal money and those determining the growth of real money, as well as the impact that these factors have on the economy. As noted above, nominal monetary growth is largely dependent on the actions of the monetary authorities. By purchasing or selling large amounts of government securities, the Federal Reserve has the power to alter the growth in nominal money. When nominal monetary growth increases, the money assets of individuals and institutions rise. As these individuals and institutions attempt to rearrange their portfolios and acquire other nonmonetary assets, the demand for a whole range of items goes up, thus leading to a further increase in spending. Just the opposite happens when there is a slowdown in monetary growth.

How do changes in the real money supply work into this scenario? At first blush it appears simple. For an individual, a rise in his own real money supply can occur in one of two ways. First, and most commonly, his money holdings may suddenly rise faster than prices. This may show up in the form of a wage increase, resulting in larger real income. Second, the rate of rise in prices may be slower than the rate of rise of his money balances. In either case, the ratio of money to prices (real money) rises, and this leads the individual to adjust his portfolio by increasing expenditures on real assets.

Unfortunately, we can't generalize from the behavior of an individual to the total economy. We can't conclude that when the ratio of money to some price index rises, monetary policy is therefore stimulating business activity, or that when the real money supply declines, monetary policy is necessarily restrictive. The problem is that the monetary authorities do not control the ratio of money to prices. The public controls this ratio, and hence decides what the real money supply will be. Although monetary action can have a lasting effect on nominal money, it has only a temporary effect on real money. Let's see why this is so.

The potentially misleading character of real money as an indicator of monetary policy can be seen most readily when adjustments occur very quickly in the economy instead of with the usual lag. Suppose that the Federal Reserve promotes an expansionary monetary policy, and that the nominal money supply rises sharply. If economic units in society could fully and immediately adjust their portfolios and expenditure habits to the excess money holdings, prices and interest rates would change immediately to equate the demand for money to the larger amount of money supplied. Prices would rise instantly so that the measures of real money balances supplied by the monetary authorities would always be equal to the amount of real money balances that are actually demanded in the economy. As a result, changes in real money balances would tend to be directly related to the total demand for real goods and services.

In the real world, however, prices do not adjust instantly, and actual movements in the real money supply often reflect the temporary effects of this adjustment process. As we will see in Chapter 5, it takes time for prices to respond to an increase in the nominal money supply. In the meantime, the observed ratio of money to prices cannot in and of itself reveal anything about the state of the actual adjustment. If there is a rapid upward adjustment in the nominal money supply, and price adjustments lag, an increase in the stock of money would result in a temporary increase in the real money supply.

Later, when prices begin to rise, real money balances will fall back toward their former level. This decline in real balances does not represent a conscious tightening in monetary policy; it simply represents a delayed adjustment brought about by a prior increase in monetary growth. The price rise is finally catching up with the previous rise in the money supply! Prices would continue to rise, and real money balances to fall, until people are no longer willing to increase expenditures by exchanging money for assets and goods and services. Hence people end up holding the increased stock of money. Unless we know how far the price adjustment has proceeded, we can be misled by the existing measure of real money.

Let's look at one more complication in trying to view monetary policy by referring to the change in the real money supply. Take the above instance, in which the initial increase in the nominal money supply led first to an increase in the real money supply but as prices rose, resulted in a decline. Some argue that if we are to maintain an economic stimulus, it is necessary to maintain growth in the real money supply. For example, they argue that if prices are increasing at 7 percent, it is necessary to increase the nominal money supply at a faster rate, say, 10 percent. But this 10 percent growth in the money supply would then lead to an even greater rise in prices, and before long it would be necessary to speed up the growth in the nominal money supply to more than 10 percent in order to maintain a constant growth rate of the real money supply. It is unnecessary to go through an infinite set of periods to realize that this approach would lead to an exploding system. The more the nominal money supply increases, the greater the rise in inflation; but the greater rise in inflation would necessitate an even greater rise in the nominal money supply to maintain a stable growth in the real money supply. If we followed this method to its logical conclusion, we would be in a period of runaway inflation similar to that observed in post-World War I Germany and in many South American countries since World War II.[3]

---

[3] For a more detailed discussion of the role of the real money supply, see Denis S. Karnosky's article "Real Money Balances: A Misleading Indicator of Monetary Actions," *Federal Reserve Bank of St. Louis Review,* vol. 56, no. 2 (1974), pp. 2-10.

Let's summarize the arguments up to now. There are essentially two reasons why it can be misleading to use the real money supply as an indicator of monetary policy. The first is that we cannot be certain whether an increase in the real money supply represents an actual stimulative policy whereby the Federal Reserve is causing a rapid growth in money, or whether it represents a downward adjustment in prices reflecting previously tight monetary policy. It would be even worse to use changes in the real money supply as an indicator of what the Federal Reserve should do. This could very easily lead to a system of runaway inflation, such as occurred in Germany in the early 1920s, or progressive deflation, which would occur if real money is increasing because prices are dropping faster than monetary growth.

So much for the theory; let's look at the data. Which has the better record as an indicator of subsequent trends in economic activity—the nominal money supply or the real money supply? Which indicator would you prefer to use as a measure of what is likely to happen to the economy? You will note by a quick glance at Chart 4-2 that during most periods, changes in the nominal money supply and the real money supply show similar patterns. Prior to a recession, when nominal money growth slows, real money tends to decrease, and therefore tends to provide an accurate indication of the oncoming recession. Similarly, prior to an expansion, when nominal money is growing more rapidly, real money tends to increase, thus correctly forecasting the recovery. However, on some occasions there can be considerable differences between the signals given by nominal money and those given by real money.

It was noted earlier that real money provided a misleading guide to the economy during the early 1930s, the Korean War, and the recovery from the 1974-75 recession. These important exceptions argue against automatically assuming that changes in real money will soon be followed by similar changes in real output. Hence, in making predictions concerning probable future trends of economic activity it is much safer to rely on changes in the nominal money supply as an indicator of changes in nominal spending than to rely on changes in the real money supply as an indicator of changes in real spending. Furthermore, investors should be particularly leery of any attempts by the monetary authorities to maintain a stable growth in the real money supply when prices are

Chart 4–2
Money and real money

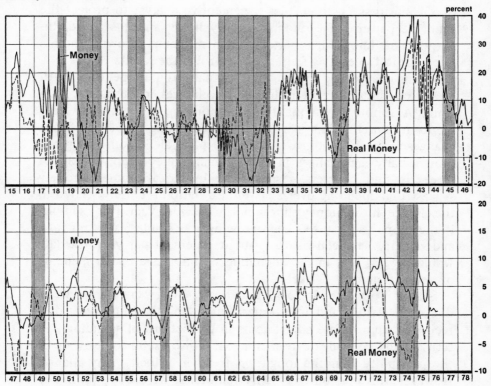

Shaded areas: Peak to trough of business cycle.
Money is defined as currency plus demand deposits (seasonally adjusted). Real money is calculated by dividing money by the consumer price index.
The data are six-month annual rates of change plotted at the midpoint of the interval.
Source: Board of Governors of the Federal Reserve System; National Bureau of Economic Research; U.S. Department of Labor, Bureau of Labor Statistics.

rising rapidly. Such a policy would surely lead to an explosive situation marked by hyperinflation.

USING MONEY TO IMPROVE YOUR FORECASTING RESULTS

Most business forecasters use an eclectic approach in attempting to estimate future trends in economic activity. They tend to be pragmatists and will use any technique which has a good track record and hence promises to have a better than average chance of accurately forecasting the future. Knowledge concerning the stage of the business cycle enables a perceptive analyst to project the probable pattern of economic activity in the months ahead. Incorporating knowledge pertaining to monetary growth and its impact into forecasting frequently improves the results.

In this chapter we argued that fluctuations in monetary growth are often the dominant influence on changes in business conditions. A simple technique for incorporating monetary developments into a forecast is to use the knowledge that significant changes in total spending, in the form of a sales boom or a recession, usually lag changes in the nominal money supply by about three or four quarters, respectively. Empirical studies strongly suggest that spending over a six-month period is closely related to the change in the money supply in the previous year. For example, if the money supply has been growing at a stable 5 percent rate, and velocity has been rising at about 3 percent per year, the data would suggest that in the upcoming six months a rise in spending of about 8 percent is likely.

Since velocity tends to systematically underperform its trend during recessions and to overperform during the initial year of a recovery, appropriate adjustments in predictions of spending patterns should be made at these times. It is also useful to be aware of the possibility that the long-term trend in velocity may change. However, this possibility is fairly remote. If we use M_1 (currency plus checking account balances) as our measure of money, the last change in the long-term velocity pattern occurred just after World War II; for M_2 (the broader definition of money), the last fundamental change occurred in the early 1960s.

While past changes in the money supply are often able to give a reasonably accurate view of spending patterns for the next six months, most of us are interested in a horizon which extends at least a year into the future. The farther our forecast horizon, the more important it is to anticipate the developing pattern of monetary growth. Until recently it was necessary to play the game of placing oneself in the position of the Federal Reserve Board, with its known biases, and thereby attempt to estimate how it would conduct monetary policy in the next six months. For example, if inflation were becoming a more serious matter, and you were aware that the Federal Reserve usually tightens monetary policy in such a period, you might have been inclined to estimate a declining trend in monetary growth in the six months ahead. Conversely, if the economy were entering a recession, you would have been likely to expect that the Federal Reserve Board would ease monetary policy, and that in the months ahead the rate of monetary growth would accelerate. Since in the past a persistent trend toward monetary restraint has brought on business recessions, this knowledge should be applied to recent and prospective changes in monetary policy. Conversely, since an upward trend in monetary growth has tended to precede recovery in the business cycle by an average of eight months, this knowledge should also be used in making forecasts for the period ahead.

Beginning in 1975, the Federal Reserve Board was required to establish public targets for monetary growth in the upcoming year. To the extent that the observer has confidence that the targets will be achieved, they can be a useful input in any forecast of monetary growth. Unfortunately, the ranges established by the Federal Reserve Board have been fairly broad, almost covering the extremes of monetary growth over the past decade. In May 1975 Arthur F. Burns, chairman of the Federal Reserve Board, indicated that the money supply (currency plus demand deposits) was targeted to grow at a rate of 5 percent to 7½ percent in the 12 months ending in March 1976. A year later the range was reduced to 4½ percent to 7 percent. If monetary growth is at the upper end of the target, the spending pace will be hectic, while if monetary growth is at the lower end, the spending pace will be moderate. Consequently, in forecasting the period ahead, it is necessary to take into account whether the Federal Reserve Board is attempting to achieve growth at the upper or the lower end of its target range.

Of course, the fact that a target has been set does not necessarily mean that it will be achieved. In the past, the Federal Reserve has tended to alternate between underachieving and overachieving its monetary targets. This has been a result of the Fed's practice of purchasing securities in an attempt to stabilize interest rates. The implications of this policy for monetary growth targets were discussed in Chapter 2.

Needless to say, projecting future monetary growth trends is a hazardous business. Nonetheless, it appears to be easier now that public targets are established and the Federal Reserve is required to report those targets at a quarterly public forum. The Fed discloses what policy it has been conducting and why, as well as its target rates of growth for the next year. This information, if assimilated in an organized and continuous fashion, can be of considerable aid in determining the future pace of expenditures.

Once total spending has been estimated, it is necessary to separate nominal or dollar spending into the amount that is likely to be real and the amount that represents inflation. Projecting inflation is a somewhat different feat, and in recent years it has been a difficult task. Nonetheless, here too the behavior of the money supply can significantly improve your forecasting record, as will be shown in Chapter 5.

To summarize. We argued in this chapter that changes in monetary growth are the major factor inducing changes in economic activity. Past experience shows that, on average, a slowdown in monetary growth precedes a recession by many months and that a speedup in monetary growth precedes recovery by a lesser number of months. Several explanations were given to indicate why more money leads to more spending and a tendency toward business expansion, while conversely, reduced monetary growth leads to less spending and eventually results in a contraction in economic activity. Real money, or money adjusted for inflation, was considered as a potential indicator of real business activity. We concluded that it could be extremely misleading to assume that real money is an automatic guide to real economic performance. Finally, we argued that knowledge of the typical lead-lag relationships between the money supply and economic activity can be a useful input to the challenging and perplexing task of forecasting business trends. Careful observation of past monetary trends and a knowledge of the Federal Reserve's intentions for the months ahead can improve forecasts of economic activity and financial markets.

5

Inflation—Whoever thought we could have too much money?

"Don't take any wooden nickels!"
Full many a wag still hollers;
What soon may rate more up to date's
"Don't take any paper dollars."

S. S. Biddle

In recent years high rates of inflation have become a primary factor influencing production, jobs, investments, government policies, and even governments themselves. The problem has not respected political or philosophical boundaries. It has affected every major industrialized country, and has permeated democracies, dictatorships, and totalitarian governments as well as capitalistic, socialistic, and communistic economies.

There is evidence that inflation has existed ever since the invention of money.[1] Since the problem is of ancient origin, the current high standard of living is proof that society has met and overcome this problem on numerous occasions. However, such assurances offer small comfort to the individuals whose income and savings are destroyed in the victory.

Within the past decade the problem has become progressively worse for the United States as well as for many other countries.

---

[1] Anna J. Schwartz, "Secular Price Change in Historical Perspective," *Journal of Money, Credit, and Banking*, vol. 5, no. 1, part 2 (1973), p. 264.

Whether the victory over inflation in subsequent years comes with a whimper or with a bang, or not at all, will have a significant effect on the value of various investments. A thorough understanding of inflation and money and their role in the economic process is essential for investors who wish to avoid being the victims of future economic developments.

A key problem that has often plagued societies is that of viewing inflation in the perspective of longer-term trends. One reason for the decline in the money supply which aggravated the depression of the 1930s was a fear of inflation. This fear prevailed despite the fact that prices were stable in the latter 1920s and declined in the early years of the depression. Unfortunately, the 1930s were not the only period when observers found it difficult to place inflation in perspective. During the latter part of the 1950s inflation was viewed as a debilitating economic evil that was rapidly eroding the value of the dollar. At the time, consumer prices were rising an average of 2 percent to 3 percent a year. Again, in the early 1960s, inflation was viewed as a major problem. Presidents Kennedy and Johnson resorted to jawboning and guidelines in an effort to hold the line on prices when increases reached the then intolerable rate of 2 percent a year. Since the mid-1960s the problem has become progressively more serious.

Historically there has been no shortage of explanations for inflation. Businessmen tend to place the blame on higher wages and union power, while labor leaders and many workers blame big business and the market power it wields. Many observers not closely associated with either group cite both business and labor as important causes of higher prices. More recently, the responsibility has been shifted to the government, with huge deficits cited as the culprit. In a democracy, however, government policies should represent the desires of the people. Could it be that the people themselves are accountable for inflation? A more popular explanation would hold that neither the people nor their representatives would have undertaken the policies which resulted in inflation had they been fully aware of the consequences. Since those consequences should have been clearly and forcefully explained by economists, the blame for inflation could be shifted quite logically to the economics profession! Suffice it to say that there is plenty of blame to go around.

The main purpose of this chapter is not to uncover a scapegoat for the inflation problem, but rather to analyze that problem in a manner useful to investors. A thorough understanding of inflation and its effects on the economy is indispensable for protecting incomes, assets, investments, and profitability in the years ahead. It may also serve to determine whether or not capitalism and democracy will remain viable institutions. The first step is to understand what is meant by inflation and to be able to place inflationary developments in a proper perspective.

INFLATION—WHAT IS IT?

Much of the confusion and complexity that surrounds discussions of inflation stems from either a misconception of the problem or a lack of perspective. Basically, inflation is a continuing rise in the overall price level of an economy. A rise in the price of one or more items does not necessarily amount to inflation, at least not so long as the rise is offset by declines in the prices of other items. In a dynamic economy, price changes occur constantly. Increases in the overall price level for several months, followed by offsetting declines, would not be classified as "inflation" and "deflation." A minimum of six months to a year is necessary to establish a trend, and for many practical purposes, such as analyzing effects on investments, even longer-term trends are more useful.

Just as the alternative measures of the money supply show different growth rates, so too do the alternative measures of inflation. Although many inflation series tend to move in the same direction, there is often a discrepancy among the various measures. This is an important point to remember. There is no single correct measure for inflation. In addition to inaccuracies and measurement problems which can serve to distort a particular inflation index, the different scope of the indexes will often lead to different inflation rates.

The most comprehensive measure of the overall price level is known as the gross national product price deflator. This measure encompasses the behavior of prices paid by consumers, by businesses, by the government, and by purchasers of U.S. exports. Less exhaustive measures of inflation include the consumer price index

(CPI), which tracks the prices paid by consumers, and the wholesale price index (WPI), which tracks prices paid by businesses for various goods. Chart 5-1 shows the behavior of these price indexes from some of the earliest data available through the mid-1970s. As can be seen, the latter part of the 19th century was generally characterized by deflation—a decline in the overall price level. Since the turn of the century, however, prices have declined significantly on only two occasions. The first occurred during 1920-21, and the second occurred during the depression in the early 1930s. Relative price stability has occurred only briefly during this century. It existed as recently as the period from 1959 to 1964, when price increases averaged less than 2 percent per year. Still, aside from a limited number of years, to one degree or another inflation has characterized the U.S. economy during the 20th century. The most severe inflationary periods were those which accompanied

Chart 5-1
Historical price trends

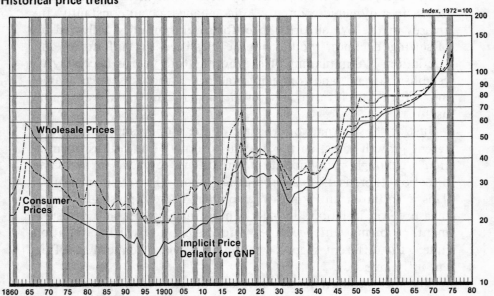

Shaded areas: Peak to trough of business cycle.
Prior to 1929, the implicit price deflator for GNP was estimated, based on Kendrick's series for the deflator.
Source: U.S. Department of Commerce, Bureau of the Census; U.S. Department of Labor, Bureau of Labor Statistics; U.S. Department of Commerce, Bureau of Economic Analysis; National Bureau of Economic Research.

the two world wars. During World War I wholesale prices doubled within a three-year period, while a similar doubling of prices required seven years in the 1940s. The worst inflation in U.S. history that has not been associated with a war or its aftermath, is the one we have been experiencing in the late 1960s and the 1970s.

Chart 5-2 shows inflation rates (changes in prices) from one period to another. These are the figures that usually appear on the

Chart 5-2
Alternative measures of inflation

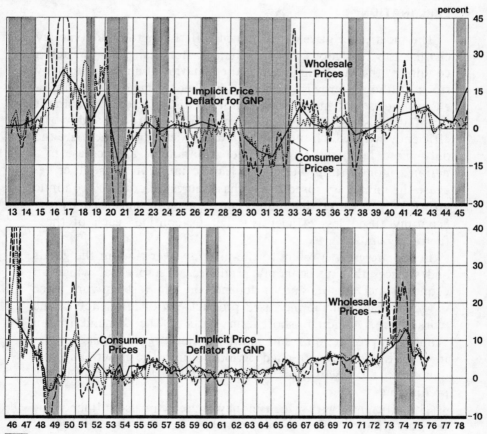

Peak to trough of business cycle

Wholesale and consumer price data are 6-month annual rates of change.
Implicit price deflator for GNP data prior to 1948 are annual rates of change. Thereafter data are 2-quarter annual rates of change.
Prior to 1929, the implicit price deflator for GNP was estimated based on Kendrick's series for the deflator.
Rates of change are plotted at the midpoint of their interval.

Source: U.S. Department of Labor, Bureau of Labor Statistics; U.S. Department of Commerce, Bureau of Economic Analysis; National Bureau of Economic Research

front pages of newspapers. As in the previous chart, it is apparent that the alternative price measures move in a similar pattern. However, they often reveal differences. This lack of consistency among the inflation numbers highlights an important aspect of economics. It is seldom possible to obtain precise measures of economic concepts. As a result, when viewing the evidence presented in this book, the reader should not expect to find perfect relationships among the various series.

WHAT CAUSES INFLATION—THE BARE BONES EXPLANATION

The most descriptive definition of inflation is too much money chasing too few goods. While several factors can lead to such a condition, the most important is the behavior of a nation's money stock. Although growth in money has been a major factor influencing the rate of inflation, it is not the only factor. The amount of inflation is also influenced by an economy's growth and by the efficiency with which money is used. By definition, these are the only three factors that can affect inflation. If an increase in a nation's money supply does not lead to inflation, it is either because the money was used to purchase increased output (economic growth) or because the money was somehow absorbed by the economy (used less efficiently). Let us consider each of these factors separately.

Economic growth refers to the increase over time in the goods and services that an economy produces. The speed at which an economy increases its output depends on how fast its work force is growing and on the increased productivity or efficiency of the work force. Although short-term shifts in the demand for an economy's production result in alternating surges and slackenings in output, over any extended period of time, the growth and productivity of the work force have been fairly constant and highly predictable.

The efficiency with which money is used can also influence the rate of inflation. This factor, which is termed the velocity of money, merely refers to the number of times a nation's stock of money is used for purchases of goods and services during a particular time period. For example, if the nation's production of goods and services totals $500 billion a year, and the stock of money in use is $100 billion, then each dollar must be used an average of five times during the production of the $500 billion worth of output. Hence, the velocity would be five. If a larger amount of money is used in the same number of transactions, this would not lead to higher prices, but rather the velocity of money would be lower. For example, if production totaled $500 billion and the stock of money in use totaled $200 billion, the velocity would be 2½.

Fortunately, the factors influencing the velocity of the money supply as well as those affecting economic growth tend to be fairly stable over time, and the degree of inflation in an economy tends to be dominated by the behavior of the economy's money supply. Hence, a speedup in the growth of a country's money supply tends to be followed by a speedup in inflation.

But why should more money mean more inflation?

Although the view that more money leads to more inflation has intuitive appeal, the actual process by which this happens is neither direct nor obvious. The first step in increasing the supply of money can occur in different ways. Prior to 1914, and to some extent afterward, newly mined gold was sold to the U.S. Treasury, which, in turn, paid for it with Treasury notes (currency). Today the most common method of increasing the money stock is for Federal Reserve officials to purchase government securities held by the public. The payment for these securities ends up as an addition to the money supply.

Those who sell government securities to the Federal Reserve typically do so because they are offered a higher price than had previously been paid for those securities. Once those who sell the government securities receive payment from the Federal Reserve, they are quite anxious to exchange their new funds, which do not earn interest, for some asset that will yield them a return. However, in order to bid such assets away from their current owners, those with newly created money (money they have just received from the Federal Reserve) normally find that they have to offer a price for those assets which is higher than the going price. (If they don't, the asset holders won't sell.) Of course, no matter how many times individuals in the private sector exchange money for other assets, someone ends up holding the extra money that has been put into the economy. As prices of financial assets—securities, notes, bonds, stocks—are bid up, nonfinancial or real assets become relatively more attractive. Eventually, unless there is an increase in output equal to the value of the new money, or unless the new money is absorbed into the system because the public uses its money balances less efficiently than in the past, the prices of goods and services must be bid up, thus generating an increase in the price level.

The inflation process is neither highly predictable nor instantaneous. In modern complex economies, a faster increase in the money supply does not immediately lead either to a greater demand for goods and services or to more inflation. The effect of such an increase has to be transmitted through financial markets before it can affect the demand for goods and services. Historically it has taken several months for an abrupt change in monetary growth to have a perceptible impact on the demand for goods and services. The time that elapses between increased money growth and inflation is determined in a more complex manner. It depends on such factors as the economy's ability to increase output, past price behavior, and the extent to which labor and product markets are free to adjust to economic pressures.

In the short run, a monetary stimulus can appear to be anti-inflationary. If available labor and machinery are not being utilized, higher rates of monetary growth can stimulate demand and lead to an increase in output. The sharp gains in productivity (output per hour worked) which accompany a cyclical expansion in output reduce labor costs per unit of output and therefore make it possible for businesses to increase profits and wages without raising prices. It is only after the idle labor and machines have been put to work that large productivity gains become more difficult, unit labor costs rise, and businesses find that they must raise prices in order to increase wages and profits.

Past price experience is also a major factor affecting the time that elapses between changes in money and changes in inflation. In an economy free from inflation, a sharp increase in the money supply will tend to boost demand and output first, with inflation lagging behind. If this increased rate of monetary growth is maintained, then prices will also increase. Eventually, inflationary expectations will develop, and labor agreements, contracts, business and investment plans, and financial decisions of all types will begin to incorporate premiums to allow for inflation. Once these premiums are included, it will take several years (or however long the contracts run) to remove their effects from wages and prices. This is why a particular rate of inflation, say, 5 percent per year, could not be ended immediately even if monetary growth were stopped. The initial effect of that action would be a sharp reduction in actual demand as compared with expected demand, but the contractual arrangements incorporating the previous inflation would still be in effect.

If various contractual arrangements and expectations of future inflation prevent wages and prices from adjusting rapidly to reduced demand, then the impact of slower monetary growth must first affect real output. As unsold goods pile up in the hands of businesses, the income received for those goods tends to be lower than expected, and profits decline. In addition, workers are laid off, unemployment rises, and in this way aggregate wage increases begin to slow. As long as the adjustment to reduced demand is mild, businessmen will be tempted to cut output instead of prices in the hope that the demand for their product will soon pick up and that they will again be able to realize their previously expected income. Similarly, workers will be inclined to accept temporary unemployment rather than immediately reduce wage demands. As might be expected, the more severe the drop in demand, the quicker the expectations of future inflation will decline.

Although a logical explanation for the relationship between money and inflation exists, the real test is past experience. To what extent have changes in the rate of inflation accompanied or followed changes in the money supply? In other words, how often has excess money been absorbed into the system by either increased output or changes in velocity? We now turn to the historical experience in an attempt to answer these questions.

The evidence

The relationship between money and inflation may be viewed in many ways. One way is to observe the extent to which changes in the utilization of money (velocity) have accounted for the difference between money and inflation. Chart 5–3 shows the relationship between inflation, as measured by the consumer price index, and the money supply, as measured in terms of both M_1 (currency and checking account deposits) and M_2 (M_1 plus most savings deposits at banks). In order to remove the impact of economic growth from the relationship, the money supply measures are divided by real output. As a result of this adjustment, the difference between the money measures and the consumer price index shows the extent to which the changing usage of money has accounted for inflation.

As can be seen from the chart, the money measure which includes savings deposits (M_2) shows the more stable relationship to inflation. When money increases relative to real output, the price level shows a corresponding increase. Since the 1930s the money measure which excludes savings deposits (M_1) has not shown as consistent a relationship with inflation as has the measure which includes savings deposits (M_2). There is a technical

Chart 5-3
Money per unit of output and prices (index 1967 = 100)

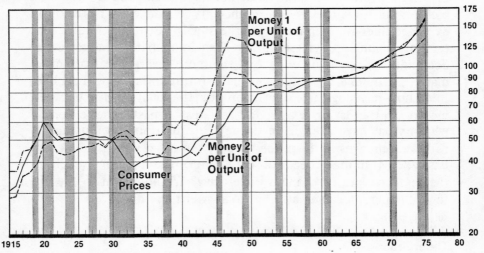

Shaded areas: Peak to trough of business cycle.
Consumer price data are plotted annually for calendar year.
Quantity of money is for fiscal year ending June 30, while output (real GNP) is for calendar year. Prior to 1929, real GNP was estimated based on Kendrick's series for real GNP.
Source: National Bureau of Economic Research; Board of Governors of the Federal Reserve System; U.S. Department of Labor, Bureau of Labor Statistics; U.S. Department of Commerce, Bureau of Economic Analysis.

reason why M_2 is more meaningful in Chart 5-3. The reason is that up to the 1930s banks were permitted to pay interest on checking account balances as well as on savings accounts. As a result, both checking and savings accounts grew at a similar rate. Hence, up to the 1930s both measures of money showed similar growth. However, since that time banks have been prohibited from paying interest on checking account balances. As interest rates moved up in the 1950s, the public placed a much greater amount of its increased money assets in interest-bearing savings accounts than in non-interest-earning checking accounts. This resulted in an artificially slower growth rate for the measure of money which excludes savings accounts, a slowing that helps explain the downward trend in the M_1 measure relative to the M_2 measure which is shown on the chart. Since the M_2 measure in essence, is, less influenced by the prohibition of interest on checking accounts, it shows a much more stable velocity pattern over the entire period.

The only time that a rise in money (M_2) per unit of real output does not adequately explain inflation is during and after World War II. During the war, prices did not rise as much as might have been anticipated from the substantial increase in the money supply. Essentially, two factors accounted for this surprising result. First, price controls were in effect during World War II. When the controls were dismantled after 1945, the price level spurted, and as the chart shows, the money supply per unit of output fell. Second, the velocity of money declined from 1942 until 1946. There were undoubtedly many reasons for this, but these were intricately tied to the fact that during World War II many previously available consumer durable goods were not being produced. Hence, there were incentives to build up other kinds of assets, especially cash and war bonds. Also, throughout World War II and into the early postwar years, it was widely believed that money would become more valuable, as it had following World War I and during the Great Depression. This expectation was never realized, and after World War II the influence of velocity in explaining inflation was substantially reduced.

A different way of viewing the evidence on money and inflation is to observe changes between the two series. Chart 5-4 shows annual rates of change over six-month periods. A six-month period is chosen in order to smooth some of the erratic month-to-month movements in each of these series. Even with this adjustment,

86

Chart 5-4
Money and inflation

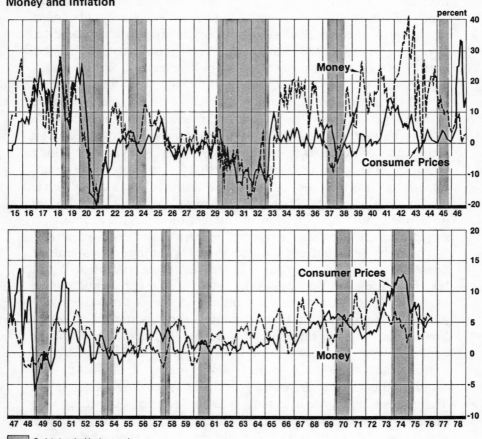

Peak to trough of business cycle
Money is defined as currency plus demand deposits.
Data are six-month annual rates of change plotted at the midpoint of the interval.

Source: Board of Governors of the Federal Reserve System; National Bureau of Economic Research; U.S. Department of Labor, Bureau of Labor Statistics

both series are highly volatile. One factor which should be noted is the relative stability of monetary growth and inflation since the beginning of the 1950s relative to the extreme variations prior to this period. Although inflation rates briefly exceeded 10 percent at the outbreak of the Korean War in 1950, and again in the aftermath of price controls in 1974, for the most part they have been more stable since 1950 than in prior years. For example, during World War I both inflation and the money supply were increasing at about 15 percent to 20 percent a year. Note also the rapidly falling prices in the early 1920s and early 1930s, and the sharp absolute declines in monetary growth during those periods. Also of interest is the period of price stability in the mid-to-late 1920s, when the money supply remained virtually stable.

The widest divergencies occur in the mid-1930s and during World War II and its aftermath. During the former period, monetary growth averaged between 15 percent and 20 percent over a three-year period, while inflation was relatively low. At that time a sharp rise in real output absorbed much of the increase in money. Industrial production rose by almost 18 percent per year during the 1933–36 period, since huge amounts of idle labor and machines were available for use following the severe decline in business activity of the early 1930s. During World War II a similar rise in output occurred from 1939 to 1944, absorbing much of the increase in money. Rationing and a strict system of price controls also contributed to the enormous gap between the reported rates of inflation and the explosive monetary growth that occurred at this time. Although the relationship is far from perfect, in all other instances a fairly close and consistent relation exists between major changes in money growth and changes in inflation.

The chicken or the egg—Which came first? A close relationship between money and inflation does not necessarily mean that money causes inflation. Some observers have argued that inflationary conditions determine the amount of monetary growth. And, as we saw in Chapter 2, to some extent the money supply can be influenced by business conditions and inflation. During a period of hectic business activity and sharply rising prices, the monetary authorities may be increasing the money supply to accommodate a greater demand for it. The main question is not whether business activity and inflation influence the money supply—they do. Rather, the key question is: Which factor initiates changes in the other?

One way to help resolve this "chicken-egg" dilemma is to observe situations in which changes in the money supply are clearly independent of changes in inflation.[2] Such situations

---

[2] This approach and the following examples are used in Milton Friedman and Anna Schwartz, *A Monetary History of the United States, 1867-1960* (Princeton, N.J.: Princeton University Press, 1963), pp. 686-95.

would provide evidence that inflation did not cause the money supply to change, and would thereby reinforce the possibility that the relationship is the other way around. This was the case during at least three major inflationary periods in the United States. First, in the period from 1897 to 1914 the money supply expanded rapidly as a result of substantial discoveries of gold in South Africa, Alaska, and Colorado. In the United States, the gold stock began to increase substantially in 1897, and had more than tripled by 1914.[3] Since the money supply was directly backed by gold during these years, it is clear that the increase in monetary growth was primarily the result of the worldwide pickup in gold production, and not of business conditions or inflation.

Similar examples of largely independent monetary expansions occurred during the inflation accompanying both world wars. In the early stages of these conflicts, gold flowed into the United States as the belligerent nations purchased war materials. In both instances the rise in the U.S. gold stock accounted for virtually all of the rise in the money supply. Once the United States became directly involved in the wars, the Federal Reserve System purchased the bulk of the government's debt, and thus engineered an increase in the stock of money. During the latter stages of each war, the rise in the money supply was almost entirely the result of these purchases of government debt. Business activity, confidence, and bank lending policies played an insignificant role in the sharp increases in the money supply.[4] These three episodes provide convincing evidence that money has been and can be an independent factor in initiating inflationary developments.

A second test for independence is to analyze the timing between changes in money and changes in prices. In Chart 5-5 each observation shows changes in the money supply for the previous two years (at a yearly rate) plotted at the same point as the inflation rate for the coming year. Although that sounds complicated, all it involves is taking the growth in the money supply for the previous two years and comparing this rate to the inflation rate for the next year. The relationship is presented in this way to allow for the time lag between changes in the money supply and the impact of those changes on prices. This arrangement has the further advan-

---

[3] Ibid., p. 137.
[4] Ibid., p. 687.

Chart 5–5
Forecasting inflation with money

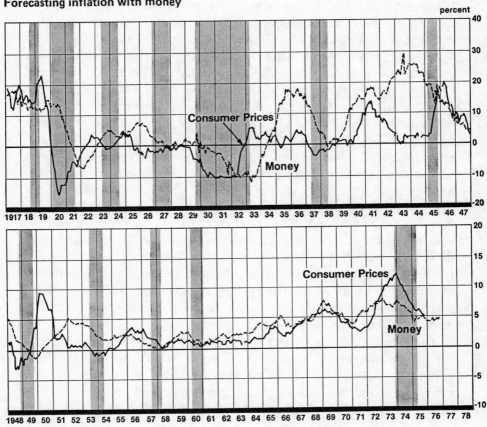

Peak to trough of business cycle
Money data, defined as currency plus demand deposits, are two-year seasonally adjusted annual rates of change plotted at the end of the second year.
Consumer price data are one-year rates of change plotted at the beginning of the year.
Source: Board of Governors of the Federal Reserve System; National Bureau of Economic Research; U.S. Department of Labor,
Bureau of Labor Statistics

tage of providing a guide to forecasting inflation for the coming
year. The distance between the two lines at any time represents
the error that would have been made if one had forecast inflation
for the coming year on the basis of the growth in money over the
previous two years.

Some of the largest errors that result from using this procedure
would have occurred during the mid- and late 1930s and the early
1940s, when the huge increases in money were met with substan-

tial gains in real output because of the availability of unemployed labor and machines. Other substantial errors in forecasting inflation would have occurred during periods when monetary growth changed very dramatically, for example, in 1920-21, 1930-31, 1933, and 1950. During these periods, the substantial change in inflation and money occurred at approximately the same time (see Chart 5-4), and the use of a two-year average for money growth does not allow for this quick response. In 1950, when the inflation rate greatly exceeded the increase in money, prices appeared to be influenced largely by psychological factors, such as a fear of shortages associated with the outbreak of the Korean War, rather than monetary factors. For most of the remaining periods, there is an extremely close relationship between the rate of inflation and previous monetary growth. Use of this relationship during the past 25 years would have led to inflation forecasts for the upcoming year that were often within 2 percentage points of the actual rate. Over this period the largest errors would have occurred if the forecaster had not adjusted the inflation forecast for the impact of price controls, which held prices down in 1971-72, and the catch-up inflation in 1973-74, which occurred when the controls were removed.

The relationship between money and inflation is also evident in foreign economies. As is shown in Chapter 7, by simply taking the growth in the money supply of many foreign economies over a two-year period, an individual can often get a fairly accurate indication of the inflationary trend for the subsequent year.

CAN WE TRADE MORE INFLATION FOR LESS UNEMPLOYMENT?

Until recently, it was popular to argue that if a nation were willing to accept a little more inflation, it could lower its unemployment and reduce the wastage of resources, thereby improving everyone's standard of living. Widespread unemployment is an economic waste for the nation as a whole and carries with it the inevitable personal costs that must be borne by the unemployed. Therefore, a change in the economic environment which permanently lowers the level of unemployment also reduces wasted resources and increases real output. Furthermore, many individuals are willing to settle for a little more inflation in order to achieve a reduction in unemployment, rather than have stable prices at a higher level of unemployment. This is especially true for those currently among the unemployed. Not only is the argument for substituting inflation for unemployment attractive from a humanitarian point of view, but there has also been serious academic research which appeared to substantiate the validity of such a trade-off.

In 1958 Professor A. W. Phillips, an English economist, published an article suggesting that for the United Kingdom there had indeed been a trade-off.[5] Phillips measured inflation in terms of wage rates and concluded that the periods of higher inflation were accompanied by lower levels of unemployment, while higher levels of unemployment existed when inflation was lower.

Although Professor Phillips' argument was very persuasive when it was first presented, it has become much less convincing in light of recent developments. During the late 1960s and early 1970s many countries suffered from both accelerating inflation and high unemployment. Why doesn't this potentially attractive trade-off between a little more inflation and a little less unemployment hold true?

Speaking from experience: Short run versus long run

Actually, there usually is a trade-off between more inflation and less unemployment, but only for a relatively short period of one to three years. There is no permanent trade-off! As is typical of many arguments in economics, a viewpoint may be correct for a limited time span but completely wrong over a longer period. This should have been apparent from Professor Phillips' own figures, which show that for the United Kingdom an unemployment rate in the vicinity of 2 percent was consistent with falling wage rates in 1875, and with wage increases of 2 percent in 1913, 7 percent in 1952, and over 28 percent in 1919.[6]

---

[5] A. W. Phillips, "The Relation between Unemployment and the Rate of Change of Money Wage Rates in the United Kingdom, 1861-1957," in *Readings in Macroeconomics*, ed. by M. G. Mueller (New York: Holt, Rinehart and Winston, Inc., 1966), pp. 245-56.

[6] Ibid., pp. 248-53.

The existence of a trade-off between inflation and unemployment over even a limited time period is dependent on the premise that the public can be temporarily fooled about the rate of inflation. As we have seen, it takes about two years for an economy's inflation rate to adjust to a more rapid increase in the money supply. This delayed adjustment has a significant effect on employment. In the labor market there exists a real wage rate which equates the number of workers whom business would like to hire with the number of qualified workers who are willing to work for the going real wage. When the number of workers who are willing to accept the prevailing real wage is the same as the number whom businesses actually employ at that wage, the unemployment rate is at its "natural" or "market" rate. There are strong economic forces which tend to push unemployment toward this natural rate. If the unemployment rate happens to be higher than the natural rate, this means that there are not enough workers to satisfy the demand for output at the going wage rate. Faced with this situation, businesses will raise the real wage rate to encourage more workers to take jobs, and the unemployment rate will fall back toward the natural rate. In contrast, if the actual unemployment rate is lower than the natural level, this indicates that there are too many workers employed at the going real wage, and therefore that wages must be reduced in order to discourage some of those workers from offering their services. Whether we like it or not, this is the way a market system operates.

Dissatisfied customers. Very often, labor leaders and politicians are not satisfied that the existing natural unemployment rate is low enough, or they believe that progress toward a natural unemployment rate is too slow. If we observe what often happens in the labor market under these conditions, we can see why the trade-off between unemployment and inflation is only temporary.

Let's start by assuming a simple example in which prices have been stable, and the real wage and unemployment rates are at their natural levels. Let us also assume that the natural unemployment rate is 5 percent, which is higher than the public or the policy-makers want it to be. How can the unemployment rate be lowered? One possibility would be to increase the rate of monetary growth. As previously explained, a rise in the rate of monetary growth would soon lead to an increase in total spending. Faced with a greater demand for their products, businesses would find it desirable to hire more people and produce more goods and services. In order to induce some of the 5 percent unemployed to work, business must raise the real wage. Therefore, since prices tend to adjust very slowly, the initial impact of the increase in the money supply would be to create more demand for goods and services, a higher real wage, and finally, a boost in employment to meet the increased demand. So far, so good. Unemployment has been reduced below its natural level; there is very little inflation to show for the move; and there is a great deal of back-slapping by policymakers who honestly believe that they have succeeded in replacing fundamental economic laws with their own.

Unfortunately, this is only the initial effect; the game is far from over. As we noted at the beginning of Chapter 4, prices will eventually begin to rise, since an increase in money does not permanently increase any factors which contribute to the economy's potential for producing goods and services. Over time, real output is going to remain about the same, regardless of how much money is poured into the economy. Since output cannot be permanently raised by an increase in the money supply, the increase in spending will have to end up in the form of higher prices.

As prices rise, the real wage begins to fall back to its starting point. Those who were hired to increase output are no longer needed, since rising prices tend to reduce the demand for real output and therefore the need for additional workers. In short, when prices begin to rise, powerful economic forces work to push the unemployment rate back up to its natural level, which we assumed to be 5 percent.

If the authorities wanted to maintain unemployment below the natural level somewhat longer, then it would be necessary to increase monetary growth at a faster rate. Once again, this would fool the public by creating incentives that would only temporarily raise the real wage rate. Hence, economic theory suggests that to trade more inflation for less unemployment, we have to continuously speed up the rate of inflation. Moreover, this method will only work as long as the public is continually fooled into believing that the most recent inflation rate will continue in the future. If the public were not fooled, and prices immediately adjusted to the increase in money, then unemployment would not drop below the natural rate at all.[7]

Recent evidence. A good example of the politics of the inflation-unemployment trade-off is the experience of the U.S. economy in the late 1960s and early 1970s. Monetary growth began to speed up in the mid-1960s, as efforts to support the Vietnam War and reduce unemployment governed economic policies. By 1968 the unemployment rate was below 4 percent, but the lagged impact on inflation was becoming apparent. Eventually the voters became more concerned with rising inflation than with unemployment, and monetary growth was curtailed. This brought on the 1970 recession, with the unemployment rate rising to 6 percent.

Although inflation began to slow in 1971, impatience with the amount of easing and with the continued high unemployment rate led to a speedup in monetary growth and the institution of price controls. Initially, the results were favorable. Sales rose, production and employment surged ahead, and by 1973 the unemployment rate had dropped to 5 percent. Then came the lagged effect of rapid monetary growth, but this time it came with a vengeance. Not only did inflation rise to a rate consistent with prior monetary expansion, but it rose even further, completely offsetting the earlier impact of price controls. Although controls may hold the line on prices temporarily, eventually economic forces, not legal forces, will determine the rate of inflation. As Table 5-1 shows, despite a fourfold increase in oil prices, worldwide crop failures, and an extensive system of price controls, the inflation rate over the first half of the 1970s continued to approximate the rate of monetary expansion.

The price explosion in 1973 and 1974 led voters to demand an end to inflation. At this point, the only effective policy for containing inflation was pursued—slower monetary growth. Since the inflation response tends to lag on the downside as well as on the upside, the initial impact of slower monetary growth was a decline in production and employment, bringing on the recession of 1974-

---

[7] For an excellent discussion of the concept of the natural unemployment rate and the Phillips trade-off, see Milton Friedman, "The Role of Monetary Policy," *American Economic Review,* vol. 58, no. 1 (1968), pp. 1-17.

Table 5-1
Money and inflation (annual rates of change)

	Money (percent)	Inflation (percent)
1955-65	2.2	1.7
1965-70	5.1	4.2
1970-75	6.2	6.7

Money is currency plus demand deposits. Inflation is measured by the consumer price index.
Source: Board of Governors of the Federal Reserve System; U.S. Department of Labor, Bureau of Labor Statistics.

75 and an unemployment rate of 9 percent. Taken as a whole, the period in the late 1960s and early 1970s represents one more example of the futility of attempting to trade more inflation for less unemployment. The end result was more inflation, more unemployment, and economic hardship.

Public policies which attempt to reduce unemployment below the natural level by stimulating the economy are doomed to failure. If such policies are checked soon enough, it is likely that a mild recession will be sufficient to undo the damage and restore either price stability or the previous rate of inflation. However, the longer such policies go unchecked, the more difficult and costly it becomes to undo the damage.

What is the natural rate of unemployment?

Having seen the foolishness of using stimulative policies in an attempt to reduce unemployment below the natural rate, the next logical questions are: What is the natural unemployment rate? Is it 3 percent, 4 percent, 5 percent, 6 percent, or higher? Frankly, we don't know. To begin with, it is different for different time periods. It changes with changes in the structure of the labor force, in the ability of unions to raise wages above a free-market level, in the profitability of businesses and the amount of investment stimulated by that profitability, in governmental regulations, and in a host of other ever-changing factors. Careful analyses of the behavior of these factors can help us to monitor shifts in the natural unemployment rate, but we can't know for sure whether our estimate is right until we have experienced that rate for several years and observed the behavior of prices. Investors should be particularly leery of attempts to legislate unemployment targets. Given the nature of the political process, legislation will often focus on what people believe the natural rate should be rather than accepting what it is.

This is not to say that there is something sacred about a natural rate of unemployment. No particular rate is inevitable. The rate can be permanently reduced or increased—not by running the printing presses and turning out more money, but by influencing real factors. One of these key factors appears to be the mobility or turnover of U.S. workers. Unlike the workers in many foreign countries, U.S. workers are not wedded to their jobs, and U.S. businessmen do not usually feel impelled to act as patriarchs. The net result is more freedom for both workers and managers in the United States, and probably more efficiency. Many of us wouldn't want it any other way, but the higher resulting turnover in the labor force tends to raise the U.S. unemployment rate above otherwise comparable foreign rates.[8]

Another factor which tends to raise the natural unemployment rate is unemployment compensation and related aid, which encourage individuals to shop around instead of taking the first available job. Also, the minimum wage laws tend to price low-skilled workers out of beginning jobs and to deprive these workers of valuable on-the-job training which is necessary to develop skills and increase earning potential. The list goes on, but by now it should be apparent that permanently reducing the unemployment rate is not as easy as printing more money. It involves real choices which policymakers often fail to face. If economic policies avoid these real choices and opt instead for increased monetary growth to reduce unemployment below its natural rate, then the investor can be fairly certain that a speedup in inflation lies ahead.

WHAT'S SO BAD ABOUT INFLATION?

At first blush, the answer to this question seems obvious enough. However, as with so many questions concerning eco-

---

[8] Robert J. Flanagan, "The U.S. Phillips Curve and International Unemployment Rate Differentials," *American Economic Review,* vol. 63, no. 1 (1973), pp. 114-31.

nomics, the answer is neither simple nor straightforward. Knowledge of the psychological impact of inflation is virgin territory which economists and sociologists have only recently begun to tread. The obvious negative impact of inflation on those with fixed incomes—retired individuals, pensioners, welfare recipients, and so on—could conceivably be offset by its impact on individuals who benefit from a continuous rise in prices. If those who profit from inflation gain more than those who suffer from it, then redistributing some of the benefits would make everyone better off! Does society as a whole gain or lose from inflation? The answer is important not only for policymakers, but also for investors who have to evaluate the prospects for either very high or very low rates of inflation in future years.

Benefits?

Few, if any, observers argue that inflation is beneficial in and of itself. However, in the late 1960s it was popular for many economists to defend inflationary policies on the ground that the developing inflation was not a particularly high price to pay for the extra production and jobs that tended to accompany inflationary pressures. It was argued that providing continuous pressures to stimulate or "fine-tune" the economy whenever growth appeared to be slowing, would result in a greater output of all goods—consumer items as well as plant and equipment—than would be obtained without those pressures. Since productive capacity would be increased, more jobs would be created in future years, and everyone would be better off.

The key factor in determining the validity of the above reasoning is the time period under consideration. In measuring the potential benefits of inflationary policies, observers should view not only the rise in output and jobs that accompanies the initial stage of such policies, but also the behavior of output during subsequent periods which include the containment of inflation. For example, no one denies that over a short time period, a year or two, inflationary policies can lead to seemingly wondrous events—sales boom, production increases, demand for workers with minimal skills increases, and job security is greater than ever. From the perspective of the unemployed or low-skilled worker whose main objective is getting a job, and for those whose time horizon places a great deal of emphasis on near-term developments, such inflationary policies are desirable since they fulfill an immediate need. Politically, it has proved all too easy to gear economic policies toward meeting short-term objectives. However, to maintain the attractive conditions that accompany the initial thrust of an inflationary policy, greater and greater upward pressure must be brought to bear on prices.

If monetary growth speeds up for awhile and then holds steady, rising inflation causes production and employment to slow down as a greater proportion of total spending goes toward inflation and a smaller proportion goes toward real growth. The only way to avoid this situation is to continually speed up monetary growth, which would lead to a continuous acceleration of inflation and, eventually, an economic collapse. For this reason, evaluations of the possible benefits that might accompany inflation should incorporate the time period necessary to contain or halt the speedup in inflation.

The inclusion of a longer time horizon is reasonable from other viewpoints as well. After all, the long run is made up of a series of short runs that we inevitably live through. At some point, accelerating inflation inevitably has to be contained. As inflation becomes unbearable to more and more individuals, the policies that brought it about will have to be stopped or reversed. The only effective way to do this is to slow the growth in the money supply and thus put a damper on demand. This, in turn, results in rising unemployment and lower production. Once the time horizon is lengthened to include not only the benefits that accompany an initial speedup in inflation but also the difficult period necessary to contain the inflation, the obvious advantages of inflationary policies disappear entirely.

Costs

Although the shift from economic boom to recession represents the most dramatic cost of pursuing overly expansive policies, inflation itself is costly. During a period of inflation, money cannot be held as a store of value without losing some of its purchasing power. As a result, efforts must be made to protect wealth by holding assets in alternative forms. Also, in a period of rising prices, various plans and decisions must be altered in an effort to adjust money income to real values. The resources devoted to these tasks—the time spent by accountants, statisticians, economists, corporate planners, and others—represent the true direct cost of inflation to society. Without inflation, these resources could have been used to produce additional output.

A key problem in developing a scientific approach to economic policy concerns the value of production that is lost because of inflation. This value is probably small if the inflation rate has been minimal or stable for an extended period of time. The higher and more unstable the rate of inflation, the more resources society has to devote to deal with the problem. Prospects for variable rates of inflation increase the risks of long-range financial commitments. This, in turn, raises the true cost of such commitments. As a result, the prospect of highly variable rates of inflation will tend to discourage longer-term commitments to save and invest. It will tend to encourage the purchase of consumer items and to discourage spending on facilities for future production. Unfortunately we have no dollars-and-cents estimates of the actual cost of inflation to an economy in terms of lost output. This cost would vary, depending on how successful the economy is in avoiding distortions. For example, allowing wages, contracts, interest rates, and other financial agreements to adjust automatically to changes in an appropriate price index would help offset some of the redistribution problems associated with a high and variable rate of inflation.

One main problem in isolating the cost of lost production that results from a high rate of inflation is that numerous other factors appear to have far more influence on an economy's growth than does inflation. Table 5-2 shows that there is little direct relationship between a country's average increase in output and its inflation rate. However, as we noted in Chapter 4, there is a strong direct relationship between output growth and the average amount of current income that is plowed back into the formation of productive facilities. To the extent that inflation discourages the formation of productive capital, society as a whole is clearly worse off.

When all is said and done, is inflation really all that bad? From a theoretical viewpoint, there is a cost to society in terms of the

Table 5-2
Inflation and growth in selected countries, 1960-1974 (annual rates of change)

	Real gross national product*	Inflation†
Canada	5.2%	3.8%
Chile	4.0	58.7
France	5.5	5.2
Germany	4.3	3.6
Italy	5.0	5.6
Japan	9.4	7.4
United Kingdom	2.8	5.8
United States	3.6	3.7

*For Chile, Italy, and the United Kingdom, gross domestic product was used.
†Inflation is measured by the consumer price index.
Source: International Monetary Fund; Federal Reserve Bank of St. Louis; U.S. Department of Commerce, Bureau of Economic Analysis; U.S. Department of Labor, Bureau of Labor Statistics.

resources that are used to cope with inflation. From a practical viewpoint, the disruption and higher unemployment that result from containing a speedup in inflation probably more than offset any of the temporary benefits that accompany the early stages of a boom. Nonetheless, in terms of actual experience, it is not at all clear that inflation or inflationary policies have necessarily resulted in a significant net loss of output. Over extended periods of time, real output and productivity have advanced at a fairly constant rate during periods of deflation and stable prices as well as during periods of inflation. The evidence, both from the U.S. experience and that of other countries, suggests that factors other than inflation rates have a far more powerful effect on growth and production than does the performance of the overall price level.

Hyperinflation can lead to a temporary collapse of the economic system, as it did in Germany in the 1920s and in Chile in 1974. However, it is possible to contain extremely rapid rates of inflation with minimum disruption to the economic system, as was witnessed recently in Brazil, where the inflation rate fell from 96 percent a year in 1964 to about 13 percent by 1973, while economic activity continued to boom. All in all, it would appear that even very rapid rates of inflation can be tolerated if an economy makes the appropriate adjustments, such as indexing various contracts and actively stimulating business investment. It can be con-

cluded from the available evidence that at best inflationary policies need not result in a substantial reduction in real output and
that at worst, if the business and financial structure of an economy cannot adapt to substantial changes in the inflation rate, then
the potential cost of inflation may be an economic collapse.

Who wins and who loses?

Although society as a whole does not gain, and might well lose,
from inflation, various groups in society fare differently. Income is
redistributed, and the rise in the general price level changes the
value of various assets. Those who receive the fruits of this redistribution—the winners—do so at the expense of others—the losers.
Anticipating whether inflation will speed up or slow down is only
one part of living with inflation. An equally significant task is
adjusting your financial position so as to line up with the winners
instead of the losers.

In the table below, those whose fortunes are boosted by an
unexpected rise in prices are compared with those who lose out.

Inflation's redistribution of income and wealth

Winners	Losers
Debtors	Creditors
Owners of real assets	Owners of financial assets
Worker with low skills or job mobility	Individuals on fixed incomes
Government tax collectors	Most taxpayers

Debtors gain because they can pay off their debts with dollars that
are worth less than they had anticipated. However, for each debtor
who finds himself in this situation, there is a creditor who is being
repaid in less valuable dollars and is therefore losing out. By definition, during inflation real or tangible assets gain in value relative to
inflated dollars, while financial assets, such as currency, bank
deposits, and other close substitutes for money, lose value.

While the average worker's wage tends to adjust to higher prices,
workers with low skills or high mobility tend to benefit indirectly
from unexpected inflation. The increased demand for goods and
workers means that higher wages will be offered both to already

employed workers and to those who might otherwise have been unemployed. At the same time, individuals with the least mobility who are on fixed incomes will lose out. With a progressive tax structure, inflation pushes more individuals into higher tax brackets, whether or not their real incomes have increased. The beneficiary in this case is the federal government, which ends up with more money to spend.

The problem of deciding on specific investments for inflationary periods is more involved. What assets should be added to or eliminated from a portfolio depends on a number of factors—the nature of the inflation, whether it is speeding up or slowing down, the extent to which it is anticipated, and the investor's aggressiveness or daring. Such factors are best considered after one is familiar with the historical performance of specific assets, a topic which is treated in Chapter 6.

MONITORING INFLATION

As will be seen in Chapter 6, financial gains and losses can be substantial during inflationary periods. While broad shifts in monetary growth are a major force in influencing and anticipating basic swings in inflation, the timing and magnitude of these swings can be influenced significantly by nonmonetary factors. Excess capacity, price controls, speculative price changes, international developments, and other factors can alter the basic inflationary trend— at least for a limited number of years. Since timing is crucial in developing a winning inflation strategy, the investor who wishes to protect his holdings should develop a system for monitoring price movements that will both confirm the occurrence of anticipated changes and spot unexpected influences on price trends.

One useful approach in confirming inflationary movements is to view price developments at various stages of production. For example, prices of basic materials and raw foodstuffs can be considered separately from prices at the intermediate and final stages of production, and these prices, in turn, can be considered apart from the price of the final product. The wholesale and retail prices of the final product can also be examined individually. Prices of crude materials tend to be extremely sensitive to changes in demand. At the intermediate stage of production, the costs of labor and machinery, as well as the wider variety of products, damp the volatility of price movements. Nonetheless, the tendency has been for prices at this stage to move in line with broad changes in the prices of crude materials. Lastly, the prices of final products show the least price sensitivity because labor costs (associated with shipping, retailing, and so on) play a dominant role. Since these costs are fixed by labor agreements, at least in the short run, an abrupt reduction in demand for a final product is more likely to lead to reduced orders for that product than to a sharp reduction in price. Similarly, with so many costs fixed by contract or competition, a significant increase in demand is more apt to cause a surge in new orders and production than a sharp increase in prices.

Unfortunately, the timing of price changes between raw materials and final product prices has provided little, if any, advance notice of price trends. The volatility of sensitive prices is such that many months must pass before the existence of an upward or downward trend can be confirmed.

Another issue in tracking inflation trends is whether or not to include food prices in the data. The problem with food prices is that they have cycles all their own and are highly influenced by such factors as crop production and foreign demand. For example, the continued high rates of inflation in late 1957 and early 1958 and the abrupt slowdown in price increases later in 1958 are attributed in part to rapidly rising and then sharply falling prices for farm products. The slowdown in inflation in late 1966 and early 1967 also appears to have been influenced by a sharp decline in the prices of farm products after almost two years of substantial increases. Since short-term changes in inflation are influenced by what happens in the farm sector, additional insights into inflation during relatively short time intervals of about a year or less can be gained by observing the behavior of food prices separately from that of nonfood prices. However, neither movements in farm prices nor movements in the prices of sensitive commodities have provided any consistently reliable insight into future inflationary developments. For better or worse, there is no magic price index which the investor can use to successfully anticipate future price trends.

FORECASTING INFLATION TRENDS

Month-to-month changes in prices are so erratic that they can often be a misleading guide to the developing inflation rate. We have found that the most useful guide to the future inflation rate is the average monetary growth over the past two years.

As indicated in Chart 5-5, this guide lacks precision. On some occasions it has to be supplemented with information on unemployed resources. For example, if the unemployment rate is high and the economy is recovering from a recession, real growth will tend to increase rapidly and to be accompanied by lower price increases than monetary growth alone would suggest. Observe the relationship between money and inflation in the early 1960s in Chart 5-5 (page 89).

On other occasions, such as wartime periods, the money rule may be highly misleading. However, on the whole it is the single most important guide that we know of for evaluating future inflationary trends. Monitoring price developments can be a useful supplement to confirming an inflation forecast, but the forecast itself is best arrived at by utilizing information on prior monetary growth.

PRICE CONTROLS—CAN WE DECLARE INFLATION ILLEGAL?

Our final comment concerns price controls. Virtually all economists agree that inflation cannot be successfully contained by using controls. The use of price controls has no basis in economic theory, and it has not worked in practice. Many economists who favor price controls realize that they will not contain inflation but believe that such controls will redistribute incomes in a more equitable way. Even so, price controls are a useful out for politicians and monetary authorities who have overstimulated the economy. They can then blame inflation on labor, business, and other causes!

The investor should not be fooled by the implementation of price controls to lower inflation. Once controls have been imposed, it is best to assume that prices would have continued to rise in line with prior monetary growth. In these circumstances, the difference between the reported inflation rate and your estimates represents a potential surge in prices which is likely to occur when the controls are removed. In all likelihood, the price controls will not last. They represent an attempt by legislators to end inflation by declaring it illegal—a good trick if it could be done. What the controls actually do is encourage consumption and discourage production, a combination which leads to shortages. Once the shortages become apparent, the only alternatives to price controls are either a complete, centrally controlled, communistic economy or removal of the controls. When faced with this choice, the people of the United States have consistently chosen to remove the controls.

Up to this point, we have considered those elements of economics that are important to the investor. The nature of money, and the influence of the money supply on the economy and on inflation, can have a significant impact on the value of various investments. Just what that impact is, and how it can affect the returns to different assets, will be taken up in Chapter 6.

6

Money, inflation, investments– Putting it all together

> The actual, private object of the most skilled investment to-day is "to beat the gun," as the Americans so well express it, to outwit the crowd, and to pass the bad, or depreciating, half-crown to the other fellow.
>
> *John Maynard Keynes, 1935*

The preceding chapters were designed to show that changes in the money supply exert a powerful influence on business activity and inflation. This in and of itself is an important reason for investors to place a good deal of emphasis on monetary developments. However, there's an even more important reason to heed such developments. Financial markets are the mechanism through which money impacts the economy. In this sense, the money supply can have a direct impact on the value of investments as well as an indirect impact through its influence on the economy.

This chapter deals primarily with investments and their behavior. The influence of money, both direct and indirect, is of key importance, and is discussed at length. Of course, other factors also affect the behavior of investments, and the role of these factors is also considered. Among the more basic ingredients for a successful investment strategy is knowledge of how various investments have performed in the past. While there is no guarantee that future returns will be the same as historical returns, it is helpful to use past investment returns as a starting point in evaluating future prospects. With this in mind, the first section of this chapter presents a long-term look at the returns to various financial assets, namely stocks, bonds, and commercial paper, as well as the returns to certain real assets, including houses, farmland, gold, and silver. This long-term view is designed to present a broad perspective on the rewards or returns that have accrued to different assets over time. While the long-term performance of various investments is a logical starting point, most investors are concerned with a much shorter time horizon. This is where changes in the money supply are important, and subsequent sections discuss the influence of such changes on the prices of various investments. Finally, the effects of inflation on financial markets and on the value of real assets are considered.

THE INVESTMENT DECISION

Before we review the performance of different investments, some preliminary comments are in order. First, many factors need to be considered when determining the best investment vehicle. One of these factors is the time period over which funds will be committed. Is the investor likely to need some or all of these funds during the upcoming year, during the next 5 years, or not for 20 or 25 years? The longer the funds will be committed, the more important the return becomes, and the less important short-term changes in the asset's value are. For funds which may have to be used in emergencies, short-term swings in value are of the upmost importance since the investor may be forced to cash in securities which have temporarily fallen in value. On the other hand, securities may happen to have risen substantially at the time of conversion. Whichever way it goes, for an asset with substantial price changes, the risk and the potential reward increase as the time interval for holding the asset becomes shorter.

Closely related to the time period and the risk involved in an investment is the liquidity of the asset. Liquidity refers to how readily the asset may be converted into cash without the possibility of a loss in principal. For example, most savings accounts can be withdrawn on demand with no loss in principal or interest. However, the value or market price of securities that earn a fixed income, such as commercial paper or corporate bonds, will change as interest rates change.

Securities which earn a fixed rate of interest for a short time period before maturing are fairly liquid. For example, if you were to purchase one-month commercial paper (an IOU from a corporation) for $1,000, and the interest rate were 6 percent per year throughout the year, you could continually repurchase the monthly commercial paper with little risk of a change in its value (assuming that the corporation were financially healthy). At the end of the year you would have received $60 in interest, and your initial $1,000 would still be intact.

Generally speaking, the longer the period before your security matures and the face value or principal is repaid, the more risk there is that a change in market interest rates will alter the value of your initial $1,000. Notice that even the value of a one-month security can change if you need your funds immediately. For example, if the market interest rate jumps to 12 percent, the day after you have committed $1,000 for one-month commercial paper earning 6 percent per year ($60 a year or $5 a month), you cannot sell your commercial paper for $1,000. The paper you bought will still yield only $5 during that month (that was the agreement), while in the marketplace those wanting to purchase one-month paper now find that they can get paid $10 per month for each $1,000 they commit. Obviously, if you had to sell your commercial paper, which pays only $5, you would have to accept a lower price than the $1,000, (approximately $995 in this example). Hence, as interest rates go up, the market price of an outstanding fixed-income security goes down. By the same token, as market interest rates fall, the price of a fixed-income security which yields a higher return is increased.

In the case of one-month securities, changes in interest rates would have to be substantial before there is any appreciable change in the price, since the investor will soon be able to cash in the security for his initial $1,000. However, the longer the time period before maturity, the greater the impact even a small change in the interest rate will have on the price of a security. For example, if you were to purchase a corporate bond for $1,000 which promised to pay 6 percent per year for the next 20 years, and the following day the market rate on bonds of similar quality rose to

8 percent, your bond would have fallen in value to about $800. You would have lost $200 in one day! This is because no one (other than a beneficent uncle) will give you $1,000 for a security yielding $60 a year for the next 20 years when one of comparable quality yielding $80 a year can be obtained for the same price. Hence, as interest rates change, the market value of outstanding bonds will also change.

It should be apparent that certain assets, such as short-term commercial paper, can be readily sold for cash without fear of a sharp reduction in their value. Such assets are said to be highly liquid. Fixed-income securities of a longer-term duration, such as corporate bonds, tend to be less liquid since changes in interest rates could change their value significantly. As a rule, stocks are even less liquid than fixed-income securities, owing to the substantial changes in value which occur from year to year.

Unless there are special circumstances, we would anticipate that the greater the volatility or risk associated with a particular asset, the greater potential return it will yield. If similar returns were expected for assets with different risks, then investors would all attempt to buy the asset with the lower risk and to avoid the one with the higher risk. However, this very action would bid up the price and lower the return on the asset with the lower risk while lowering the price and increasing the return on the asset with the greater risk. Hence, before even looking at the evidence, we would anticipate that over time a relatively secure investment in short-term fixed-income securities would yield the lowest return, that bonds would be more volatile and hence yield a higher return, and that stocks with their extreme volatility would yield the highest return.

But what type of returns are we talking about? How much of a difference is there likely to be in the returns for stocks relative to those for bonds or some other asset? The question of expected return is extremely difficult to answer; it depends on many different factors. As a starting point it is helpful to look at the historical returns to various assets over an extended period of time.

A LONG-TERM PERSPECTIVE

If today's investor were able to turn the clock back 50 years or even 100 years and were given a choice among a broad category of investments, where should he put his funds? Should he purchase stocks, bonds, short-term fixed-income securities, real estate, or precious metals? Unfortunately, the question is not easy to answer precisely, even though the period is over. The difficulty is compounded by a number of problems, one of which involves the data.[1] Generally speaking, the information on prices and on returns to financial assets is available over a longer time period and is far more reliable than the information on real assets, such as real estate. For this reason it is useful to start by considering investments in financial assets before turning to investments in real assets.

The performance of financial assets

Three groups of financial assets were chosen for analysis: (1) short-term fixed-income securities represented by commercial paper, (2) long-term fixed-income securities in the form of high-grade corporate bonds, and (3) equities or common stocks. In measuring the performance of these assets, total returns were considered. These include not only the change in market price, if any, associated with the asset from one year to another, but also the income it earned in the form of interest or dividends. As a result, the difference in values between any particular years represents the total gain or loss from holding that asset during those years. For example, at the end of 1975 an investment in common stocks was worth 37 percent more than at the end of 1974. This means that $1,000 invested in a representative group of stocks at the end of 1974 would have been worth $1,370 by the end of 1975 as a result of the change in stock prices plus dividend payments. All changes in market values exclude taxes and transactions costs, and assume reinvestment of income. Chart 6-1 shows the returns to financial assets as well as the change in the cost of living since 1871.[2]

---

[1] In reviewing various studies on returns to investments, we found that it was often difficult, if not downright impossible, to get consistent information on investment returns for extended periods of time. As a result, the information on prices and returns referred to in this section was compiled by the authors. A description of the data, original sources, assumptions, shortcomings, and methodology, as well as the series themselves, is presented in the Data Appendix.

[2] Chart 6-1 is plotted on a semilogarithmic or ratio scale where equal percentage changes are represented by equal lengths on the axis. For example, 20 to 40 and 40 to 80 are both 100 percent increases; therefore, the distances between 20 and 40 and between 40 and 80 are the same. A straight line on this chart indicates a constant percentage change over time. The key on the left side of the chart shows the inclination or slope of a line consistent with various percentage returns. By using this key as a guide, it is possible

Chart 6-1
Return to financial assets

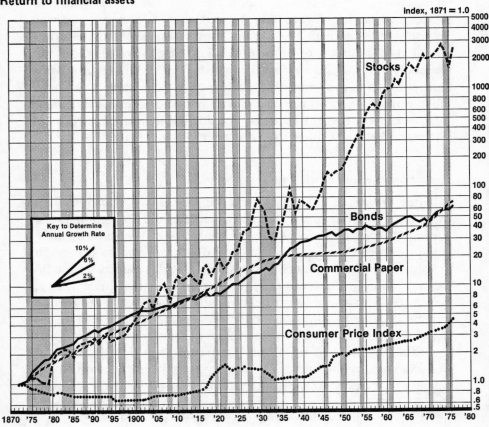

Peak to trough of business cycle
All data are end of period figures.
Source: Data Appendix

Long-term returns. For the 104 years between 1871 and 1975, common stocks have clearly given the highest return. At 7.8 percent, the yearly compound return to stocks was approximately twice that of the other financial assets. Surprisingly, the returns to

to determine the approximate returns to the various assets for different time periods. To estimate the average annual percentage return for stocks during a certain period, approximate the slope of the line for stock returns during the period with a ruler, and then attempt to match this slope to the slope of a line in the key. If the slope of the stock return line is the same as the slope of the 10 percent line in the key, the average annual percentage return for stocks during that period is approximately 10 percent. If the slope of the stock return line is not as steep as the 10 percent slope, yet not as flat as the 6 percent slope, the average annual percentage return would be approximately 8 percent.

bonds and six-month commercial paper were similar, with commercial paper actually producing a higher compound return of 4.2 percent per year, versus 4.1 percent for bonds, over the 104-year period. We argued above that bonds represent a greater risk than do short-term securities, and hence should yield a higher return to reflect that risk. Actually, this was the case from 1872 to 1900, and again from 1920 to about 1950, when investments in bonds outperformed those in commercial paper. However, in the latter part of the 1800s and during the 1920s and early 1930s, consumer prices were either stable or falling, while during the 1940s government policies were geared toward keeping interest rates low. For all other periods, which to one degree or another were characterized by inflation and during which interest rates tended to rise, bonds proved to be a relatively poor investment.

Despite the extended time period covered, annual rates of return can often be unduly influenced by the values in the beginning and ending period. The influence of the starting and ending values on the growth rate can be minimized by a statistical procedure known as the least squares growth rate. Using this procedure gives an annual compound return of 8.2 percent for stocks, 3.7 percent for commercial paper, and 3.9 percent for bonds over the entire 104-year period. Measured on the same basis, the annual compound rate of inflation was 1.5 percent over the entire period. Even with this adjustment, the returns to bonds are roughly the same as the returns to short-term securities.

Volatility. The data show that investments in the various financial assets behaved as anticipated with respect to volatility — commercial paper was the least volatile, with stocks on the other end of the scale. Since interest rates were positive during the entire period, an investment in commercial paper inevitably increased from year to year. Regardless of the year chosen, an investor could always have increased his principal by purchasing commercial paper. An investment in corporate bonds would have been less certain. In one out of every six years, an investment in high-grade corporate bonds would have declined in value, but the average yearly decline amounted to only 2½ percent, while the average increase was 5½ percent. For stocks, a loss occurred one out of every three years, and the average yearly loss amounted to a substantial 12½ percent, while the average yearly increase was a whopping 19½ percent.

Why have bonds performed so poorly? In view of the risks associated with a bond portfolio, the returns to bonds have been relatively low. One reason for this poor performance may be our insistence on showing the market value of a bond portfolio for each year. It might be argued that bonds are bought for income and are generally held to maturity so that it isn't fair to give their market value year by year. An alternative approach would be to compare the average interest rates paid on short-term securities with the average interest rates paid on long-term bonds for the entire period. In this case we are not dealing with the market value of the bond holdings at any particular time, but are assuming that bonds are held to maturity. This change in assumptions has little effect on the returns to either six-month commercial paper, whose interest rates averaged 4.2 percent, over the 104-year period, or to bonds, whose interest rates also averaged 4.2 percent.

Another reason that might explain the relatively low return to bonds is that for most of the 104-year period, stocks were not viewed as a "prudent" investment. Bonds were the main vehicle for investments by pension funds, trusts, and insurance companies. This competition for bonds would be expected to lower the return. Also, from the point of view of an insurance company or a pension fund which has fixed obligations for an extended period of time, the purchase of bonds for the purpose of meeting those obligations might represent less of a risk than would continually purchasing short-term securities at the market rate.

Finally, the general trend toward rising interest rates between 1900 and 1920, and again between 1950 and 1975, may not have been sufficiently anticipated by bond investors, thus contributing to a lower market return than might have been expected. Whatever the reasons, for a little over a century the returns to commercial paper have been about the same as either the holding period or the market-valued returns to bonds. Over the same period, the average annual return to common stocks was about twice that earned from fixed-income securities.

Why have stocks done so well? The 8.2 percent a year return for an investment in stocks represents twice the return that would have been earned on average from either bonds or commercial paper. Had $100 been invested in the stocks included in the Standard and Poor's (S & P) composite stock price index in December 1871 and all dividends reinvested, and had the proportion of stocks remained the same as that of the index, the initial $100 investment would have been worth about $254,500 in December 1975.[3] This compares very favorably to the returns on $100 continually reinvested in six-month commercial paper, which would have been worth about $6,900 in December 1975, or to the returns on $100 invested in high-grade corporate bonds, whose total value in December 1975 would have been about $6,400. The absolute dollar values are not very meaningful except to highlight the effects of compound rates of return. Even so, the difference between an average yearly return of 7 percent or 8 percent and one of 4 percent is substantial, and raises the question of why stocks have performed so well relative to fixed-income securities.

One reason has already been mentioned—stocks are risky. On average, at the end of one out of every three years during the past century the investor would have found that his assets in stocks were worth less than they had been at the end of the previous year. In many years there was a considerable decline in value. Risk alone, however, is not a sufficient reason for a superior return. The key to the substantial returns to stocks over this extended period is profits!

Long-term economic growth and business expansion characterized the bulk of the period considered, and the fruits of this expansion were shared by workers and by those who supplied the funds for creating businesses. The performance of the stock market over an extended period of time reflects the return to business

---

[3] This overstates the case for stocks for at least two reasons. First, the transactions costs of maintaining the S&P index could cost an additional fraction of a percent a year, but more important, there appears to be a selection bias present in choosing stocks from the S&P. The data used for stock market returns are for stocks included in the Standard and Poor's composite stock price index. In order to determine how the use of this index may have biased the results, we compared our data to the returns to all common stocks presented in the extensive Fisher-Lorie analysis whenever overlapping data were available. The comparison shows that the returns presented in our analysis are approximately 1 percent per year higher than those reported in the Fisher-Lorie study. Part of this difference is no doubt attributable to an allowance for transactions costs, while some may be due to an upward bias in the S&P index as compared to an index of all common stocks. See Lawrence Fisher and James H. Lorie, "Rates of Return on Investments in Common Stocks," *Journal of Business*, vol. 37 (January 1964), pp. 1-21; "Rates of Return on Investments in Common Stock: The Year-by-Year Record, 1926-65," *Journal of Business*, vol. 41 (July 1968), pp. 291-316; "Some Studies of Variability of Returns on Investments in Common Stocks," *Journal of Business*, vol. 43 (April 1970), pp. 99-134.

Chart 6–2
Stock prices and profits

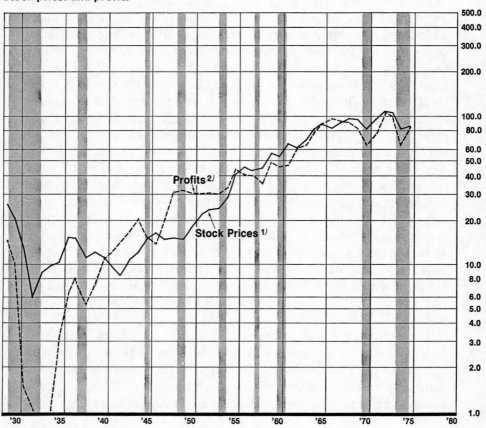

■ Peak to trough of business cycle

1/ Standard & Poor's composite stock price index, 1941-1943=10.
2/ After-tax corporate profits excluding inventory profits and valuing depreciation at replacement cost. (Multiplied profits by the mean of the price/earnings ratio from 1940 to 1975)

Source: U.S. Department of Commerce, Bureau of Economic Analysis; Standard & Poor's Corporation

in the form of profits or earnings. After all, the only reason for owning stocks is the expectation that, given an allowance for risk, the return from future profits will be greater than the return from any other investment. The greater the increase in profits, the more valuable stocks become. When economic expansion and profits become depressed, as occurred in the early 1930s, and again in the late 1960s and early 1970s, stock prices will be depressed. (The profit situation during this latter period is discussed below in the section on inflation and financial assets. See pages 131–32.)

The relationship between stock prices and profits is shown in Chart 6–2. Although occasionally stock prices have deviated considerably from trends in profits, over an extended period of time the growth rates of stock prices and profits tend to be very similar. This supports the view that profits are the major determinant of the rapidity with which stock prices are likely to increase.

The performance of real assets

It is often useful to distinguish "real" or tangible assets, such as real estate and precious metals, from financial assets. From an investor's viewpoint, the most useful data would be the total returns over time to an apartment building, an office building, or some other commercially feasible enterprise. Unfortunately, we were unable to obtain any data which would give even a rough measure of such returns. As an alternative, we attempted to measure the total returns to investments in a single-family house and in farmland. Neither of these items is normally considered an investment vehicle, but each is closely associated with the value of property.[4]

As with stocks and bonds, the total investment return from a house, farmland, or property in general has two components—the change in the price of the asset over time and the income earned from the asset while it is held. Even if an individual owns his own home, a rental return associated with that ownership is considered income. The rental return is an allowance for income from the house after all expenses—taxes, insurance, operating costs, and depreciation—have been paid. Of course, property may have a negative income in the sense that it may not be rented for a positive return after allowance has been made for all expenses. While much of the property purchased for speculative purposes falls into this category, the data included in our study indicate that the rental income from an average house or an average acre of farm-

---

[4] Unfortunately, there are significant limitations in the available data which should be recognized. The reader who is particularly interested in our approach to measuring the returns to housing and farmland is urged to read the Data Appendix. Those who wish to use or refer to the data are required to read the appendix.

land is usually positive. For both an average house and an average acre of farmland, rental income has averaged about 3 percent per year.

Two warnings should be given at this time with regard to returns to property. First, it may be difficult to find the "average" house or the "average" acre of farmland. Just as individual common stocks often diverge from the overall average, so too do particular houses or farmland often vary considerably from the national average. Although an investor in financial assets can often diversify his holdings to approximate an average portfolio, this is far more difficult to accomplish with investments in property. Second, in calculating returns, we have assumed that the rental income is earned each year. To the extent that a house or farmland is not occupied or worked for a particular period, our figures overstate the actual returns.

Other real assets, such as precious metals, diamonds, commodities, and so on, do not earn a rental income. (In fact, there are usually costs associated with holding such assets.) Hence, the returns to these assets must be measured entirely in terms of changes in their price. Unfortunately, we were unable to obtain historical prices for diamonds or other precious stones, and were able to examine only the returns to gold and silver. Any historical analysis of the returns to these metals is hampered by the extensive governmental control of their prices for most of the period.

Long-term returns. Several different starting points have been used to indicate long-term returns to real assets. The longest period, 1890 to 1975, shows an average yearly return to housing of almost 7 percent, while the average return to both silver and gold over this period was only 1 percent per year. Since prices rose an average 2 percent per year over this period, housing represents the only profitable investment in real assets, with a return after inflation of almost 5 percent per year. Beginning in 1912, information on farmland is available. This shows a total return averaging 1 percentage point per year less than housing. As of 1929, the information on rental income to housing becomes more reliable. Interestingly enough, the returns to housing after inflation remain in the vicinity of 5 percent per year throughout each of the long-term periods selected. Comparisons since 1929 show a greater total return to farmland than to housing. However, the returns to farmland were greatly influenced by the depressed conditions of farm income in the 1920s and early 1930s and by the subsequent recovery.

Volatility. It is far more difficult to evaluate the volatility of real assets than that of financial assets. For example, the agricultural depression in the 1920s and early 1930s resulted in negative returns to farmland for 13 consecutive years. In all other years since 1912, the returns to farmland have been positive. Part of the problem with farming in the 1920s was a boom in productivity which led to an overabundance of output and extremely low prices for farm products. This particular problem highlights an inherent risk—and opportunity—associated with an investment in a particular real asset, namely, that the effect of factors unique to that asset can have an enormous impact on returns. For this reason, the historical volatility of real assets can be a misleading guide to their potential volatility in the future.

A recent example of this point was the behavior of gold prices, which soared dramatically in the early 1970s after the United States had officially abandoned its commitment to exchange gold for U.S. dollars held by foreign central banks. This potential for developments that are unique to a particular real asset plays a large role in increasing both the prospective risks—and rewards—associated with that asset.

Returns to housing have behaved more reliably than have returns to the other real assets that were analyzed. Housing returns have shown substantial declines in only 2 of the past 85 years. These declines, which averaged 14 percent, were associated with the severe recessions of 1921 and 1931. Since 1933, the returns to housing have been positive every year.

Despite the warning noted above, it is interesting to look at the average volatility that has been observed for returns to real assets. Housing is clearly the least volatile, with returns declining on average in only one out of 12 years. The average decline has been 5 percent per year, compared to an average increase of 8 percent per year. Returns to farmland declined on average one out of every five years, with the average decline amounting to 8 percent. The average of all yearly increases in farm returns has been 11 percent.

Silver prices fell on average in half of the years studied, with an average decline of 8 percent per year and an average increase of 13 percent per year.

A comparison

Table 6–1 shows the returns to various assets over selected long-term periods. Stocks consistently outperform all other investment vehicles; however, returns to housing or farmland often run a close second. Bonds or commercial paper have a lively battle going for fourth and fifth place, with each showing a return above the cost of living when the longer time periods are used. For these periods, gold and silver tend to show the worst returns.

Table 6–1
Long-term returns to alternative assets (log linear least squares annual growth rates)

	Consumer price index	Housing	Farmland	Gold	Silver	Commercial paper	Bonds	Stocks
1890-1975	2.0%	6.8%	n.a.	1.3%	1.1%	3.3%	3.6%	8.8%
1912-1975	2.1	7.0	6.0%	1.5	2.1	2.7	3.5	9.9
1929-1975	2.9	7.8	9.4	1.9	4.6	2.5	2.6	11.2

n.a.—not available.
Source: See Data Appendix.

While long-term trends provide useful insights into the potential rewards from various investments, most investors are concerned with shorter-term swings in the value of their assets. Short-term swings in asset values are significantly influenced by changes in the money supply. It is to this influence that we now turn.

HOW MONEY AFFECTS INVESTMENT VALUES

The nation's money supply can influence the values of investments in several ways. As was noted in previous chapters, interest rates and financial markets represent the mechanism by which changes in money influence changes in the economy. By altering interest rates, changes in money have an immediate and direct influence on the value of financial assets. Moreover, once the effect of a change in money has been transmitted to the economy, the impact on business activity causes changes in the demands for credit, which also influence the prices of financial assets. In this sense, money has a secondary, indirect effect on investment values. Finally, too large an increase in the nation's money supply eventually leads to rapid inflation, which, in turn, influences the value of various investments. The impact of inflation on various assets is considered later in the chapter. At this point we will consider the more direct impact of money on investment values.

Why should money affect investments?

In order to understand how changes in money affect investments, it is helpful to look at the relationships among financial assets, real assets, and money. All assets are related to money, and to some extent all assets are substitutes for one another. As a result, a change in the price of any particular asset affects the prices of all other assets. Some assets are very closely related to money, while others are less closely related. For example, short-term fixed-income securities, such as commercial paper, are very close substitutes for money, since they can be exchanged readily for cash with little fear that their value has changed significantly since the time of purchase. Bonds, which earn a fixed interest rate for an extended period of time, represent an asset which is less of a substitute for money. As noted earlier, an increase in interest rates would significantly lower the market value of a bond which paid a lower rate. Stocks may be viewed as an even more remote substitute for money, but still a substitute. The risks and potential rewards of stocks tend to be greater than those for bonds, and hence a need to convert stocks to money at a particular time may result in a very significant loss.

Within each of these broad categories of financial assets is a spectrum of assets which are close substitutes for one another. For example, fixed-income securities range from 30-day Treasury bills to 30-year bonds, each of which has a substitute which is closer to money and one which is more remote. The same is true for various bonds and stocks. There are even some very high-quality preferred stocks which are closer substitutes for money than are some lower-quality bonds. This continuum of assets extends beyond the realm of financial assets into the realm of tangible or real assets. After all, stockholders can be viewed as owners of a company's real assets, and purchases of a significant portion of stock in a highly speculative venture can be viewed as a close substitute to having purchased the land and equipment needed for that venture.

Nor does the spectrum of assets end here. Investment in such assets as land, or a factory, or an apartment building, can be viewed as a close alternative to the purchase of a house. Whether the house is rented to others or used by the person who bought it makes little difference—it can still be viewed as an alternative to some other asset. Finally, to round out the spectrum, the purchase of a house, which is simply a highly durable good, can be considered a fairly close substitute for the purchase of another slightly less durable good (a $30,000 Rolls Royce?), and so on down the line. At the very end of the goods spectrum, we wind up with something like a cigarette or a piece of candy, an item that in one sense has no substitute which is more remote than money, and is also of no interest to the investor. At the other end of the spectrum, money, the ultimate source of purchasing power, is the only asset which doesn't have a substitute more liquid than money.

The reader is probably wondering where all this is leading. So far, the main idea of this section has been that the prices of all assets are interrelated. As such, each is influenced by changes in the prices of other assets, particularly close substitutes. In this scheme of things, the price of one asset, namely money, is unique. Its price, or value, depends on the prices of all the other assets. As the overall price level moves up, the value or price of money goes down.

When the Federal Reserve acts to increase the money supply, this sets into motion a whole series of changes in the prices for various assets which ends up increasing total spending. If we lived in a world of perfect knowledge and instantaneous adjustments, an increase in the money supply would immediately raise the prices of all other items, and thereby lower the price of money. Obviously, we don't live in such a world. Adjustments to an increase in the money supply do not raise all prices at once. The first price to rise when the money supply is increased is the price of government securities. When the Federal Reserve purchases government securities, it must offer a price for those securities that is higher than the currently prevailing market price.

Raising the price of government securities causes the interest rate to go down.

Hence, the immediate result of an increase in the money supply is to raise the price (lower the interest rate) of government securities. Since the prices of all assets are interrelated, increasing the money supply throws many relationships awry, and the effect on the economic system as a whole has just begun. Those who sold the government securities to the Federal Reserve have no intention of holding their newly acquired money in the form of cash—they would prefer an asset that produces some income. When they look around the marketplace they find that since the price of government securities has gone up, the prices of close substitutes, such as commercial paper and other short-term securities, have become more attractive. When they use the money they received for their government securities to purchase close substitutes, the prices for those substitutes rise (short-term interest rates decline). This process continues throughout the whole range of financial assets because (1) there continues to be an excess amount of money relative to its price, and (2) as the prices of various assets are bid up, the demand for close substitutes, such as bonds and stocks, increases.

Once the financial markets have adjusted to the increase in the money supply, the process continues in the real sector of the economy, first with increases in the demand for highly durable assets, such as houses and cars, and later with increases in the demand for other goods and services. As the impact of more money reaches this stage it has a secondary effect on financial markets. Efforts to provide more goods and services usually involve borrowing funds to support the higher level of activity. At the initial stage of a business cycle, attempts to raise money are concentrated in the short-term market, and the increased supply of short-term debt acts to reduce its price (in other words, to raise short-term interest rates). This is why, although short-term interest rates usually fall when the money supply begins to grow rapidly, once business activity picks up, they tend to rise.

In the end, the increase in money brings about an increase in total spending. The extent to which this increase in spending consists of an increase in goods and services as opposed to higher prices will depend largely on the amount of unutilized resources, such as labor and machines. If there is a large amount of slack in the economy, such as existed in the mid-1930s, an increase in the demand for goods can result in greater output without a rise in prices as unutilized resources are brought into use. If, at the other extreme, the economy is operating all out, with high utilization rates for labor and machinery, there would be little, if any, increase in output, and the increased demand for goods and services would lead primarily to higher prices as individuals bid against one another for a limited amount of output. In either instance, the rise in business activity or prices will absorb the increased supply of money and bring the markets back into balance.

In summary, an increase in the money supply unleashes powerful economic forces which increase the demand for a whole range of assets. In the process, short-term and long-term interest rates initially decline, and stock prices increase. Once the demand for real assets increases, the expansion in business activity increases the demand for credit, and interest rates tend to rise. If the economy has a sufficient amount of unutilized capacity, economic activity and profits will rise. The prices of fixed-income securities initially increase (when interest rates fall) and later decline (as interest rates move back up). The prices of stocks, which increased along with the prices of fixed-income securities, would not be expected to fall back as the economy expands. More often than not, stock prices would continue to increase since the positive impact of rising profits associated with a business expansion often offsets the negative influence of higher interest rates.

Does money really work this way?—The evidence

So much for theory. What evidence exists to show that various prices actually respond to changes in money in this manner? Ideally, if the previous explanation of the influence of money is correct, we would expect a sharp sustained rise in monetary growth to be followed, at least initially, by a rise in the price of fixed-income securities (a decline in interest rates) and by a rise in stock prices. Once total spending is affected and business activity increases, the prices of fixed-income securities would be expected to reverse their rise and begin to decline. Unfortunately, many problems arise when we attempt to observe this relationship.

First, a problem which applies to most of our historical experience is particularly relevant in this instance, namely, the extreme volatility of movements in money. Since at any given time interest rate movements incorporate not only the most recent influence of changes in money, but also the influence of prior changes, it is very difficult to isolate which influence interest rates are responding to. A second, more basic problem is that interest rates are influenced by many factors other than money—credit demands, inflation, and expectations. So long as changes in money move interest rates above or below what they *would otherwise have been,* the effect on the prices of various assets will be as expected. Since we can never know for sure what interest rates would have been without the influence of changes in money, it is difficult, if not impossible, to determine what actual move in interest rates is consistent with changes in money.

Despite these problems it is instructive to view the behavior of various asset prices with respect to money. The relationships are shown in Chart 6–3. The shaded areas represent periods of contracting liquidity—periods when the growth in the money supply tended to contract. Interest rates are plotted on an inverted scale so that their movements on the chart correspond to a rise or a fall in the price of a fixed-income security. Despite the problems noted above, in a substantial number of instances the prices of the various assets increased at the initial stage of an expansion in money and decreased at the start of a sustained contraction.[5]

Although the historical evidence tends to support the previous explanation of how money affects financial assets and the economy, in several important instances factors other than money appear to have had a strong or even dominant influence on interest rates and stock prices. Note that in 1925–26, money growth

---

[5] Further evidence that changes in money produce the type of response discussed in the previous section has been presented by David Mieselman and Thomas Simpson. They have shown that once money affects the economy, its initial impact is on highly durable items—housing, then autos—while its subsequent impact is on less durable goods. See "The Historical Record of Consumption and Monetary Policy," in *Consumer Spending and Monetary Policy: The Linkages,* Monetary Conference Series (Boston: Federal Reserve Bank of Boston, 1971), pp. 229–78.

Chart 6-3
Money and financial asset prices

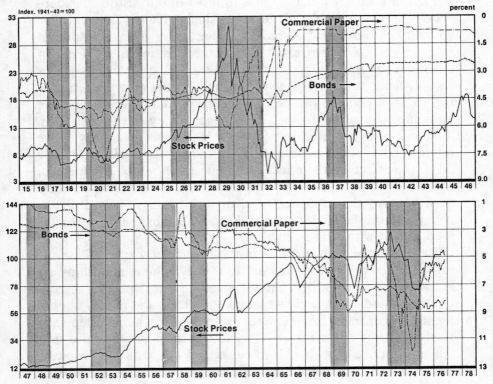

Shaded areas: Contracting liquidity.
Bond yields and commercial paper rates are plotted on an inverted scale; hence, a rise corresponds to a rise in prices.
Source: See Data Appendix.

declined while stock prices were increasing. Also, stock prices rose phenomenally in 1928 and 1929, although monetary growth was declining at the time. More recently, stock prices failed to undergo a sustained rise from the late 1960s to the mid-1970s even though the money supply was growing at the fastest rate since the end of World War II.

These instances serve as a reminder that factors other than money play a key role in determining the value of financial assets. We have already considered one of these factors, profits, which help explain many moves in stock prices that are not directly related to expanding monetary growth. In the next section we deal with the impact of another factor—inflation—on the prices of various assets.

INFLATION AND INVESTMENT RETURNS

In an economy characterized by inflation, financial markets operate in a manner similar to that described on pages 121-24, except that all decisions tend to incorporate an "inflation premium" which is equal to the generally expected rate of inflation. If the expected rate of inflation is 5 percent, then both creditors and debtors recognize that a year from now their money will only be worth about 95 percent of today's value. Creditors would like to be compensated for this loss in value, and debtors, realizing that they will be repaying dollars which are worth less, tend to be willing to pay an additional allowance to offset the expected rate of inflation. If inflation turns out to be different than anticipated, one of the parties has an unexpected gain while the other has an unanticipated loss.

Short-term fixed-income securities

Although over time the expected rate of inflation is incorporated into short-term securities, it is less important in this market than in the stock or bond markets, for two reasons. First, the debtors and creditors are only committing themselves for a short time period, and consequently no windfall gain or loss will result from a change in inflation. Second, those dealing in short-term securities may be doing so to avoid other assets and are therefore likely to accept market rates which differ from their preconceived expectations.

For example, if a creditor believes that inflation in future years will move from 5 percent to 10 percent, and therefore that long-term rates will rise to more than 10 percent, he will be unwilling to commit his funds at a long-term rate of less than 10 percent. However, he might decide to sit tight and loan out his funds for short time periods at very low rates until the market adjusts to his long-term expectations (or until his expectations change).

During periods of weak economic activity the demand for funds is generally weak and the debtor is king of the short-term market. Those supplying funds might have to do so at interest rates which are below even the expected rate of inflation. Once economic activity perks up and the economy is riding high, the creditor is in the driver's seat as debtors find themselves bidding against one another for funds in an effort to meet their commitments. Despite the wide swings that often occur in short-term interest rates, the average rate throughout a business cycle should tend to incorporate an allowance for the expected rate of inflation.

Bond yields

As noted previously, bond prices are extremely sensitive to changes in long-term interest rates. Also, the inflation allowance can be crucial for investments which will pay a fixed dollar return over an extended period of time, such as 20-year bonds. As a result, for bonds the potential gains and losses resulting from the influences of inflation on interest rates can be so large as to dominate movements in these rates. For example, the election of officials who favor rapid monetary growth over officials who desire moderate growth could conceivably change inflationary expectations overnight and bring about a rise in bond yields.

The evidence—Inflation and interest rates

Attempts to show the possible influence of inflation on interest rates run into a major problem. At any given time there is no ideal measure of the inflationary expectations of investors. One way to handle this problem is to assume that inflationary expectations result primarily from past experience. In Chart 6–4 the average inflation rate for the past five years is plotted with interest rates. To the extent that this measure accurately captures investors' expectations of future inflation, it can be viewed as the inflationary premium discussed previously.

It is apparent from the chart that interest rates have tended to move in the direction indicated by previous inflationary experience. However, prior to the past 20 years this adjustment was incredibly slow! The experience up to the end of World War II

Chart 6-4
Interest rates and inflation

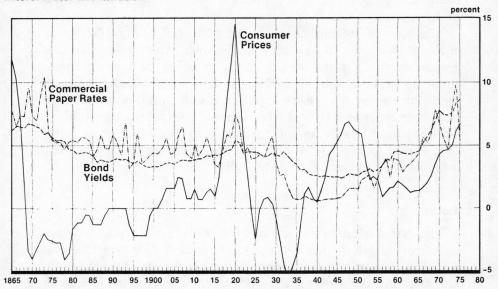

Price data are five-year annual rates of change plotted at the end of the interval.
Source: See Data Appendix.

tends to confirm Irving Fisher's observation that investors were incorporating the inflationary experience of an extremely long period to form their expectations of future rates.[6] While interest rates moved higher following the rapid inflation experienced during the Civil War and World War I, on neither of these occasions did the upward movement come even close to offsetting the increase in prices in the economy. The same is true for periods of deflation. Although interest rates often moved lower during these periods, they never came close to fully adjusting for the behavior of prices in the economy. The evidence suggests that investors seldom believed that recent price experience which differed from that of the preceding few decades would continue to exist in the future. This may have been particularly true of the experience during World War II, when interest rates failed to rise significantly

---

[6] Irving Fisher, *Appreciation and Interest,* American Economic Association (New York: Macmillan Co., 1896), pp. 66-76.

despite an increase in money and inflation. That experience had been preceded by two decades during which prices fell by a total of 20 percent.

The most interesting development in interest rates is the experience of the past 20 years, when interest rates appear to have responded much faster to the changing inflationary environment than had previously been the case. During the 1960s and the early 1970s the prior five year's experience with inflation appears to have been sufficient to lead to substantial changes in interest rates. This apparent change in the formation of expectations indicates that future interest rates may respond much faster to changing inflation than has occurred historically.

Stocks

The effect of inflation on stock prices is more complicated than its effect on other financial assets. The extent to which the total return on stocks will completely incorporate a standard inflationary premium depends on the performance of profits. So long as prices and costs increase in the same proportion to reflect the new rate of inflation, then the increase in profits will also reflect the inflation. If costs rise faster than prices, and profit margins decline, then the total real return to stocks will be lower. This would be true whether profit margins declined due to inflation, lower productivity, or any other reason.

Assuming no change in profit performance, and an economy without inflation, fixed-income securities might earn 2½ percent per year while stocks might earn a total return of 6½ percent. Stocks would be expected to yield a greater return than fixed-income securities as long as the potential for increased profits existed and the risks associated with holding stocks were greater than those associated with holding fixed-income securities. If a 5 percent rate of inflation were to characterize the economy for an extended period of time, fixed-income securities would be expected to adjust to the situation by returning 7½ percent, with five percentage points compensating for inflation. So long as other factors, such as profits and risk, remain unchanged, stockholders should also receive a real return amounting to about four percentage points above that on fixed-income securities. With 5 percent inflation, this would suggest a yearly total return to stocks of 11½ percent.

But shouldn't inflation reduce profits? Actually, there are some technical reasons why inflation may misstate profits. Various accounting practices can lead to illusory "inventory profits" which may deceive businessmen into believing that profits are higher than they actually are. An inventory profit results from purchasing materials at one price and selling the final product at a price which reflects a new and higher cost for those materials. If a company lists as its cost the original, lower price of the materials, then the difference between the original cost of the materials and the current inflated cost of the final product looks like gravy. From the point of view of economic analysis, the assumed gravy should not be viewed as profit since it will all have to be spent to replace the inventory at the new, higher prices. As long as the business is an ongoing concern which must replace its inventory, the "inventory profit" is never realized. Yet, to the extent that these illusory profits are reported, and taxes paid on them, the effect is to make realized profits lower than they would have been without the inflation. Also, inflation tends to raise the replacement value of plant and equipment above the amount that businessmen allow for depreciation. When depreciation expenses are understated, profits appear to be larger—until the time comes to replace the worn-out equipment at new and higher prices.

Although inflation may depress realized profits, it does not have to. Businessmen who recognize the illusoriness of inventory profits can opt for accounting practices which list recent prices—not original prices—of materials as their cost. Furthermore, tax reductions can be legislated to compensate for the higher replacement cost of new plant and equipment. Actually, there is no reason why corporate profits cannot prosper in an inflationary environment as long as businessmen and legislators anticipate the inflation and adjust their policies to cope with it.

By the same token, profits and stock prices can become depressed without the existence of inflation. Low productivity, a lack of economic growth, stringent government regulations, and a host of other factors can adversely affect profit performance.

Inflation, profits, stock prices—The evidence

In recent years the widespread view concerning the impact of inflation on the stock market has taken a 180-degree turn. Prior to the past ten years, stocks were viewed as a hedge against inflation—an investment whose value would rise as inflation increased. However, during the late 1960s and early 1970s, when the stock market underwent its worst period since the Great Depression, and when inflation rose considerably, the poor performance of the market was blamed on inflation. In terms of historical experience, neither of these inflation-oriented explanations is convincing.

There have been three extended periods of rapid inflation in the United States during the 20th century—the two world wars and the late 1960s and early 1970s. In addition, a brief period of rapid inflation, from 1949 to 1951, was associated with the Korean War. The poor performance of stock prices during the most recent inflationary period and a decrease in stock prices at the time of World War I stand in contrast to a rise in stock prices during World War II, and a rapid surge from 1949 to 1951. A moderate inflation rate in the 1950s and the early 1960s was accompanied by a surge in stock prices, but a similar inflationary experience at the start of the century was accompanied by only a moderate advance in stock prices. During the price stability of the 1920s, stock prices soared, yet from 1934 to 1940, when price stability again occurred, stocks gained only slightly. During the two brief periods of deflation experienced in this century stock prices declined, whereas during the extended deflation that existed at the end of the 19th century they showed little movement.

These examples show that there has not been any consistent relationship between inflation and stock prices. Those who look upon inflation as the key to an understanding of movements in stock prices will have to look again. This is not to say that inflation has not been a key factor affecting stock prices, only that its effect has been neither direct nor consistent.

THE INFLATIONARY ENVIRONMENT AND FINANCIAL ASSETS

In order to compare the returns to various financial assets during periods of alternative inflationary pressures, the periods are classified as: (1) deflation, when consumer prices in the economy were generally falling; (2) stability, when prices showed no tendency to either rise or fall; (3) moderate inflation, when consumer prices tended to increase by less than 2 percent per year; and (4) rapid inflation, when consumer prices rose in excess of 5 percent per year. As in previous sections, the returns to financial assets will be considered first. The results are summarized in Table 6-2.

Table 6-2
Inflation and returns to financial assets (end of year, log linear least squares annual growth rates)

	Consumer price index	Commercial paper	Bonds	Stocks
Deflation:				
1871–96	−1.3%	5.3%	6.2%	5.4%
1919–21	−4.4	7.2	6.7	−3.5
1929–32	−8.7	3.3	4.1	−27.8
Price stability:				
1921–29	0.1	4.4	5.2	21.4
1934–40	0.6	0.8	6.2	4.8
Moderate inflation:				
1896–1915	1.2	4.8	2.7	7.6
1951–65	1.4	3.2	2.0	13.9
Rapid inflation:				
1915–19	16.9	4.9	0.4	3.6
1940–47	6.7	0.7	2.3	14.7
1949–51	5.8	1.7	−0.8	26.9
1965–75	5.6	6.7	3.1	3.0
1871–1975	1.5	3.7	3.9	8.2
1950–1975	2.7	4.4	1.9	9.9

Source: See Data Appendix.

Deflation

During the periods when prices were falling, bonds tended to slightly outperform other financial assets, with commercial paper a close second. Since recessions and declining profits tend to be associated with periods of falling prices, stocks tend to perform very poorly in this environment. However, for the period from 1871 to 1896, when the economy expanded in spite of falling prices, the return to stocks averaged 5.4 percent per year. If we allow for an average decline of 1.3 percent per year in consumer prices, it becomes apparent that the return to stocks was approximately 7 percent per year in real terms. While stocks may not yield the best returns, during deflation the returns can still be attractive as long as the economy and profits are expanding.

Price stability and moderate inflation

During the periods of price stability and moderate inflation, stocks usually showed superior returns. Commercial paper outperformed bonds in the 1896–1915 period and the 1951–65 period. However, during the periods of price stability, bonds did better, particularly in the 1934–40 period. During these periods of moderate or stable prices, fixed-income securities earned a positive return after allowing for inflation. The real return to bonds averaged 3.2 percent, while the real return to commercial paper averaged 2.5 percent.

Rapid inflation

During the periods of rapid inflation, stock returns ranged from only 3 percent to 27 percent per year, while bonds tended to produce their worst returns. Returns from bonds never came close to keeping pace with the higher cost of living during the periods of rapid inflation. In real terms, when the effects of inflation have been elimin..ted, the best return from bonds amounted to a *negative* 2.5 percent per year. Returns to commercial paper outperformed bonds in three of the four rapid inflationary periods, but in only the most recent were the returns to commercial paper positive after allowing for the effects of inflation.

In short, the data show that none of the financial assets have performed consistently well during periods of rapid inflation. Stock returns have varied considerably during such periods, indicating that there has been a tendency for factors other than high inflation to dominate stock market performance. Fixed-income securities have tended to perform poorly during these periods, with bonds showing the worst performance and short-term securities doing slightly better.

THE INFLATIONARY ENVIRONMENT
AND REAL ASSETS

As with financial assets, the performance of real assets was viewed in different inflationary settings.[7] By definition, real assets should decline in value during periods of falling prices and increase in value in periods of inflation—this is what inflation is all about.

As Table 6-3 indicates, this basic pattern has occurred. When prices were falling, returns to real assets were almost always negative. In contrast, returns were consistently high during periods of

Table 6-3
Inflation and returns to real assets (annual averages, log linear least squares annual growth rates)

	Consumer price index	Housing	Farmland	Gold	Silver
Deflation					
1890–1899	-1.7%	2.7%	n.a.	*	-6.8%
1920–1922	-8.5	-11.2	-12.1%	*	-18.2
1929–1932	-7.4	-3.9	-12.3	*	-19.8
Price stability					
1922–1929	0.3	4.4	-2.8	*	-3.3
1932–1940	0.8	7.2	3.9	6.3%	1.0
1948–1949	-1.8	0.0	9.3	*	-3.3
Moderate inflation					
1899–1915	1.3	5.7	n.a.	*	-0.5
1951–1965	1.4	5.5	6.7	*	3.0
Rapid inflation					
1915–1920	15.2	21.3	15.5	*	16.3
1940–1948	6.6	12.2	18.5	*	12.1
1950–1951	5.9	10.2	21.7	*	20.5
1965–1975	5.3	11.4	13.0	17.3	11.7
1950–1975	2.6	7.6	8.9	3.9	5.9
1912–1975	2.1	7.0	6.0	1.5	2.1
1890–1975	2.0	6.8	n.a.	1.3	1.1
1871–1975	1.5	n.a.	n.a.	1.0	0.2
1860–1975	1.2	n.a.	n.a.	0.9	-0.1

*Due to government regulation, the U.S. market price of gold did not change during this period.
n.a.—not available.
Source: See Data Appendix.

---

[7] The reader should note that the table is not directly comparable to the previous one on financial assets. The time periods are slightly different to allow for the fact that the time period for financial assets refers to year-end data, while real asset returns are *averages* for the whole year.

rapid inflation. The high returns experienced during inflationary periods suggest that the potential for protecting the value of an investment by moving into real assets may provide an added boost to the value of these assets during such periods.

TIMING AND INVESTMENT RETURNS

Studying the returns to alternative investments under different inflationary assumptions helps to place them in some perspective. However, for many assets there is a difference of night and day between the returns experienced during the initial stages of a price cycle, when inflation is speeding up, and the returns experienced during the later stages of the cycle, when inflation is slowing down. While it appears unlikely at present that the U.S. economy will experience an extended period of falling prices, it's a fairly sure bet that there will be alternating periods of rising and falling inflation over the coming years.

Although the historical evidence seldom reveals precisely the same pattern for various investments, it does reveal some tendencies. For example, in the initial stage of an inflationary period, when business activity and profits tend to rise, stocks tend to outperform all other assets. Bonds tend to be the least attractive financial asset under these conditions, since the higher interest rates which usually accompany the upturn tend to depress bond prices. Shorter-term fixed-income securities, which earn a steady, safe return, have generally outperformed bonds in the initial stages of an inflationary cycle.

In the intermediate stage, performance has been a mixed bag, with stocks often playing a leading role, bonds usually second, and short-term fixed-income securities third. However, at this stage the order is no longer as consistent as it was in the initial stage.

In the final stage of an inflationary cycle, prior to a slowdown or an actual decline in consumer prices, stocks tend to be down substantially, with bonds and short-term securities vying for top honors among the financial assets. So long as the rapid increases in inflation continue, real assets provide a good, consistent hedge against an erosion of principal.

When inflation slows or prices actually decline, fixed-income securities, such as bonds and commercial paper, tend to produce the best returns. Stocks tend to do very poorly in this setting, since the slowing in inflation is often accompanied, at least initially, by a recession and falling profits. Once the economy and profits show signs of recovering, stocks tend to do very well.

SUMMING UP—WHAT THE EVIDENCE SUGGESTS FOR THE FUTURE

The historical evidence on investment performance provides many useful insights for the future. For fixed-income securities, it was shown that returns varied considerably in different inflationary settings. One reason for this extreme variation was the failure of interest rates to respond adequately to changes in inflation. There has been some indication in recent years that interest rates have been responding much more rapidly to changes in inflation than had previously been the case. At 8 percent–9 percent in 1975, the interest rate on bonds had fully adjusted to an expected inflation rate of about 5 percent–6 percent. Once this adjustment has been made, future inflation would have to advance more rapidly than the expected rate for fixed-income securities to perform poorly. On the other hand, an inflation rate below the expected rate would be likely to lead to even lower interest rates and therefore to extraordinary gains for holders of fixed-income securities.

Successful investment in fixed-income securities is likely to hinge on the accuracy of the investor's perception of future inflation. Since inflation is strongly influenced by monetary growth, investors should be able to get a jump on fundamental changes in interest rate levels by closely monitoring monetary growth and its implications for future inflation.

With respect to stock returns, the evidence shows that business activity and profit performance can be far more important than the inflationary environment. For the entire 104-year period, the return to stocks after stripping the effects of inflation has been about 6½ percent. This suggests that with the same type of profit performance and economic considerations which were experienced during this period, investors might expect a similar real rate of return. Hence, if the inflation rate were 5 percent in coming years, investors could expect a total return to stocks of 11½ percent per year.

Since returns to stocks can and do adjust for inflation, individuals should key their efforts toward analyzing corporate profits. From a cyclical viewpoint, current and prospective changes in the money supply can often provide insights into cyclical movements in the economy and therefore in profits. Over longer time periods, profits can be adversely affected by government regulation, price controls, poor productivity, and countless other factors. By closely monitoring these factors and their impact on the environment for profits, an investor should be able to improve the performance of his stock portfolio.

For real assets, the implication of past experience is less persuasive. While we have seen that real assets do well consistently in periods of rapid inflation, would this superior performance continue if inflation were fully anticipated? Unfortunately, we cannot look to historical experience for a guide to the answer. The relatively brief or mild inflations prior to the mid-1960s, combined with a very sluggish response in inflationary expectations, do not provide a good example of the response of real assets after an economy has fully adjusted to a rapid rate of inflation. However, from a theoretical viewpoint we might expect the response to be similar to that of financial assets. Once an economy adjusts to a 5 percent rate of inflation, it is reasonable to assume that the prices of real estate, property, and various other real assets will be bid up in anticipation of future price hikes. The prices of real assets could then be viewed as also incorporating an expected rate of inflation. Should the future inflation rate be less than the expected rate, real assets might lose some of their "inflationary premium," and hence could underperform. Conversely, if future inflation exceeds current expectations, real assets would continue to yield superior returns in future years.

Regardless of the investment under consideration, past experience reaffirms the importance of the money supply and the implications of changes in money for the prices of alternative assets. The investor has to be aware that volatile monetary policies will lead to wide swings in the prices of various investments, and if such policies are continued long enough, to volatile rates of inflation. In such an environment the investor has to remain alert to developing trends if he is to protect the value of his assets. We have discussed the procedures involved in following and interpreting the implications of monetary developments as well as the impact of these developments on investments. One further area should be discussed before we attempt to apply our knowledge toward winning the money game. This is the area of international influences on money and investments, and it is to this topic that we now turn.

7

Does foreign money speak the same language?

The money of a particular country is divided amongst its different provinces by the same rules as the money of the world is divided amongst the different nations of which it is composed.

David Ricardo, 1810

Events which only a decade ago seemed foreign in both time and space now appear to be occurring in our own backyard. Japanese inflation, a German recession, the indebtedness of Zaire—events which appeared to be irrelevant in the mid-1960s—are now followed closely by all who have a serious commitment to manage investments. During the 1950s and the early 1960s, most U.S. investors were content to concentrate their efforts on domestic developments. There was little concern that overseas events could significantly alter a carefully designed investment strategy. As a result of developments in the late 1960s and early 1970s, investor concern has broadened to include worldwide analysis.

The reasons for the switch from a domestic investment approach to an international approach are varied and complex, but a key factor has been the growth in the importance of international trade to the United States. In the mid- to late 1960s, exports accounted for less than 5 percent of U.S. sales. Even a relatively severe recession abroad would have had only a minor impact on business activity in the United States. By the mid-

1970s, however, exports accounted for almost 10 percent of all business activity in the United States. One reason for the sharp expansion in U.S. trade in the early 1970s was the recovery of the European and Japanese economies from wartime destruction. By this time, both had grown enough in size to effectively compete with many U.S. producers. With the recovery of productivity in foreign economies and with relatively low trade barriers, the growing interrelationship in trade gave rise to the rapid growth of multinational companies (companies with business operations in more than one country).

The growing integration in the production of goods and services among various economies has been matched by increased integration of flows in capital markets. Capital flows include any transfer of funds from one country to another. This transfer can be in the form of loans, investments, or even gifts to foreigners. The receipts from these transactions can take the form of foreign stock certificates, bonds, securities, or bank deposits.

Since in terms of volume the United States has long dominated world trade, there is a tendency for firms in other countries to hold dollars or dollar deposits for trade purposes. This preference for dollars has contributed to the development of foreign markets for dollars. The markets in Eurodollars (dollar deposits in European banks) and Eurobonds (dollar-denominated bonds issued in Europe) are the most commonly mentioned examples of this development. In the span of a decade, business activity and capital markets abroad have become highly integrated with those in the United States.

In the late 1960s and early 1970s, movements in interest rates, stock prices, and inflation followed a similar pattern throughout most major economies. Stock prices in various countries tended to perform well until the mid- to late 1960s or the early 1970s (Chart 7-1). Previously, inflation had been relatively low. However, in most countries it rose during the latter 1960s and soared during the first half of the 1970s. Soaring inflation was accompanied by declining stock markets and finally a worldwide recession. As Chart 7-2 indicates, interest rates also followed a similar pattern among the major economies of the world.

The growing interdependence between the U.S. economy and foreign economies in both production and capital flows has raised

Chart 7-1
International stock price movements

index. 1967 = 25

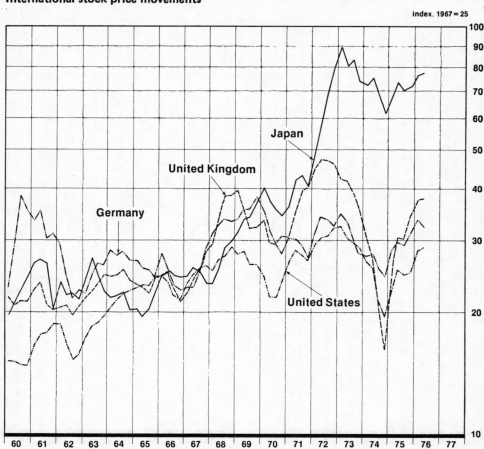

Source: International Monetary Fund.

questions that are crucial to investors. To what extent is inflation an international phenomenon which defies management by an individual country? Since many goods are traded on the world market, where their prices are determined by world supply and demand, aren't the prices of these goods beyond the control of domestic policymakers, even if a country's money supply can be controlled? Furthermore, is it possible to control the money supply of a particular country, given the growing integration of inter-

Chart 7-2
International short-term interest rate comparisons

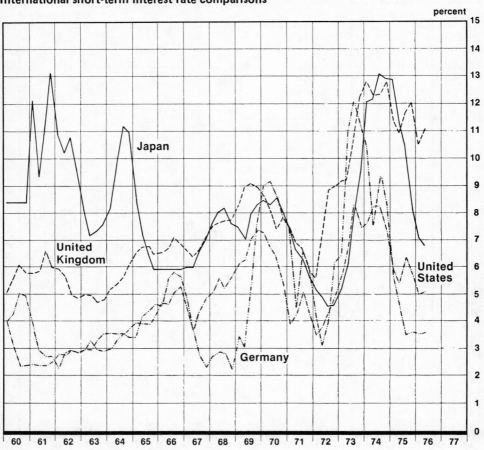

Source: International Monetary Fund.

national capital markets? Will an attempt to slow monetary growth in the United States merely push up interest rates and attract dollars from abroad, thereby preventing the monetary authorities from exercising control? Can the United States avoid inflation and recession if the policies followed by our trading partners produce inflation and recession abroad? If interest rates soar and stock markets plummet in foreign countries, is the United States likely to suffer the same fate? More than ever before, it is important for the U.S. investor to understand the implications of developments abroad for the U.S. economy and, in turn, for his investments.

This chapter is concerned primarily with these issues. Its main objective is to assess the impact that international developments can have on investments. The first step in approaching this objective is to determine the extent to which the monetarist framework that was used to analyze the U.S. economy can be employed to explain broad movements in foreign economies. To do this, changes in the money supply for a number of countries are related to changes in inflation and total spending in much the same way that the data for the United States were analyzed. Relationships similar to that found in the United States are also shown to exist in many foreign economies. Nonetheless, the broad similarities in business activity, inflation, and financial markets among the various countries suggest that the interrelationships among countries may be a key factor in explaining various developments in domestic economies. Consequently, we consider the nature of international economic relationships—the purpose of trade, the meaning of capital flows, and the role of an international monetary system. Next, we analyze the evidence on worldwide inflation and worldwide spending trends in light of interrelationships among nations and capital markets. Finally, we discuss the implications of international factors for economic activity, for inflation, and for investments in particular countries and under alternative monetary systems.

To begin with, let's look at the impact of money.

MONEY, BUSINESS ACTIVITY, INFLATION— THE EVIDENCE FOR FOREIGN ECONOMIES

In earlier chapters we discussed the relationships among the money supply, business activity, and inflation in the United States. We concluded that changes in the money supply had a significant impact on the U.S. economy. With a short lag, monetary changes were followed by changes in total spending; with a longer lag, there was a significant influence on the rate of inflation.

For a number of reasons the relationship between money and the economy may not be as close for foreign economies as for the U.S. economy. First, we might expect that the larger the role of exports in a country's economy, the more that country's business activity would be influenced by conditions among its trading partners. For example, as shown in Chart 7–3, exports account for approximately half of all final sales in the Netherlands. A severe recession among its trading partners would be expected to have a major impact on business activity in the Netherlands, regardless of its own domestic policies. In contrast, U.S. exports have amounted to less than 5 percent of all final sales during most of the past 20 years, and hence the influence of domestic policies would be expected to play a far more significant role in changing U.S. business conditions. Since international trade is more important to

Chart 7–3
Exports as a percentage of total spending

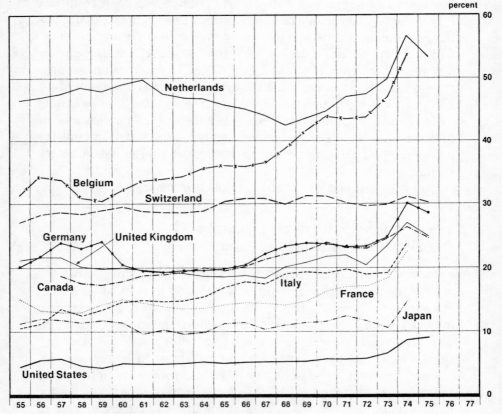

Total spending as measured by gross national product.
Source: International Monetary Fund.

many foreign economies than to the United States, many argue that changes in the prices of imports would have a more significant impact on inflation in those countries. If this is true, the relationship between a country's own money supply and inflation may not be as close for some foreign countries as it is for the United States.

There are other reasons why the relationships established for the United States may not apply to particular foreign countries. In France, the citizens hoard gold, which they sometimes use as money. Changes in such holdings, which are not reported in the money supply of France, may affect the relationship between money and the economy. Also, such problems as national strikes, price controls, and the overall poor quality of foreign data may serve to alter an otherwise good relationship.

Money and total spending

In spite of all the potential problems in relating money to business activity in various countries, the following set of charts shows that a relationship similar to that noted for the United States exists in many other countries. Changes in money are plotted along with changes in business conditions. Annual changes in total spending or GNP are used, since consistent quarterly data are not generally available until the late 1960s or the early 1970s.

It should be noted that it is extremely difficult to get a good relationship by comparing percentage changes, since these changes are far more volatile than the original series. Also, differences in the banking regulations of different countries often mean that some measures of the money supply are more closely related to business activity than are other measures. While these qualifications can be crucial for a specific analysis of the monetary relationships in the nine countries considered, the purpose here is to indicate whether or not any reasonably reliable pattern exists. Consequently, all monetary data presented consist of currency plus demand deposits.

In such countries as Belgium, Canada, West Germany, Japan, the Netherlands, Switzerland, and the United Kingdon, the relationship between changes in money and changes in business activity is fairly consistent. Slower rates of monetary growth are associated with a slower pace of business activity, while faster increases

Chart 7-4A
International: Money and total spending

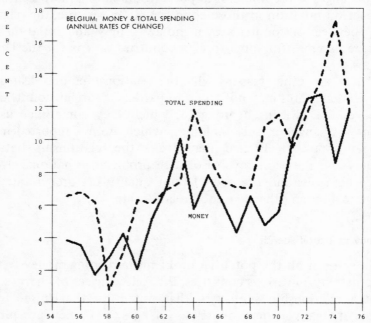

BELGIUM: MONEY & TOTAL SPENDING
(ANNUAL RATES OF CHANGE)

TOTAL SPENDING

MONEY

Money supply data are defined as currency plus demand deposits.
Total spending data are measured by gross national product.
All data are one-year rates of change plotted at the midpoint of the interval.
  Source: Federal Reserve Bank of St. Louis; International Monetary Fund; Harris Trust & Savings Bank.

in the money supply generally correspond to a faster pace of business activity. In Japan, where increases in the money supply from 1957 to 1974 averaged 18 percent per year, the largest in all the countries considered, changes in total spending or GNP averaged 16 percent per year, also the largest. For Italy, the relationship between changes in the money supply and changes in business activity appears to be very bad. Actually, it's much better than is indicated by the chart. For Italy, apparently, a greater change in money is normally required to produce a certain change in spending than is the case for most other countries. If we allowed for this by plotting changes in Italy's business activity on its own axis, the relationship would appear somewhat better. The worst relationship between changes in the money supply and changes in business ac-

Chart 7-4B

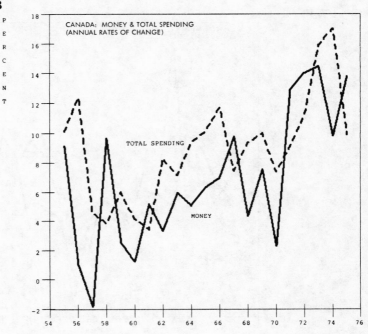

P
E
R
C
E
N
T

CANADA: MONEY & TOTAL SPENDING
(ANNUAL RATES OF CHANGE)

TOTAL SPENDING

MONEY

Chart 7-4C

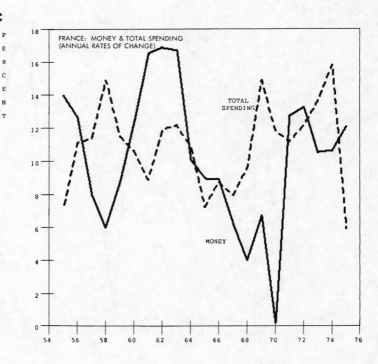

P
E
R
C
E
N
T

FRANCE: MONEY & TOTAL SPENDING
(ANNUAL RATES OF CHANGE)

TOTAL
SPENDING

MONEY

Chart 7-4D

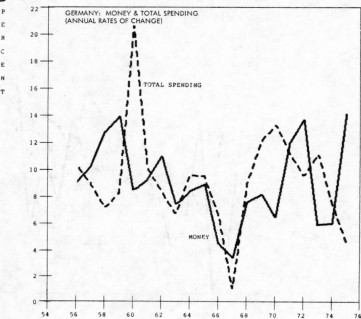

GERMANY: MONEY & TOTAL SPENDING
(ANNUAL RATES OF CHANGE)

TOTAL SPENDING

MONEY

Chart 7-4E

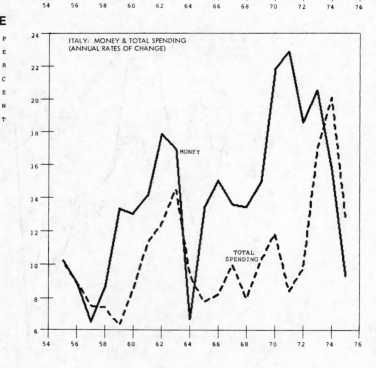

ITALY: MONEY & TOTAL SPENDING
(ANNUAL RATES OF CHANGE)

MONEY

TOTAL
SPENDING

Chart 7-4F

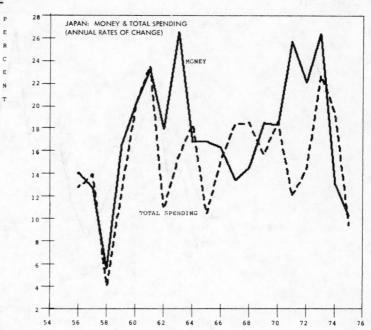

JAPAN: MONEY & TOTAL SPENDING
(ANNUAL RATES OF CHANGE)

MONEY

TOTAL SPENDING

Chart 7-4G

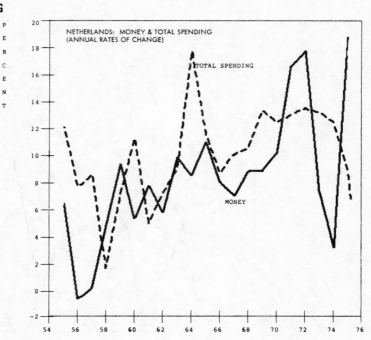

NETHERLANDS: MONEY & TOTAL SPENDING
(ANNUAL RATES OF CHANGE)

TOTAL SPENDING

MONEY

Chart 7-4H

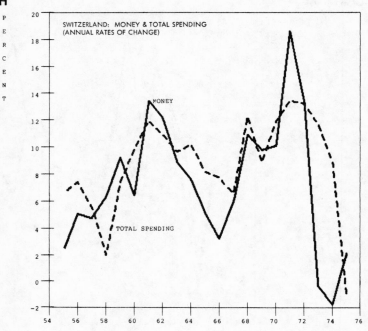

SWITZERLAND: MONEY & TOTAL SPENDING
(ANNUAL RATES OF CHANGE)

MONEY

TOTAL SPENDING

Chart 7-4I

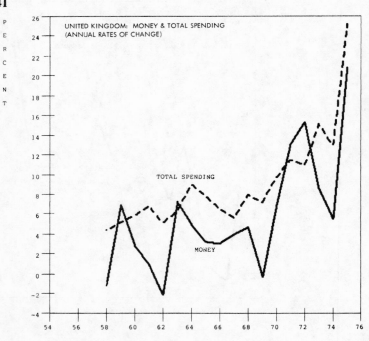

UNITED KINGDOM: MONEY & TOTAL SPENDING
(ANNUAL RATES OF CHANGE)

TOTAL SPENDING

MONEY

tivity is found for France. Here the relationship in many years was just the opposite of what we might have expected. One possible explanation may be that the hoarding and dishoarding of gold by French citizens render annual changes in the conventional money supply a less effective indicator of business conditions. Whatever the reason, apart from France, the evidence shows that the general relationship between money and business activity which exists in the United States also exists in many foreign countries.

Money per unit of output and prices

Charts 7-5A-I show the relationship between money and prices. In each of these charts a price index is compared to the amount of

Chart 7-5A
International: Money per unit of output and prices

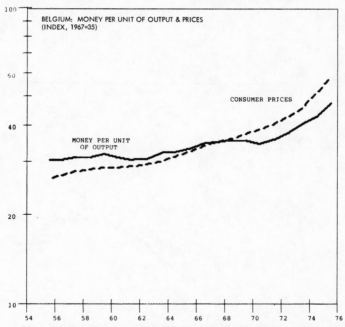

The quantity of money, defined as currency plus demand deposits, is for the fiscal year ending June 30, while output, measured by real gross national product, is for the calendar year. For Italy, output was measured by real gross domestic product.

The consumer price data are calendar year averages.

Source: Federal Reserve Bank of St. Louis; International Monetary Fund; Harris Trust & Savings Bank.

Chart 7-5B

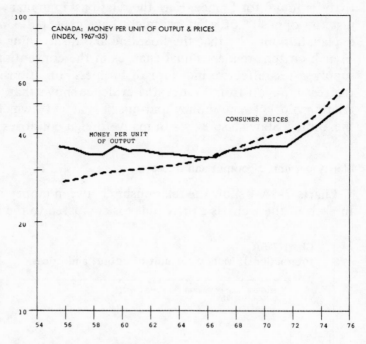

CANADA: MONEY PER UNIT OF OUTPUT & PRICES
(INDEX, 1967=35)

CONSUMER PRICES

MONEY PER UNIT
OF OUTPUT

Chart 7-5C

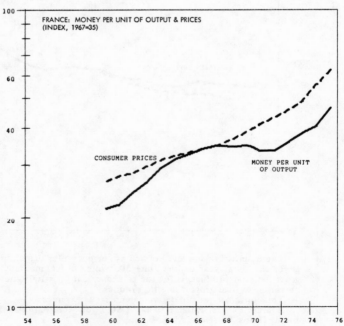

FRANCE: MONEY PER UNIT OF OUTPUT & PRICES
(INDEX, 1967=35)

CONSUMER PRICES

MONEY PER UNIT
OF OUTPUT

Chart 7-5D

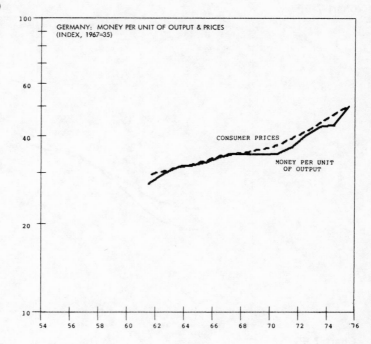

GERMANY: MONEY PER UNIT OF OUTPUT & PRICES
(INDEX, 1967=35)

CONSUMER PRICES

MONEY PER UNIT
OF OUTPUT

Chart 7-5E

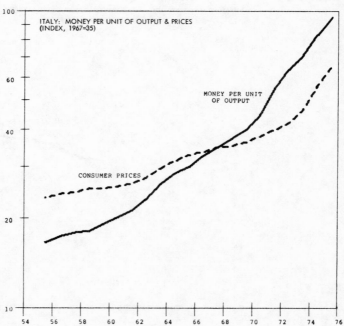

ITALY: MONEY PER UNIT OF OUTPUT & PRICES
(INDEX, 1967=35)

MONEY PER UNIT
OF OUTPUT

CONSUMER PRICES

Chart 7-5F

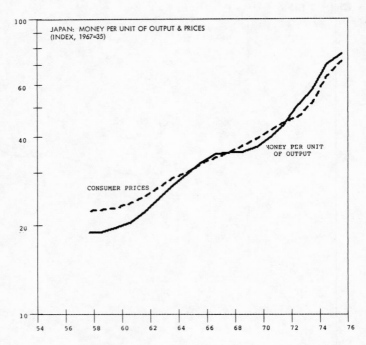

JAPAN: MONEY PER UNIT OF OUTPUT & PRICES
(INDEX, 1967=35)

MONEY PER UNIT
OF OUTPUT

CONSUMER PRICES

Chart 7-5G

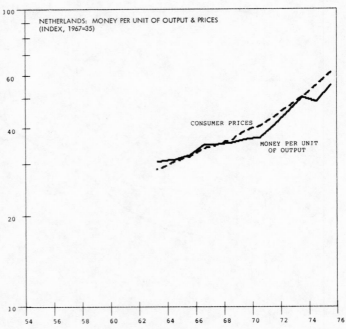

NETHERLANDS: MONEY PER UNIT OF OUTPUT & PRICES
(INDEX, 1967=35)

CONSUMER PRICES

MONEY PER UNIT
OF OUTPUT

157

Chart 7-5H

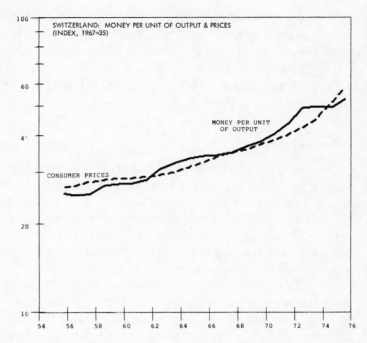

Chart 7-5I

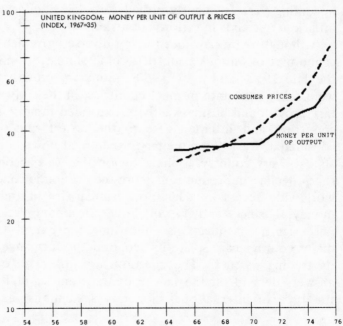

money per unit of real output for a specific country. As more money is created relative to real output, prices would be expected to increase. The greater the amount of money per unit of output, the higher we would expect prices to go. The charts show that this basic pattern, which exists in the United States, also exists in many foreign countries.

Money and inflation

Finding a general relationship between increases in monetary growth and higher prices is one thing; attempting to forecast the rate of inflation is another. Although numerous forces influence the rate of inflation in any particular year, we argued in Chapter 5 that in the United States the main factor affecting the rate of inflation over the coming year has been the average growth in the money supply over the previous two years.

As Charts 7-6A-I show, the relationship between monetary growth and inflation is closer for some countries than for others. But on the whole, the charts suggest that using money supply growth for the previous two years to project inflation for the upcoming year frequently provides a reliable guide to developing inflationary trends in various countries.

Although there have been many diverse movements among the economies of various countries, some similarities are evident. In the late 1950s and early 1960s, monetary growth and inflation were fairly moderate in most countries. In the early 1970s, monetary growth and business activity expanded rapidly in virtually all countries, and inflation rose to the fastest rate of the period considered. By 1974, monetary growth had slowed dramatically in almost every country, a phenomenon that was accompanied by a sharp decline in production, depressed economic conditions, and a worldwide recession. The broad similarities in the behavior of money, business activity, and inflation among various countries raise significant questions concerning the extent to which any major country can isolate its economic performance from that of its trading partners. The questions are not easy to answer. The answers depend on the nature of trade and capital flows and on the type of international monetary system that exists. The following section explores the nature of trade and capital flows among nations, the meaning of an international monetary system, and how such a system can influence the relationships among economic policies and investments in different countries.

Chart 7-6A
International: Money and inflation

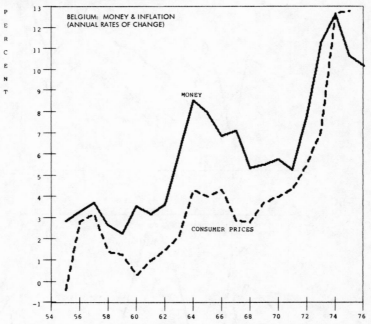

The money supply data, defined as currency plus demand deposits, are two-year annual rates of change plotted at the end of the second year, while the consumer price data are rates of change for the upcoming year.

Source: Federal Reserve Bank of St. Louis; International Monetary Fund; Harris Trust & Savings Bank.

Chart 7-6B

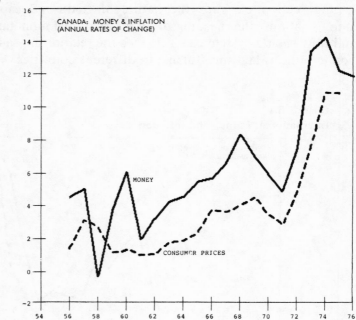

CANADA: MONEY & INFLATION
(ANNUAL RATES OF CHANGE)

MONEY

CONSUMER PRICES

Chart 7-6C

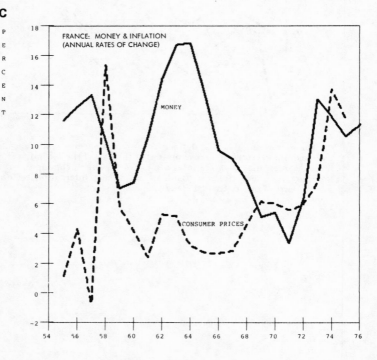

FRANCE: MONEY & INFLATION
(ANNUAL RATES OF CHANGE)

MONEY

CONSUMER PRICES

Chart 7-6D

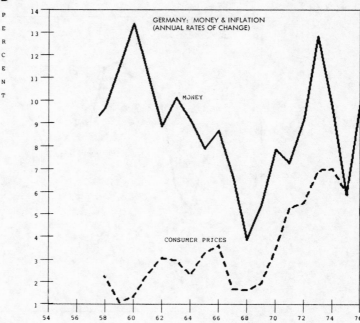

GERMANY: MONEY & INFLATION
(ANNUAL RATES OF CHANGE)

MONEY

CONSUMER PRICES

Chart 7-6E

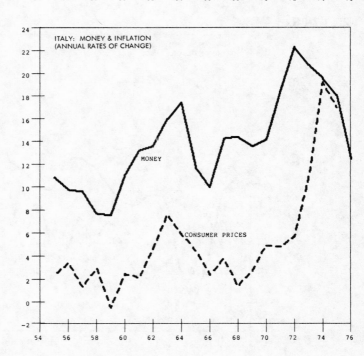

ITALY: MONEY & INFLATION
(ANNUAL RATES OF CHANGE)

MONEY

CONSUMER PRICES

Chart 7-6F

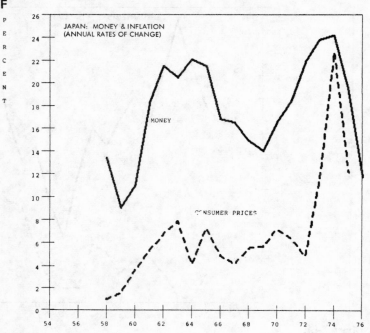

JAPAN: MONEY & INFLATION
(ANNUAL RATES OF CHANGE)

MONEY

CONSUMER PRICES

Chart 7-6G

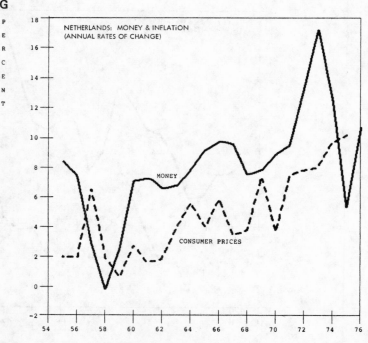

NETHERLANDS: MONEY & INFLATiON
(ANNUAL RATES OF CHANGE)

MONEY

CONSUMER PRICES

Chart 7-6H

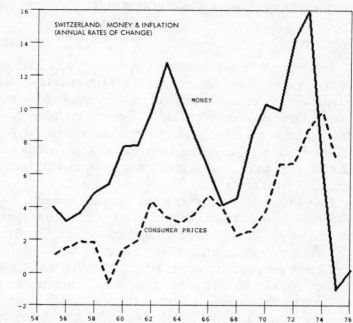

SWITZERLAND: MONEY & INFLATION
(ANNUAL RATES OF CHANGE)

MONEY

CONSUMER PRICES

Chart 7-6I

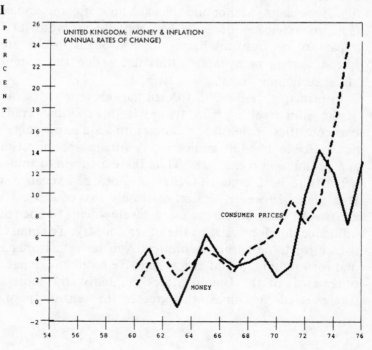

UNITED KINGDOM: MONEY & INFLATION
(ANNUAL RATES OF CHANGE)

CONSUMER PRICES

MONEY

INTERRELATIONSHIP AMONG COUNTRIES

Why trade?

The international experiences of recent years have led some investors to question the net benefit of transactions with foreign economies. Worldwide inflation, oil embargoes, devaluations, international monetary crises, the general interdependence among trading countries, and a greater economic sensitivity to developments in foreign countries have led some to reexamine whether the benefits from further growth in international trade are worth the additional costs.

One problem encountered as a country expands its trade with others is an added dimension for instability. To some extent, this is true of any extension of trade. Economic difficulties in a town five miles away had little, if any, effect on the lifestyle of the self-sufficient pioneer. However, as specialization and trade increased among individuals and geographic areas, the effects of economic difficulties in one area spread to other areas. Even so, this potential for economic instability has been far outweighed by the benefits of specialized labor and the exchange of goods and services. In fact, an extension of trade can actually promote stability. The impact of a bountiful harvest or a drought in one area can be spread among many areas, thus decreasing the potential for a "feast or famine" standard of living.

In principle, trade with foreign nations represents an extension of the gains resulting from trade within a country. Trade between two countries enables each country to acquire products which are not available at home and permits a further specialization of labor and production techniques. Thus the expansion of trade results in benefits to both countries. If it did not, the exchange would not take place. However, the more closely two countries' economies are tied to each other, the more developments in one country will influence developments in the other country. To some extent this is true for trade within a country. A major catastrophe in California, for example, would have a negative economic impact on many other areas of the United States. Similarly, the more important foreign trade becomes, the greater the sensitivity of the U.S.

economy to catastrophes abroad and, in turn, the greater the sensitivity of foreign economies to developments in the United States.

There is, however, a greater potential for instability in foreign trade than in domestic trade. Even apart from political differences, language and trade barriers, and social factors, a key economic distinction adds to the potential for instability. This exists because each country controls the creation of its own currency and therefore has control over its own economic policies. As a result, inept economic policies which lead to an economic boom followed by a severe recession in one country, will also have an impact on that country's trading partners, even if the economic policies of the trading partners are highly responsible. The greater the interdependence of trade among the countries, the more disruption we would expect. Some degree of interdependence among trading partners exists, regardless of the system for exchanging one country's currency for another. However, different international monetary systems provide for greater or lesser dependence among trading partners.

What is an international monetary system?

There is often a great deal of disagreement over the type of international monetary system that should exist. The whole point of the debate is how to exchange one country's currency for another's. Just how this problem is solved has tremendous implications for the conduct of economic policies, for the interdependence among various economies, and in turn, for the prices of various investments. Essentially there are two basic ways of coping with the problem, and hence two basic international monetary systems:

1. A system of freely floating or flexible exchange rates in which market forces determine the relative value of each country's currency.
2. A system of fixed rates in which countries agree to fix or control the exchange rate for their currencies.

All the hue and cry over different international monetary systems is about the extent to which currency values should be controlled by some authority as opposed to the extent to which market forces should determine their values.

The distinction between the two systems is crucial. With flexible exchange rates, each country has control of its money supply and, in turn, of its inflation rate. Under a system in which exchange rates are fixed by some authority, the country that defends the fixed rate by buying or selling its currency relinquishes control of its monetary policies. As a result, the country's monetary growth and eventually its inflation rate will be largely determined by policymakers in other countries.[1] On the surface, it's not at all obvious why this should be true. An explanation involves discussing the nature of balance of payments adjustments, international trade, capital flows, monetary creation, and a multitude of other awesome-sounding matters. In order to present the essence of international adjustments, it is useful to begin by discussing the nature of adjustments in trade and capital flows.

First, however, some definitional problems must be settled.

THE BALANCE OF PAYMENTS

What is it?[2]

In a strict sense, the balance of payments refers to the total of all financial transactions undertaken between one group (or individual) and another during a certain period. These transactions include the purchase and sale of commodities, services, and investments or debt instruments; the receipt or payment of interest, profits, rents, and gifts; and any other transactions between two entities.

---

[1] Although two (or more) countries may agree to a fixed rate of exchange, it is always possible for one of the countries to experience a fixed rate without taking any positive action. So long as its trading partner or partners have the ability and inclination to maintain the agreed-upon currency value, it will be maintained. In this case, those countries which actively defend their rates will do so at the expense of controlling their own money supplies since they must stand ready to buy or sell their own currencies to support the fixed values. The remaining country, which takes no effective action to stabilize its rate (but nonetheless finds it stabilized by the actions of others), is the country which determines monetary policy.

[2] For a more detailed insight into alternative balance of payments measures, see Donald S. Kemp, "Balance of Payments Concepts—What Do They Really Mean?" *Federal Reserve Bank of St. Louis Review,* vol. 57, no. 7 (1975), pp. 14-23.

However, the balance of payments can be viewed in any number of ways. One is merely definitional, in the sense that in double-entry accounting the books must balance. All purchases by either an individual or a group must be paid for. Whether by sales, the use of savings, borrowings, gifts, or whatever, any individual or group must balance its payments with the individuals or groups it does business with. It doesn't have to balance its payments with each and every one of these individuals or groups, but in total it cannot spend, invest, or give away more than it has received. In this definitional sense, the concept of a balance of payments is neither very interesting nor very meaningful.

Since total transactions must balance, a surplus or deficit in the balance of payments refers to something other than the total. It may refer to any number of transactions, such as those including goods and services and those including capital items.[3] Capital in this sense refers to credit items which represent the exchange of current buying power for buying power sometime in the future. The capital balance can be viewed simply as the transfer of credit necessary to offset the balance for goods and services. For example, if more goods and services are being bought (or imported) than are being sold (or exported), then this deficit in the balance of goods and services must be paid for by borrowing the difference. By borrowing, the deficit group is accepting buying power in the present. Those who provide this buying power do so in exchange for promises of buying power sometime in the future. In exchange for their extension of credit they receive claims to future purchases which take the form of debt instruments (bills, bonds, IOUs), investment certificates (stocks), or even money in the form of international reserves (currency, official holdings of gold, and other generally accepted means of payment).

An important point to remember is that when any one group has a deficit in its balance of goods and services, it must offset this deficit with a surplus in its capital balance (that's how it pays for the deficit). On the other side of the transaction, the group supplying the credit has a capital deficit representing the outflow of credit, and this must be offset by a surplus in its balance of goods

---

[3] Transfer payments or gifts are generally classified with goods and services to make up the balance on "Current Account." Strictly speaking, this is the balance which shows to what extent a country is a net creditor.

and services. Once again, the books must balance—one group's deficit represents another group's surplus.

A deficit in a nation's balance of payments for goods and services doesn't necessarily represent a problem. It may reflect a temporary condition which will be offset with a surplus at some time in the future. It could also reflect a favorable investment climate which encourages persons or groups in other countries to invest in (provide credit to) a particular country. This would result in an inflow of credit or a capital surplus to that country, and since the books must balance, the country incurring the surplus has to have a deficit in its balance of goods and services. The reasoning behind this is fairly straightforward. When any group decides to invest in or provide credit to another group, it is really giving that group access to its own goods and services. An extension of credit has meaning only if it is accompanied by an exchange of goods and services. When individuals in the United States invest in the sense of supplying credit abroad, they are really saying, "Take some of our goods and services today, and in exchange give us a claim to goods and services that you will produce sometime in the future."[4]

What causes balance of payments problems?—Real versus monetary factors

So far we have seen no reason why the balance of payments should present any problems. This is because our discussion so far has been concerned with general concepts. We could draw up balance of payments measures for individuals, groups, or areas, and all they would normally tell us is the extent to which each entity was a lender or a borrower during a particular period of time. So long as individuals or groups are free to express their own preferences concerning the extent to which they will lend or borrow, and so long as market forces are permitted to reflect those preferences in terms of prices and interest rates, there can be no balance of payments problems! Such problems arise only when governments take an active role in the credit or capital process by

---

[4] For an excellent discussion of the nature of capital transfers see Carl Iversen, *Aspects of the Theory of International Capital Movements,* 2d ed. (New York: Augustus M. Kelley Publishers, 1936), pp. 1-81.

providing more or less credit than the market would have provided at prevailing prices and interest rates. Such action prevents prices and interest rates from adjusting as they normally would, and as a result what might have been a temporary imbalance in payments can become a chronic one. The most useful balance of payments measure for viewing the government's influence on the private credit markets has been referred to as the balance on the monetary account. This balance reflects changes in a government's international reserves and measures the extent to which that government is influencing private market decisions regarding the movement of trade and capital.[5]

When viewing adjustments to balance of payments situations, it is important to distinguish between factors which tend to initiate an adjustment in trade, capital flows, or prices, and factors which occur because of a potential imbalance in the system. The factors which cause potential balance of payments problems can be classified into two categories—real and monetary. Real disturbances originate from such developments as changes in tastes and preferences among the public, shifts in the population or the work force, and changes in the productivity of the work force. As these factors change over time, they impact trade and capital or credit flows among trading partners. Monetary disturbances can also initiate changes in trade patterns. A sharp increase in the money supply of one country relative to the money supply of other countries may initially lower interest rates in that country relative to interest rates in the other countries. A secondary effect of more money would be to increase spending and raise interest rates relative to the spending and interest rates of the country's trading partners. Eventually, too great an increase in money in one country will increase that country's inflation rate compared to the inflation rates of other countries. All of these reactions to a change in monetary growth, from interest rates to spending to inflation, will have an impact on trade and capital flows between that country and its trading partners.

A real or monetary disturbance doesn't have to lead to an imbalance in trade and capital flows. In fact, among the various areas

---

[5] See Donald S. Kemp, "A Monetary View of the Balance of Payments," *Federal Reserve Bank of St. Louis Review*, vol. 57, no. 4 (1975), pp. 14-22.

within a country, where real disturbances are continually occurring, we never hear of a balance of payments problem. This is because spending, prices, and interest rates among the different areas of a country automatically adjust to accommodate changes in consumer preferences, investment opportunities, and so on, and in so doing serve to eliminate any potential imbalances. At the same time, these adjustments serve to allocate goods and services, credit, and eventually resources to the areas where they are desired most and where they can be used most efficiently. Only when government policies prevent prices and interest rates from adjusting is it possible for a real or monetary disturbance to result in a balance of payments problem. Such government interference has important implications for monetary policies and economic activity in different countries.

How adjustments are made

Before considering these implications, it is useful to consider how adjustments are made to disturbances in trade and capital flows. The nature of the adjustments depends on the type of monetary system in existence. For our purposes we can distinguish between three monetary systems: (1) a single currency system such as exists in one country, (2) different currencies with flexible exchange rates, and (3) different currencies with fixed exchange rates.

Single currency system. With a single currency, such as the dollar within the United States, there can be only one monetary policy, and hence any disturbances to trade and capital flows among different areas of the country must result from real factors. Decisions to invest in a particular area and any resulting capital surplus in that area will immediately generate a trade deficit. Since there is usually no direct government interference with trade and capital flows among the various areas, any deficits that develop are strictly voluntary. As tastes and opportunities change in different areas, prices and interest rates in those areas also change. These changes in prices and interest rates among the different areas automatically attract or discourage goods, services, and credit so as to eliminate any undesired imbalances in trade or capital.

Different currencies: Flexible exchange rates. The fundamental economic difference between international trade and trade within a country revolves around the use of different currencies. Since each country has control over the production of its own currency (only the United States can create U.S. dollars, only Germany can create German marks), disturbances to trade and capital can result from either real or monetary factors. Let's consider the adjustments to a potential imbalance in trade that results from a monetary disturbance. We will limit our discussion to two countries and will assume for the time being that we are operating under a system of flexible exchange rates in which governments do not interfere in the trade process.

Assume for the moment that both countries are pursuing similar noninflationary policies. In the United States, importers of goods, services, and financial assets from Germany pay 10 billion dollars to exporters in Germany. In Germany, importers pay 40 billion marks for goods, services, and financial assets from the United States. Since the exporters in each country have to pay their suppliers in their own currency, they will take the dollars and marks that they have received and present them to foreign exchange dealers to obtain their own country's currency. In this case, foreign exchange dealers must convert 10 billion dollars and 40 billion marks. If the going exchange rate were four marks for one dollar, there would be no problem. The 10 billion dollars held by German importers would be exchanged for the 40 billion marks held by U.S. importers, and everyone would be happy.

Now suppose that the United States promotes policies designed to maximize employment in the immediate future by rapidly increasing its money supply, while Germany pursues policies designed to promote price stability. When this occurs, we have the makings of a first-class disturbance to trade and capital flows that is initiated by a monetary factor. Rapid monetary growth in the United States will lead initially to an increase in U.S. spending on all items, including imports from Germany. Eventually the stimulus will raise prices in the United States, thus encouraging even more imports from Germany, where prices remain stable. Should prices of U.S. goods rise, this would discourage exports of those goods to Germany. The effect of these developments will be (1) to increase U.S. purchases from Germany, hence increasing the amount German importers will receive from the United States to more than 10 billion dollars, and (2) to discourage United States' exports to Germany, hence reducing the number of marks received by U.S. exporters.

Now when traders attempt to exchange marks for dollars at the going rate of four marks for one dollar they find that a problem exists. There are too many dollars and not enough marks at this exchange rate. As long as currency values are free to adjust, this situation would cause a decline in the value of dollars in terms of marks, or on the other side of the fence, a rise in the value of marks in terms of dollars.

Let's assume that the new exchange rate ends up at two marks for one dollar. It now takes only half as many marks as it did prior to the change in exchange rate to purchase goods from the United States. This adjustment in the exchange rate means that goods produced in Germany will now be more expensive in terms of dollars, while goods from the United States will be cheaper in terms of marks. Hence, there are incentives for Americans to cut back on imports from Germany and for Germans to increase their purchase of lower-priced U.S. goods. These changes will tend to reduce the imbalances in trade and capital flows.

The inflationary implications are also affected by the new exchange rates. If prices in the United States had doubled in terms of dollars over the period being considered, this would have had no impact on German prices for U.S. products. The rise in the value of the mark would have insulated Germans from the inflation in the United States. Similarly, Americans would have been unable to take advantage of the price stability in Germany. Although prices for German goods in terms of marks may have remained stable, their prices in terms of dollars would have doubled. Thus the rapid increase in the supply of dollars would have led to inflation only where dollars were used as a means of exchange.

Therefore, a key advantage of a system of flexible exchange rates is that it enables each country to pursue independent monetary policies. A country with stable prices will find that inflation abroad will result in a continually higher price for its currency relative to the price for the currency of an inflating country. This continual appreciation of its currency will insulate that country from paying higher prices for its imports.[6]

Different currencies: Fixed exchange rates. The system of flexible exchange rates has had its share of critics. Many businessmen and bankers have expressed concern for the value of trade when importers, exporters, and investors have the added uncertainty of not knowing what the value of a foreign currency will be when delivery is made or an investment is completed. Furthermore, it has been argued that flexible exchange rates invite short-term swings in the value of currencies which are not necessarily tied to fundamental changes in their values. As a result, an alternative international monetary system attempts to fix the value of one country's currency relative to that of another country. It is often argued that such a system increases trade by eliminating the uncertainty associated with flexible rates. It is also said that fixed exchange rates help tie all currencies together, thus giving all countries advantages of a single currency similar to those enjoyed within a country. Finally, it has been suggested that fixed exchange rates help coordinate economic policies among countries, so that individual countries are subjected to external pressures which aid them in pursuing responsible domestic policies.

It is true that a system of fixed exchange rates represents the same type of system which unites the currency of a single country. However, the problem with fixed exchange rates among different countries is that each country has its own monetary authority and its own monetary policy. Hence, the adjustment mechanism to potential imbalances in payments among countries is not automatic, as it is within a country, where there is only one monetary authority.[7] For example, if a particular area of a country starts to deteriorate because of an unfavorable local business climate, other areas of the country may experience a rapid business expansion as firms relocate. As spending and investment expand in areas of

---

[6] For an excellent discussion of flexible exchange rates see Milton Friedman, "The Case for Flexible Exchange Rates," *Essays in Positive Economics* (Chicago: University of Chicago Press, 1953), pp. 157-203.

[7] For a discussion of the political implications of fixed exchange rates, see Milton Friedman, *Dollars and Deficits: Living with America's Economic Problems* (Englewood Cliffs, N.J.: Prentice-Hall, Inc., 1968), pp. 266-79.

rapid growth, it comes *at the expense* of a reduced pace of spending and investment in the area that is deteriorating. It is usually recognized that regional problems cannot be solved by faster increases in the country's money supply. Hence, regions or cities within a country are often forced to look elsewhere for a solution to their economic problems. However, few countries are willing to have shifts in trade and capital patterns determine their monetary policies, and the automatic adjustment mechanism is often rendered inoperative by the actions of the monetary authorities in each country. An individual country with independent monetary authorities is unlikely to sit idly by and witness a drain in the purchasing power of the country without actively increasing its money supply in an attempt to offset the drain.

Let's view the adjustments to a monetary disturbance under a system of fixed exchange rates. As before, assume that the exchange rate is four marks to one dollar. However, this time both countries agree to fix the exchange rate at that level. Again, assume that the United States pursues a policy of rapid expansion in its money supply, while Germany attempts to avoid such a policy. As before, the initial effect of rapid increases in the U.S. money supply would be to stimulate spending in the United States on both domestic products and imports. And once again, German exporters would receive more dollars than they had received previously. This time, however, German exporters can take their dollars to the Bundesbank (Germany's central bank), where by previous agreement they are to receive four marks for each dollar. Exchanges of marks for dollars by the Bundesbank are similar to purchases of government securities by the Fed. Purchases of foreign currency increase the monetary base, just as central bank purchases of government securities do. Hence, when a central bank exchanges an inflating country's currency for its own, this will quickly lead to rapid increases in its own money supply.

So long as Germany continues to respect the agreement to fix exchange rates at a predetermined rate, it must accept whatever monetary policy is consistent with that exchange rate. Although Germany could attempt to neutralize the inflow of foreign currency by selling government securities or raising reserve requirements on bank deposits, this would only serve to aggravate the situation by widening the price differentials between it and the

United States. An adjustment to the imbalance will only come about if:

1. The inflating country follows deflationary policies which bring prices in the two countries back toward equilibrium.
2. The noninflating country inflates its currency sufficiently to make the fixed exchange rates reflect market values.
3. The countries resort to a system of controls. For example, the deficit country may impose import quotas, tariffs, or taxes on foreign investment in an effort to raise prices in the noninflating country relative to those in the inflating country.
4. The noninflating country decides that it has had enough, and' revalues its currency relative to that of the inflating country.
5. The inflating country devalues its currency.

The two final adjustments would have occurred automatically under a system of flexible rates, but now instead of a gradual depreciation in the inflating country's currency, the adjustment is made at one fell swoop.

Without one or more of these adjustments, all of which involve the same type of change in relative prices, there is no tendency for the system to correct for an imbalance in payments. Moreover, even if the noninflating country decides to inflate, the adjustment will continue only as long as the central bank in the noninflating country is satisfied to receive pieces of paper (currency, treasury bills, and so on) from the inflating country in exchange for real goods and services.

Under a system of fixed exchange rates, smart investors who see the accumulation of unwanted financial claims on the part of a central bank realize that the buildup stems from an imbalance in payments. The longer the buildup continues, the more likely it is that the surplus country (the country receiving reserves or foreign currency) will officially revalue its currency, or that the deficit country (the country losing reserves) will devalue, thus changing from one fixed rate to another. If the devaluation is less than market forces would have allowed for, then the surplus country will continue to incur a surplus. If the devaluation is greater than market forces would have allowed for, then the surplus country will soon begin to experience deficits. Regardless of the outcome, investors who acquire assets denominated in the currency of a surplus country will experience a windfall gain when the currency is revalued and the assets are converted back to the original currency. If the expected revaluation is postponed, all the investor loses is the time, effort, and transactions expense of converting his assets. Hence, a system of fixed exchange rates provides an opportunity for substantial windfall profits for the investor who can anticipate when a country will respond to imbalances in trade by changing its exchange rate.

To summarize. In a modern day system of fixed exchange rates there is no provision for an automatic mechanism to adjust imbalances in trade and capital flows. For rates to remain fixed when imbalances occur, monetary policies must ultimately change so as to bring relative prices back into balance with the established exchange rates. Under this system, if one country follows highly inflationary policies, all countries will have to follow highly inflationary policies in order to maintain the fixed rates of exchange.

By now, the major defect of a system of fixed exchange rates should be obvious. To the extent that a country fulfills its commitment to support another country's currency at a fixed rate, it no longer controls its own money supply. Under such a system, a country relinquishes control of its monetary policy and, in turn, of its inflation rate.

There have been numerous proposed variations of a fixed rate monetary system. One variation permits flexible rates within a certain range of a fixed rate, with intervention to prevent the value of a currency from going outside the range. Another variation calls for an automatic change in the value of a currency when one country's holdings of "reserves" or foreign financial claims, such as currency or gold, reach a certain point. There can be as many variations as there are imaginative individuals to work up the plans. However, all such systems have to handle the basic problem of correcting for an imbalance in payments among countries and, ideally, to do so gradually and efficiently so as to minimize the costs of such an adjustment.

After analyzing the essential principles involved in various international monetary systems, it is useful to look at recent international monetary developments and to view them in light of these principles. We'll begin by briefly describing the evolution of our present system.

OUR INTERNATIONAL MONETARY SYSTEM:
FROM GOLD TO BRETTON WOODS TO JAMAICA

The classical international monetary system consisted of currencies which were backed by gold and therefore, tied to each other in a system of fixed rates. Under this system, monetary policy for all countries was determined by the rate at which new gold discoveries were made. A balance of payments surplus in one country would result in an inflow of gold to pay for the surplus. However, the inflow of gold represented an increase in the money supply which served to increase business activity and prices in the surplus country. At the same time the loss of gold in the deficit country slowed business activity and lowered prices. Income and price adjustments brought about by the shifts in gold flows eliminated the surplus by discouraging exports from the country with rising incomes and prices, and encouraging imports from the country with falling incomes and prices. In this way the system automatically adjusted for any tendency toward an imbalance in international payments.

As countries abandoned the gold standard for paper currencies, the automatic income and price adjustments afforded by a gold standard were undermined. The monetary authorities now had discretion over the amount of money that existed in a particular economy and had to make difficult political decisions concerning declines in the money supply in order to offset unwanted trade deficits. As a result, there was no longer an automatic mechanism to correct imbalances in trade.

Moves toward flexible exchange rates in the early 1920s, and again during the 1930s, were designed to facilitate adjustments to imbalances in international trade and capital flows without giving up discretionary control over domestic policies. However, these moves were accused of promoting economic instability, and so, in 1944 at Bretton Woods, New Hampshire, a new system was adopted by the United States and its key trading partners. In essence, this was a system of fixed exchange rates which gave each nation the option of valuing its currency in terms of either gold or the U.S. dollar. Originally, each country agreed to limit the fluctuations in its exchange rate by 1 percent of its official value. Owing to the growing importance of the U.S. economy in world trade and finance, most countries chose to use dollars as a reserve to stabilize the value of their currencies. If a country's currency rose or fell from the fixed rate by more than 1 percent, the country would have to either sell or buy its currency to maintain the agreed-upon rate. The United States initially chose to meet its obligations with purchases and sales of gold at a price of $35 an ounce, thus further enhancing the usefulness of dollars.[8]

Given divergent trends in growth, inflation, and tastes, various countries, including the United States, could stabilize the value of their currencies only if they had sufficient reserves. To assure all countries of access to additional reserves, the International Monetary Fund (IMF), which was established to oversee the system, provided a pool of currencies from which countries could borrow if necessary. Initially, countries contributed their currencies to the pool on a quota basis, but in 1968 the members of the IMF agreed to create Special Drawing Rights (SDRs) as a supplement to their reserve assets. Nothing but the good faith of the participants stood behind the value of SDRs, which have been aptly termed *paper gold*.

The need for reserves was clear. If a country tended to have a persistent balance of payments deficit, its currency would fall in value. In order to defend the officially set rate, that country would have to use its reserves to purchase the "surplus" of its currency. If the balance of payments problem continued, its reserves would soon be depleted, and the value of its currency would decline. As a result, there was continued concern about a growth in international reserves or liquidity sufficient to keep pace with the growth in world trade. Actually, the fixed rates agreed upon in the Bretton Woods system were not expected to remain permanently fixed. The rates were to be changed from time to time to reflect fundamental imbalances in international payments. These changes were to be made only after other measures taken to correct an imbalance had failed. At such a time a country would request the IMF to change its rate, and the IMF could then grant permission.

The idea of the Bretton Woods system was to provide fixed

---

[8] J. Keith Horsefield, ed., *The International Monetary Fund, 1945-1965* (Washington, D.C.: International Monetary Fund, 1969), vol. 3, pp. 185-214.

exchange rates which would add stability and growth internationally as well as domestically. If an imbalance in payments did occur, the system was designed to provide sufficient time for the deficit country to adjust its internal policies gradually so as to avoid the need for abrupt changes.

As with any system of fixed rates, the decision to maintain or change an exchange rate had to be made by some authority. Since such a decision had important political implications, there was a tendency to avoid making it as long as possible. When the decision was finally made, it was usually because the problem had become so severe that a relatively large disruptive move in the existing fixed rates was needed.

The Bretton Woods system of fixed rates led to a "dollar shortage" in the 1950s, when the dollar was undervalued at the fixed exchange rates. During this period, the United Stated tended to have balance of payments surpluses. After many devaluations of foreign currencies in the late 1950s and early 1960s, the dollar became overvalued, and the United Stated experienced a chronic outflow of gold and a "dollar glut" overseas.

Despite continual minor crises as the currencies of individual countries were revalued, the Bretton Woods system survived. One reason is that monetary growth in the United States averaged a modest 2.2 percent per year in the ten years ending in 1965. This meant that as long as foreign economies pursued policies of relatively moderate monetary growth, changes in currency values would stem primarily from real as opposed to monetary disturbances. As we noted earlier, monetary growth in most key foreign economies was indeed moderate in the late 1950s and early 1960s.

The essential weakness of the Bretton Woods system became readily apparent in the late 1960s and early 1970s, when the U.S. monetary authorities pursued a policy of rapid monetary growth. At that time foreign central banks attempted to maintain fixed exchange rates by exchanging their own currency for dollars. When a central bank purchases foreign currency, the payment for that currency adds to high-powered money, just as do central bank purchases of government securities or gold! The end result was predictable. As foreign central banks exchanged dollars for deposits in marks, francs, and yen, these countries as well as the United States experienced rapid monetary growth. During 1972 the money supply rose by 7 percent in the United States, by 12 percent in Belgium, by 14 percent in Canada, by 14 percent in Germany, and by 22 percent in Japan.

Even these sharp increases in monetary growth in many foreign countries were insufficient to realign the values of their currencies at the agreed-upon rates. Rapidly expanding and highly efficient capital markets enabled investors to convert massive amounts of financial assets into currencies which appeared to be undervalued at the officially fixed rates. Many astute investors made enormous windfall gains at the expense of taxpayers in certain countries by correctly anticipating that an undervalued currency would be revalued. The German central bank alone purchased $5 billion in one week in 1973 in a vain attempt to maintain the official value of the mark. Once the mark was revalued with respect to the dollar, the $5 billion which had been purchased by the Bundesbank was worth less in terms of marks. It has been estimated that the Bundesbank, and hence the German taxpayers, lost approximately $500 million in one week in 1973 because of the Bundesbank's attempt to maintain exchange rates at the official values.[9] In all, between 1967 and 1973 an estimated $12 billion was lost by central banks in various attempts to maintain a system of fixed exchange rates.[10]

As a result of such experiences and a desire to control their own money supply, the major countries of the world grudgingly abandoned the Bretton Woods system of officially fixed exchange rates. Although central banks still sought to stabilize short-term swings in currency values, by 1973 the major countries were operating in a system in which market forces played the dominant role in setting exchange rates. Under the new system, each country was free to determine its own monetary growth without regard to the effects on the value of another country's currency. After the explosive rise in money in the early 1970s, most countries chose to reduce their monetary expansion, and the result was a worldwide recession, with output declining sharply. By the end of 1975 the inflation rates had begun to decline in most of the countries

---

[9] Charles A. Coombs, "Treasury and Federal Reserve Foreign Exchange Operations," *Federal Reserve Bank of New York Monthly Review,* vol. 55, no. 3 (1973), pp. 50-53.
[10] Robert Z. Aliber, *The International Money Game,* 2d ed. (New York: Basic Books, Inc., 1976), p. 48.

that had curtailed monetary growth. A system of flexible exchange rates had arrived. All that was left was to recognize what had happened. This was done early in 1976 at a meeting of the IMF in Jamaica. The meeting produced an agreement which officially permitted IMF members to let their currencies move up or down in response to market forces. It is interesting to note that many smaller countries, including most of the South American nations, continue to fix the value of their currencies with respect to the dollar. This may make sense for smaller countries, whose exports can be crucial to economic well-being. For such countries, the prospect of a loss in foreign markets due to a revaluation in their currency may be worse than relinquishing control of their monetary policy.

The move from fixed to flexible exchange rates leaves the major countries free to determine their domestic monetary policies. If different countries wish to pursue highly divergent monetary policies, they can now do so. Changes in the value of each country's currency will reflect the value assigned to it by market forces. As long as rates are permitted to adjust to these forces, there can be no balance of payments problem.

IMPLICATIONS OF INTERNATIONAL FACTORS FOR INVESTORS

The implications of international factors for investors depend on the type of international monetary system. Under a system in which governments agree to support a predetermined rate of exchange among various currencies, different countries tend to pursue monetary policies which lead to similar rates of inflation. Under a fixed-rate system, if a country attempts to pursue an independent inflationary policy which is not offset by other influences on exchange rates, then pressures will build for a dramatic change in the officially recognized value of that country's currency.

The possibility of such changes gives investors a great potential for experiencing windfall profits. The trick is to follow balance of payments patterns closely to determine the extent to which a central bank is accumulating foreign reserves. Since the United States dominates world trade, most foreign reserves held abroad are in the form of dollars or U.S. government securities. For the

United States, foreign reserves consist primarily of gold and foreign currencies held by the Federal Reserve.[11]

A persistent accumulation or decumulation in foreign reserves usually indicates an imbalance in payments. If a government is accumulating foreign reserves, this generally indicates the private investors do not want these claims at the agreed-upon price. For an item such as currency, it would indicate that the official price is above the free-market value. At this point, the investor who follows international trends closely would want to denominate his assets in the undervalued currency. This can be done by purchasing assets denominated in that currency or by purchasing common stock of multinational companies that have significant operations in the country whose currency is undervalued. Once the currency is revalued, the assets and operations of those companies will be worth more in dollar terms. The same principle holds true for U.S. industries which compete in a country whose currency is undervalued with respect to the dollar. Revaluation of the foreign currency means that residents of that country will get more dollars for their currency and that U.S. products will therefore appear more attractive. The opposite implications hold if a foreign currency is overvalued, and a devaluation is in order.

It is important to realize that markets are highly efficient. Stocks, bonds, and other assets denominated in a given currency are likely to adjust to the market's expectations of that currency's value. Hence, the investor who wishes to switch into assets denominated in a given country's currency or to purchase stock certificates of companies with extensive operations in that country would do well to recognize that he is assuming that the currency is more undervalued than most other investors believe. Such an investor should consider his knowledge of international financial trends to be better than the average knowledge of all other investors. There is nothing wrong with this type of assumption. To

---

[11] Although gold held by central banks is also considered part of a country's foreign reserves, the role of gold as a reserve asset has been effectively frozen. This is because central banks are only allowed to exchange gold with each other at a price which is far below the free-market price. Moreover, since the price of gold is now determined largely by market forces, it has become a speculative commodity which is no more suitable for use as reserves than are diamonds or any other real assets. If it were desirable, the government receiving foreign currency could simply exchange it for gold at the free-market price rather than demand initial payment in the form of gold.

varying degrees, the assumption of better than average knowledge is implied in every investment that promises an above average return. It is simply worth mentioning that information on international financial trends is not a deep, dark secret that is being revealed to the reader and no one else. Markets in different countries will adjust as the prospects for a change in currency values become more certain.

However, there is one market that by definition will not adjust under a system of fixed exchange rates, and that is the market for foreign exchange. As it becomes more and more apparent that a currency is undervalued (that the official price is below its market value), investors with sufficient funds should attempt to exchange an overvalued currency for one that is undervalued. At worst, the central banks of the respective countries will be able to defend the unrealistic currency values and the investor will have incurred some transactions costs for switching currencies as well as forgone the interest income he could have earned during the period in which the undervalued currency was held. At best, the central banks will respond to market forces and revalue (place a higher price on) the undervalued currency. In the latter case, the investor can now take the revalued currency and exchange it for more of the devalued currency than he started with. In this instance the investor has profited at the expense of the central banks or the constituencies which the banks represent.

Unfortunately for the investors who have the ability to play this game, the system of officially pegged exchange rates has been largely abandoned. As a result, such investors are left in a much more difficult situation, one which involves competition for profits with other investors, rather than competition with the politicians and the central bankers who influence central bank policy. Needless to say, from the investors' point of view, competition with politicians is preferable. However, the cost to taxpayers has been so large that central bankers, in part embarrassed by their large losses, decided to get out of the game. Under a system of flexible exchange rates, investors will find it far more difficult to profit from international financial developments.

What can be done about international investments under a system of flexible exchange rates? Under these conditions, our suggestions for international investors are broadly the same as our suggestions for domestic investors. These suggestions include monitoring the political sentiment and economic policies in countries where actual or potential investments are considered.

MONITORING INTERNATIONAL DEVELOPMENTS

Although political sentiment is often difficult to gauge, it is crucial to determine the prospects for expropriation of assets or income, government regulation, a trade-off between inflation and unemployment, and monetary growth. These factors are key influences on the future values of investments. In some instances, policies may be subtle rather than bold initiatives. For example, governments can usurp profits in any number of ways—government regulations, raising taxes on corporations, and supporting policies conducive to the development of powerful labor unions. By sufficiently reducing a firm's profitability, a government can legally and even unintentionally effectively expropriate the firm's assets. This is precisely what happened to Chrysler in the United Kingdom. Chrysler's profitability was destroyed to such an extent that the company offered the government all of its plant and equipment plus $70 million to simply enable it to leave the country![12]

Attempts to monitor prospective political and economic developments in various countries can be accomplished by subscribing to newspapers and magazines which deal objectively with such developments. For example, the *International Herald Tribune* (Paris), the *Japan Economic Journal*, the *Financial Times* (London), and *American Banker* contain a wealth of up-to-date information on developments in various foreign economies.

While it can be crucial to follow recent political information and economic data, it is important to place the data in some perspective. For example, a monetary growth of 10 percent per year for a country like Japan, which has experienced sharp increases in output, may be consistent with stable prices; a similar monetary growth in Switzerland, which has experienced a slower

---

[12] The government of the United Kingdom countered with various subsidies in an attempt to keep the company in the country. See Felix Kessler, "How British Cabinet Made a U-Turn to Aid Failing Chrysler U.K.," *Wall Street Journal*, February 10, 1976, pp. 1 ff.

growth in production, would be highly inflationary. To place international developments in perspective, the Federal Reserve Bank of St. Louis offers two extremely useful publications. *Rates of Change in Economic Data for Ten Industrial Countries* presents data on monetary growth, inflation, and other items for ten countries, including the United States.[13] The data in this publication can be used to update many of the charts presented earlier in this chapter. *U.S. International Transactions and Currency Review* presents data on U.S. trade and capital flows as well as the dollar exchange rates for various foreign currencies. Other useful sources include International Monetary Fund's *International Financial Statistics* and publications of the Organisation for Economic Co-operation and Development, and the European Economic Community.

The charts presented earlier in this chapter show the relationships between money and business activity and between money and inflation for a number of key foreign economies. The patterns are never perfect. Nonetheless, the data tend to show significant relationships between money and business activity, and between money and inflation, for many key nations of the world. In some instances, the relationship is better than that found in the United States; in other instances, it is worse. Judging from the long-standing historical pattern of U.S. relationships, and from the relationships found to exist in other countries, we believe that changes in monetary growth rates provide the initial thrust for a host of economic and financial adjustments.

While more extensive research may either confirm or refute the view that the monetary influence is very similar among a wide range of countries, the preliminary data suggest that the investor who ignores the behavior of money on the international stage, does so at his own peril.

WRAPPING IT UP

At the beginning of this chapter we raised a number of questions concerning the influence of international factors. Although

---

[13] Investors concerned with countries in the Pacific Basin should consult the Federal Reserve Bank of San Francisco's publication *Pacific Basin Economic Indicators*, which gives economic data on that area of the world.

these questions have been answered at one point or another in the course of the chapter, it might be useful to present our answers explicitly in this closing section.

1. To what extent is inflation an international phenomenon which defies management by an individual country? Since each country controls the production of its own currency, each controls its own inflation. However, if a government agrees to fix the price of its currency, it must be prepared to produce as much of it as is requested at the agreed-upon price, and hence will find it difficult to pursue an independent monetary policy.

2. Since many goods are traded on the world market, where their prices are determined by world supply and demand, aren't the prices of these goods beyond the control of domestic policy-makers even if the money supply can be controlled? The behavior of a nation's money supply doesn't determine the prices of *particular* goods but rather the *overall* behavior of prices. For example, a shortage of oil (real or artificial) will drive up its price relative to the prices of other items. This will occur whether an economy has overall price stability or rapid inflation. In an economy with no inflation, oil prices might go up 5 percent (and some other prices would fall), while in an economy with rapid inflation oil prices would rise much more than 5 percent. How much the price of a good traded on a world market would rise, depends on the particular currency under consideration. If currency values are free to adjust to market forces, inflation will not be transmitted across international borders.

3. Is it possible to control the money supply of a particular country, given the growing integration of international capital markets? Will an attempt to slow monetary growth in the United States merely push up interest rates and attract dollars from abroad, thereby preventing such control? The answers to both questions hinge on the distinction between capital flows and money. Although it is extremely difficult for a nation to control capital or credit flows, each country has both the ability and the responsibility to control its own money supply. The main ingredient for such control is the monetary base. As was shown in Chapter 2, it is extremely rare for monetary growth to differ substantially from the growth of its base. Only when monetary authorities decide to abandon their control over the monetary base—by fixing

interest rates or currency values—can the money supply vary extensively from the desired amount.

4. Can the United States avoid inflation and recession if the policies followed by its trading partners produce inflation and recession abroad? If interest rates soar and stock markets plummet in foreign countries, is the United States likely to suffer the same fate? Fortunately for the United States, the sheer size of its economy provides a great deal of insulation from activities abroad. Moreover, with a system of flexible exchange rates, the U.S. economy is further insulated from the influence of chaotic economic policies among its trading partners. The same is not true for many U.S. trading partners whose fortunes are closely tied to business activity in the United States. In the late 1960s and early 1970s, instability in the United States was transmitted to the rest of the world. Even under a system of flexible exchange rates, instability in the United States is likely to have a significant impact on business conditions abroad. The main contribution the United States can make to worldwide economic stability is to pursue stable non-inflationary policies at home.

In summary, worldwide integration of business activity does not represent a threat to the conduct of U.S. economic policies. If another nation pursues irresponsible policies, investors need be concerned only with the impact of those policies on their operations in that particular country. For the United States, the pursuit of orderly and stable policies to promote a healthy climate for expansion is contingent primarily on the wisdom of our future policymakers and their constituency.

8

Winning the money game as a nation

We used to think that you could just spend your way out of a recession and increase employment by cutting taxes and boosting government spending. I tell you, in all candour, that that option no longer exists, and that insofar as it ever did exist, it only worked by injecting a bigger dose of inflation into the economy followed by a higher level of unemployment. That is the history of the past 20 years.

James Callahan,
Prime Minister of the United Kingdom, 1976

The previous chapters presented a good smattering of basic economics and its implications for investors. In the final two chapters, the implications are brought together in an attempt to provide some rules for winning the money game. Winning can be viewed from the perspective of the nation as a whole or from the perspective of the individual investor.

For the nation as a whole, winning the money game involves eliminating inflation with a minimum of economic hardship and maintaining a prosperous and productive economy. The first part of this chapter applies various rules, distilled from the evidence presented in earlier chapters, for accomplishing this goal. But knowing the rules and following them are two different things. Since inflation has occurred at one time or another during most of recorded history, it would be naive to assume that it will not occur in the future. However, even if we accept inflation as an economic fact of life, it is still possible to minimize its damage by undertaking the appropriate public policies. The second part of this chapter deals with those policies. Knowing the impact of various government policies is useful for achieving various personal economic objectives and for protecting the value of one's own investments. Winning the money game from the individual's perspective is the topic of Chapter 9.

RULES FOR WINNING AS A NATION

Prescribing public policies for achieving stable growth without serious inflation is much easier than implementing those policies in practice. Difficulties in real-life formulation and implementation arise not only because of the inevitable short-run versus long-run political trade-offs, but also because of the inevitable disagreement among competing economic philosophies. Although most economists would agree with the following prescriptions, there remain irreconcilable differences concerning the star role assigned to money as well as other matters.

Rule No. 1

After analyzing inflationary patterns both in the United States and abroad, we are convinced that the cause of inflation is too much money chasing too few goods and services. Therefore, *the first rule for avoiding serious inflation is that the average yearly growth in the money supply be approximately equal to the average long-term rate of growth in real output.*

Those countries which have most nearly adhered to this rule have suffered the least inflation. Furthermore, countries which had experienced a good inflation record, such as Germany and Switzerland, found that record quickly tarnished in the early 1970s, as rapid growth in their money supplies brought on rapid inflation. Once monetary growth was restrained following the abandonment of a system of fixed exchange rates, inflation receded. A substantial body of evidence presented in previous chapters shows that higher monetary growth leads to higher spending and later to greater inflation. Furthermore, the greater the growth in the money supply relative to the growth in real output, the greater the price rise.

This rule can be refined somewhat for direct application to the

U.S. economy. For many years, the long-run potential for real growth in the United States was approximately 4 percent per year. However, recent studies suggest that this potential has slipped to 3 percent–3½ percent. In order to promote price stability, we would have to have yearly increases in spending that are consistent with the economy's ability to produce more goods and services. Hence, we need increases in money that would be consistent with increases in spending of 3 percent–3½ percent per year. What type of monetary growth is consistent with such increases in spending? It depends on what measure of money we use. For M_1 (currency plus checking account deposits), a growth of 0 percent–½ percent per year has been consistent with increases in spending of 3 percent–3½ percent per year. Hence, price stability in the United States would be consistent with a minimal increase in M_1. For the broader definition of money, M_2, which consists of M_1 plus most savings deposits in commercial banks, an increase of 3 percent–3½ percent per year has been consistent with similar increases in spending. The precise numbers given above are not carved indelibly in stone. They may not correspond to price stability forever, but they are reasonable estimates for the foreseeable future. Certainly, if these numerical guidelines had been followed in the past decade, the inflationary experience of this period would have been substantially reduced if not entirely eliminated.

Rule No. 2

Not only should the average growth rate in the money supply be commensurate with the economy's real growth, but *the growth rate in money should also be stable, not volatile.* Inflation often owes its inception to stimulative policies designed to reverse recessionary trends. As Chart 4–1 indicates, volatile monetary growth inevitably promotes volatile economic activity. Monetary growth declined prior to almost every recession in the past, just as monetary growth accelerated prior to recoveries. Volatility in economic performance goes hand in hand with volatile growth in the money supply, and very often the pattern feeds on itself.

Once an economy is in a serious recession characterized by declining output and rising unemployment, both economic reasoning and political pressures favor more stimulative policies. The short-run effects of greater monetary growth are politically attractive. As we noted in previous chapters, more money leads first to lower interest rates and higher stock prices and then to more spending and increased employment.

In the early phase of a recovery it is politically attractive to engage in massive stimulus to hasten the decline in unemployment. Patience has seldom been a political virtue, and inevitably many voices argue for more stimulus to bring about a faster decline in the unemployment rate. Easier monetary policies often become addictive, and all too soon the longer-run effects of more money are reflected in accelerating inflation. At this point renewed political pressures develop to fight inflation with tighter money, and before long another recession is in the making. This nonsensical pattern accurately describes the economic performance of the United States during the late 1960s and early 1970s. Unfortunately, each pickup tended to bring a higher inflation rate than the prior expansion, and each slowdown reduced inflation, but less than in the prior decline. In other words, volatile economic performance induced by volatile but rising monetary growth, resulted in escalating inflation.

Why isn't it possible to fine tune the money supply in such a way as to hasten the attainment of high employment of resources, yet still have stable prices? Unfortunately for "fine-tuning buffs," inflation tends to lag the growth in the money supply. If the United States pursues rapid monetary growth to attain the commendable goal of high employment of resources, subsequent attempts to reduce monetary growth tend to slow spending just as inflation is speeding up. The inevitable result is a slowdown in the economy's output. Therefore, the probability of future recessions will be substantially reduced if a stable monetary growth rate is maintained.

Although stable and moderate growth in money during the recovery phase of the business cycle would undoubtedly defer the attainment of high employment of resources, it would unlike a volatile monetary pattern, be sustainable over a long period of time. It is desirable not only to reduce the human and economic waste associated with high unemployment, but to make the reduction in waste permanent. Stable monetary growth does not necessarily mean that the business cycle will disappear, since nonmonetary factors will still inject some volatility into the economy. Money cannot offset the effects of a major strike or an Arab embargo on oil. Nonetheless, maintaining stable and moderate growth in money would greatly improve the odds of achieving stable noninflationary growth in economic activity.

Rule No. 3

Central banks can more readily achieve stable and moderate monetary growth by focusing on a monetary aggregate, such as the monetary base, rather than attempt to fix short-term interest rates. As explained in Chapter 2, the Federal Reserve has control over the monetary base, even though banks and the public can exert a moderate influence on the amount of money produced by changing the base. At the time of this writing the Federal Reserve was still establishing a monetary objective and then attempting to estimate a short-term interest rate consistent with the monetary objective. Unfortunately it is often impossible to achieve both a particular interest rate and a given rate of monetary growth. Central banks can stabilize either monetary growth or short-term rates; they can't do both simultaneously. Unless the Federal Reserve's method for achieving monetary targets is changed, volatile monetary growth is likely to continue.

Rule No. 4

Large, continuous federal deficits can be very damaging to an economy and should be avoided. There are several reasons why this is true. To begin with, large deficits can lead to pressures for large increases in the money supply. Since the Federal Reserve System is the U.S. Treasury's banker, it feels an obligation to assure that the government's debt is sold successfully. The greater the Treasury's deficit, the greater the temptation for the Federal Reserve to purchase the debt so that the deficit does not absorb funds that might otherwise fulfill private credit demands.

When cumulative deficits were small, as was the case in the decade ending in fiscal 1965, the problems posed were moderate. From fiscal 1955 to fiscal 1965, the Federal Reserve purchased half of a ten-year deficit totaling $31 billion. During this period, the money supply increased at a yearly rate of only about 2 percent. As deficits loomed larger in the next decade, the Federal Reserve purchased only a third of the federal debt of $141 billion. The result was an annual increase in the money supply of approximately 5½ percent during this period.

It should be emphasized that there is no fixed relationship between the size of the federal deficit and the amount which the Fed has to purchase. For example, in fiscal 1976 the Federal Reserve purchased about 10 percent of a $66 billion federal deficit. Actually, if none of the deficit were purchased by the Federal Reserve, it would be possible for huge federal deficits to be consistent with stable prices, since it is the increase in the money supply and not the deficit which determines the inflation rate. Nonetheless, since larger deficits create larger political pressures to increase the money supply, it's a good idea to avoid such deficits on this account alone.

In addition to their potential for increasing monetary growth, large federal deficits can be damaging to an economy in other ways. It is important to recognize that when Congres votes for federal spending amounting to, say, $400 billion a year at the same time that it votes to collect only $300 billion in taxes, it has not found a secret formula for magically supplying citizens with $100 billion more in government services than taxpayers have paid for. A federal deficit is paid for in one of two ways. First, the Federal Reserve can purchase a portion of the deficit, thereby increasing the money supply. Since increases in the money supply lead to more inflation, citizens pay for that portion of the deficit through inflation, or a decline in the value of their money. Second, the deficit can be sold to the public in exchange for the funds that citizens have decided to set aside for the future, that is, savings. In any year, only a limited supply of these funds is available for use in building factories, machines, houses, hospitals, and other major projects. When the federal government borrows from this limited supply, it usurps funds that would have been available for long-term investment purchases and uses those funds for current expenditures. Citizens pay for this portion of the deficit in two ways. First, since the funds that the government borrows are not available for major expenditures in the private sector, citizens lose the factories, houses, and other major items which might have been produced with the use of those savings. This will usually mean less private investment and will eventually lower productivity and growth.

In addition to the lost investment in the private sector, there is a further cost—the cost associated with borrowing. This cost takes the form of dividends or interest payments normally associated with the use of the borrowed funds. When the government borrows funds, as opposed to borrowings by private industry, no productive investment is associated with the funds, and the interest payments associated with the funds have to come out of the hides of future taxpayers. The impact of large budget deficits is readily apparent when we realize that net interest on the federal debt amounted to over $23 billion a year, or close to 7 percent of all federal spending in fiscal year 1975. In this sense, federal deficits commit citizens to future tax payments for servicing the debt with little or no comparable benefit to those who will be making the payments. This tends to frustrate taxpayers who feel that they are not getting their money's worth for their taxes (they are not), and also politicians who find that their predecessors have already spent a large portion of the current budget! While it is true that a subsequent generation also inherits the debt securities, the taxpayers will not share proportionately in the inheritance.

Large federal deficits do not contribute to a healthy economic climate and should generally be discouraged. However, undesirable as the deficits themselves are, the amount of federal spending can be an even more important issue in maintaining a prosperous non-inflationary economy—which leads to the next rule.

Rule No. 5

Increases in government spending should be debated on their own merits and not on the false assumption that such increases will stimulate the economy or will pay for themselves.

Ridiculous as it sounds, many politicians and even some economists continue to argue that we can get something for nothing. They consistently try to sell the public on new government expenditures by suggesting that either the expenditures or the resulting government deficit will stimulate the economy and generate more income, jobs, and taxes, thereby paying for themselves.

There's just no way around it—the public must pay for every dollar of government spending. As we noted previously, if Congress votes to spend $400 billion, then that is how much the public ends up paying for federal government services, regardless of the amount of taxes that is collected. In recent years, expenditures on all government outlays have amounted to more than 40 percent of national income. Moreover, in the five years ending in 1975, the trend accelerated, with the rise in government spending amounting to more than half of the rise in national income.

As government increases in size, it tends to usurp resources in the marketplace and to leave less for the private sector, while often telling citizens how to spend their incomes. This trend results in an inevitable loss of personal freedom and incentives. Since the authors are inclined to trust the marketplace as a server of human needs and wants, and to distrust the effectiveness of government programs, we prefer less government to more. Of course, others disagree with this view, and the disagreement over the relative size of government is an important and legitimate area of political debate. The debate should proceed on the basis of the desirability of public services versus private choice. Unfortunately, many who prefer a larger share of income for government services justify their choice by arguing that a larger budget and a larger deficit stimulate the economy. Although the argument is heard over and over again, it doesn't hold up well under close scrutiny.

Let's look at what happens when Congress votes to increase spending by $10 billion. Initially, some group winds up with an extra $10 billion to spend as a result of this "stimulative" action. Won't this $10 billion lead to an increase in demand for various items and therefore stimulate sales, production, and employment? Not necessarily. It all depends on how the initial $10 billion is paid for. Remember, if the government borrows from the available supply of savings, then that leaves $10 billion less for companies to borrow for building factories, homes, and machines. What has really happened is that the government has stimulated certain areas while draining funds elsewhere.

A similar analysis holds for a $10 billion reduction in taxes. Although at first it appears as if Congress has created an additional $10 billion for taxpayers to spend in the economy, as soon as the Treasury borrows to pay for the resulting deficit, $10 billion is drained elsewhere in the economy, and again we have a washout. If the deficit is financed with newly created money made available through the purchase of $10 billion in government debt by the Federal Reserve System, the money supply would rise and there would be an increase in national income creation, as noted in previous chapters. But the stimulus results from greater monetary growth—not a more "stimulative" budget, as some would argue.

The above arguments have been tested, and it turns out that changes in fiscal policy are not a significant determinant of subsequent income growth, whether the deficits are measured as actual deficits or as full employment deficits.[1] An increase in federal spending does have a low positive effect on total spending for two quarters immediately following the rise, but the effect washes out over a period as long as a year.[2] It is for these reasons that monetarists insist that changes in the federal budget are an inefficient means of affecting national income growth.

Those who justify large federal budgets by arguing that they stimulate the economy should be suspected of promoting more government spending for false reasons. A large government budget should be debated in terms of whether government can use resources more efficiently than can the private sector, not on the basis of providing further stimulus to the economy. If more stimulus is needed, monetarists would prefer the route of greater monetary growth, which would not have the effect of ballooning the federal budget, but would permit expansion in the private sector.

Rule No. 6

Avoid wage and price controls and other interferences with free markets. Throughout history, governments have repeatedly opted for the false security of *wage and price controls* in a vain attempt to control inflation. The appeal of controls resides in the false premise that by simply declaring inflation illegal the government can appear to be on the side of responsibility and achieve what all

---

[1] Beryl W. Sprinkel, *Money and Markets: A Monetarist View* (Homewood, Ill.: Richard D. Irwin, Inc., 1971), pp. 8-16.

[2] Leonall C. Andersen and Jerry L. Jordan, "Monetary and Fiscal Actions: A Test of Their Relative Importance in Economic Stabilization," *Federal Reserve Bank of St. Louis Review,* vol. 50, no. 11 (1968), pp. 11-23.

citizens want—a stable currency. The reason for repeated failures of wage and price controls to achieve asserted objectives is that such controls attack symptoms of the disease rather than the cause—excessive monetary growth. In fact, wage and price controls or various forms of income policies are often used as a decoy to permit governments to continue on their profligate ways. Arbitrarily reducing prices below free-market levels inevitably creates shortages by stimulating demand while retarding output. Shortages create incentives for excessive inventory accumulation based on the view that "I'll buy before the hoarders arrive." Inevitably, economic instability is fostered, and eventually the controls are abandoned amid recriminations and soaring prices. There can be no successful substitute for monetary and fiscal discipline.

So far, the discussion has been limited largely to general tools for influencing the economy. However, the economy can also be aided by numerous specific policies for reducing or minimizing interference with the free market. Estimates vary, but under present ground rules it appears unlikely that unemployment can be reduced below 5 to 6 percent without risking a speedup in inflation. The present high *minimum wage* makes the achievement of low unemployment a practical impossibility. Although the minimum wage assures that most workers will receive at least a fixed amount per hour when working, it does not assure that potential workers and producers will be able to get jobs. A high minimum wage is especially onerous for the young, whose skills are often not yet worth that wage, but would soon be worth even more if they had jobs and could acquire qualifications and skills from a working experience. So far, Congress has been unwilling to seriously consider the adverse secondary effects of a high minimum wage, and hence the unemployment rate among the young and the unskilled is roughly two to three times the national average. In the United Kingdom, a high minimum wage is one mistake that has not been made. The minimum wage is so low that the level of unemployment among the young and unskilled is near the average for the total labor force.

Other forms of interference with the free market include *restrictive labor laws* which result in artificially high wages in parts of the construction industry, thereby preventing competition and restricting employment. Detailed government *regulation* of many industries also limits competition and hence restricts output and employment. Fortunately, a serious move is now under way to reduce the deadening and costly effect of government regulation by restoring the invigorating breath of competition. However, it is often difficult to eliminate existing regulation since companies and unions often find it in their best interests to limit competition. Important social functions are served by efforts to quickly eliminate pollution, reduce safety hazards, rigorously enforce industry controls, delay introduction of possibly dangerous life-saving drugs and insist on expensive consumer disclosure, but these practices are reducing the ability of our economy to grow and provide higher-paying jobs. Recent trends suggest that the heavy costs are now being recognized and that a better trade-off will be achieved in future years.

Rule No. 7

Governments can more nearly achieve a goal of stable and moderate monetary growth with an international monetary system that allows for flexible exchange or floating rates rather than with a system of fixed exchange rates. Even with a fixed exchange rate system, very large countries like the United States can maintain a high degree of monetary autonomy so long as other countries assume the responsibility of stabilizing the value of their currencies with respect to the dollar. The dominant influence of the United States often forces other countries to adjust their domestic monetary policies and inflation rates to the U.S. pattern when the world is on a fixed exchange rate system.

In the late 1960s and early 1970s, excess monetary growth and inflation in the United States was transmitted to the rest of the world. As the dollar weakened, the Bretton Woods rule of fixed exchange rates forced foreign countries to buy surplus dollars. These dollars were purchased with newly created marks in Germany, Swiss francs in Switzerland, and yen in Japan. The result was a sharp rise in domestic money supplies in the developed free world. As always, the early results were exhilarating—a worldwide boom in production and employment quickly developed. But just as inevitably, the boom was followed by worldwide inflation, and finally restrictive policies ensued which plummeted nearly all countries into a serious recession.

The present flexible exchange rate system increases the odds that a renewed worldwide inflation will not develop. Of course, it is always possible for a nation to develop its own homegrown inflation brought on by excessive monetary growth. However, such renewed inflation is now more likely to be confined within that nation since other nations are no longer forced by the international monetary rules to absorb weak currencies and thereby inflate their domestic money supplies.

A floating exchange rate system will not insure domestic price stability. Only domestic policies can assure price stability at home. Nonetheless, flexible rates will enable independent governments to retain control of their domestic monetary policies. Such a choice was unavailable to many governments under the previous system. Under the new international system, nations will no longer be able to blame domestic inflation on the profligate policies of other nations. If they get inflation, it will be homegrown.

If the above simple rules appear to be in conflict with the prescriptions of many of the popular Keynesian economists, it's because they are! We have been told too long that money is of secondary importance; that we have sufficient knowledge to permit "fine tuning" of economic policies; that fiscal change can provide lasting stimulus or restraint; that growing government spending can bring broader public services without harming the private sector of the economy; that thrift and savings are bad, and spending is good; and that balanced budgets are passé, and deficits beneficial. The world has suffered serious inflation, recession, and slower growth by listening to these claims. As the experience of the United Kingdom shows, the more faith countries have placed in these claims, the more their economic situation has deteriorated. If we are to restore price stability and stable real economic growth, policies must veer toward the rules we have stated. A large body of empirical research supports our analyses and policy prescriptions. A better-informed citizenry and pressure on elected representatives can play a major role in restoring the dynamic character of our market-oriented economy.

Unfortunately, even if there were unanimous agreement among economists and policymakers on the above prescriptions, it would be difficult, if not impossible, to implement them in governments formed by free men and women. Short-run political advantages can often be gained by doing the opposite. Only an informed, vocal, and effective citizenry can force elected representatives to eschew the short-run, temporary gains for the longer-run benefits. To the extent that investors observe violations in the above rules, they should be on the lookout for economic instability and sharp swings in the values of their investments.

PUBLIC POLICIES FOR LIVING WITH INFLATION

The major obstacles to ending inflation and promoting stable growth are related to politics, not economics. When political will is backed up by an informed and outraged citizenry, inflation can be conquered. Serious inflation can be prevented if the central bank limits the growth of the nation's money supply to a stable rate commensurate with the long-term growth of real goods and services. Achieving stable prices in this way could readily avoid the inevitable inequities that result from volatile inflation. Borrowers and lenders would be able to execute contracts equitable to both parties. Fixed-income recipients would not suffer a constant erosion of purchasing power. Financial markets would become less volatile, thereby facilitating the financing of enterprises as well as governments. Investors would be able to choose among investment media on the basis of the asset form and income stream which best served their needs, given their risk inclinations. Retirement would be based on the personal trade-off between leisure and higher income without the fear that income might be eroded by serious inflation. Windfall losses and gains would be less frequent, strengthening the confidence of citizens in the economic system. Clearly, a stable value of money would promote a more equitable distribution of income. Yet in both ancient and modern societies, inflation has been the rule and price stability the exception. What are the overriding incentives that cause governments to promote inflation?

Political obstacles

There appear to be at least two. Just ending inflation and promoting price stability would deprive governments of revenues they obtain without the painful task of legislating tax increases. Second, halting existing inflation inevitably brings a temporary period of economic slowdown and higher unemployment of human and capital resources. Alternatively, governments are encouraged to move from price stability to inflation because tax revenues rise more than national income and because the short-run effects of economic stimulus are politically attractive—more employment, production, and profits—while the longer-run costs of inflation are delayed.

How do governments gain from inflation?[3] First of all, they issue money to pay for expenditures or debts. Newly issued money serves as a base on which the banking system creates additional money in the form of deposits. The more money a government issues, the greater its claim on resources without taxation and the greater the ultimate inflation. This is a time-honored practice. Rulers once acquired such extra resources by clipping coins (reducing their size and issuing more coins). Later, resources were acquired by replacing gold and silver with less valuable metals; and now they are acquired by issuing paper money and creating bank reserves through Federal Reserve purchases of government securities. In 1973 the U.S. government acquired about $8 billion in this way.

Governments also gain from increases in personal and corporate income tax receipts during inflation. Individuals are forced into a higher tax bracket, even though their real income (income after allowing for inflation) may not have increased. Under a fixed-percentage income tax, say 10 percent, inflation would raise both individuals' income and government revenue proportionately. However, under a progressive tax system, such as exists in the United States, the increase in taxes that results from moving into higher tax brackets is more than proportionate. Inflation sometimes results in paper gains on which taxes must be paid and inadequate charges for expenses. For example, corporations tend to pay more real taxes since inflation raises the prices of their inventories and renders depreciation allowances inadequate to replace capital. In such ways inflation causes resources to be shifted from the private to the public sector of the economy. It

---

[3] This section draws heavily from Milton Friedman, "Using Escalators to Help Fight Inflation," *Fortune Magazine*, vol. 90, no. 1 (1974), pp. 94-97 ff.

has been estimated that additional corporate and personal taxes caused by inflation amounted to about $16 billion in 1974 alone.[4]

Finally, as the largest single debtor, the government gains from inflation at the expense of its creditors because inflation decreases the real value of outstanding federal debt. The inflation of 1975 benefited the government by about $5 billion in this manner.

Indexation of public and private contracts

After inflation has become a long-established way of life, inflationary expectations tend to be reflected in interest rates, rentals, union contracts, and other longer-term agreements. Once this has happened, it takes a change in the inflation rate to bring about a redistribution of income. For example, if the expected rate of future inflation is 6 percent a year, high-grade corporate bond yields would be about 9 percent, as would wage increases. If inflation should unexpectedly slow to 3 percent a year, there would be a windfall to bondholders and wage earners. Debtors would lose, and the profits of firms that had made substantial wage commitments would be squeezed. Thus, varying rates of inflation can lead to unexpected gains and losses for those entering into contracts for future payments or receipts.

One way to reduce the inequities and uncertainty of future inflation is to establish the widespread use of price-escalator clauses in private and government contracts. Through this procedure, known as indexing, the amount called for in various contracts is adjusted in line with developing inflation rates. In addition to reducing the uncertainty and inequities that result from unanticipated inflation, indexation may actually reduce the government's incentives to inflate.

How could indexing be so beneficial? Professor Milton Friedman, a key proponent of indexing, has made several proposals. In general, he advocates that escalator clauses be legislated for the federal government and that existing legal barriers to indexation in the rest of the economy be removed. Specifically, he calls for the use of escalator clauses in personal and corporate income tax rates

---

[4] William Fellner, Kenneth W. Clarkson, and John H. Moore, *Correcting Taxes for Inflation* (Washington, D.C.: American Enterprise Institute for Public Policy Research, 1975), p. 8.

and in government securities. The proposed technical changes in income tax rates would avoid the payment of a higher percentage of income as a result of inflation. It not only would remove an incentive for government to inflate, but would also permit the private sector to retain control of more resources by avoiding automatically higher tax rates. Friedman also proposes that the payment of interest and the repayment of the principal on government securities be indexed. This would insure an equitable return to purchasers of the federal debt. The federal government has already adopted partial escalators for social security payments, retirement benefits to federal employees, and the salaries of post office employees. In addition, cost-of-living escalators have been incorporated into numerous wage agreements.

Many fear that the extension of indexation to taxes, government bonds, and private contracts would condemn us to perpetual inflation. They believe that higher costs, and particularly higher wages, cause inflation. But wages are merely the price for a worker's services since costs to the person doing the buying are actually prices to the person doing the selling. Hence, the view that higher wages or "costs" lead to higher inflation is really a view that higher prices lead to higher prices. This is hardly a substantive explanation. It does not tell us why inflation alternatively speeds up, slows down, and on rare occasions stops entirely.

If indexation becomes widespread, the normal two-year lag between changes in money and inflation will be shortened. This means that stimulative monetary policies would be followed by more inflation sooner rather than later. As a result, the short-term political benefits of stimulating the economy to artificially boost employment are likely to be less effective, Similarly, slower monetary growth could result in a much quicker slowdown in inflation, thus minimizing the recessionary effects that now inevitably follow such action.

To summarize. Inflation can be controlled and even eliminated, provided that the political will exists to accomplish the job. The only effective way to eliminate serious inflation is to eliminate rapid monetary growth. But by itself reducing or eliminating inflation won't bring continued prosperity. Productivity gains, continued investment in factories and machines, and a profitable free market for business go hand in hand as essential ingredients of prosperity. Following the rules listed at the beginning of this chapter would achieve these objectives.

If the political will does not exist to end or at least control inflation, then the second-best method for dealing with inflation would be indexation of public and private contracts. By itself, indexation won't stop inflation, but indexing the tax system and government securities would eliminate government gains from inflation and hence reduce the government's inevitable incentive to inflate. Indexation of private contracts would promote equity and reduce the distortions which result from inflation. Since costs would promptly reflect abating inflation, private escalation would tend to ease the transition from inflation to price stability. There is little reason to believe that widespread indexation would promote inflation, and in fact it might tend to inhibit inflationary pressures. The worst possible combination of affairs was represented by recent history, when policymakers promised noninflationary policies while pursuing the opposite. An inadequately escalated private and public sector resulted in widespread inequities and encouraged a widely held view that citizens were getting the short end of the bargain.

If public policies do become noninflationary, the recent trend toward escalation will disappear. In that event, existing escalators will do no harm. If, conversely, inflation increases, the recent trend toward indexation will become more pronounced, and escalators will serve a useful purpose.

Investors should not be apprehensive about widespread indexation; they should welcome it. What should concern investors are violations of the above-mentioned rules. To the extent that government spending continues to grow faster than does national income, that large federal deficits persist, and that monetary growth remains rapid and erratic, we as a nation will lose the money game. Although, on average, a citizen's well-being is reflected in the well-being of his country, particular individuals will fare differently. Just as there are individual losers in a prosperous, noninflationary economy, there are individual winners under adverse economic conditions. Regardless of the future direction of economic events, being on the side of the winners, or at least avoiding the losing side, should be an investor's prime objective. This is the topic of our final chapter.

9

Winning on your own

Ask not what your country can do for you—You may have to do it yourself.

We began by discussing money—its mechanics, its politics, where it comes from, and how it influences production, jobs, and inflation. Next, we considered the influence of money and business activity on stocks, bonds, and other investments. We went on to demonstrate that monetary relations are not purely a domestic matter, but that the same principles which govern the U.S. economy also underlie economic fluctuations abroad. Throughout the presentation we have insisted on testing our assertions against the hard touchstone of past facts. Since no one factor completely explains business and investment performance, we have consistently presented evidence so that the reader can judge for himself the extent to which our explanations have held true.

On the basis of our reasoning and the evidence, we presented various rules for winning. Hopefully, we can win the money game as a nation so that in future years a sustainable increase in productive jobs, economic freedom, and price stability will characterize the economy. As individuals, our first priority should be to fight for the types of economic policies that will accomplish these goals.

As long as there is widespread belief that hard economic problems can be solved simply by printing more money, increasing government spending, incurring large deficits, and passing legislation to outlaw unemployment and inflation, dreams of economic stability will remain impossible dreams. As investors, we cannot be tilting at windmills forever. We must recognize artificial solutions for what they are, and design investment programs to protect our assets and maximize our returns in future inflationary settings.

Our review of basic economic principles serves many purposes. If we have been successful in persuading the reader that to a large extent the behavior of the economy is geared to fundamental economic factors which are controlled essentially by the government, then he is less likely to be swayed by mass psychology into buying stocks when investor sentiment is high and selling when the headlines are most discouraging.

Furthermore, if ill-conceived economic policies are adopted, a good grounding in economic principles should help the individual investor to avoid the pitfalls arising from those policies. While we may not have the power to convince policymakers of the appropriate policies for winning the money game as a nation, we do have power over our own assets and can win the game on our own. Knowledge of past investment behavior, of the key ingredients underlying that behavior, and of the expected returns from various investments, should help the investor to formulate and meet his basic objectives.

INVESTMENT OBJECTIVES

To begin with, anyone who wants to win the money game has to play, and in order to play he must first accumulate funds. At some point, all assets were preceded by saving income. Either the investor or his rich uncle sacrificed some income by not spending it on a night on the town or some other enjoyable function. Instead, use of the money was given to someone else, and in return the investor received a bonus. Anyone who wants to badly enough can accumulate assets by giving up current pleasures derived from spending income today. Therefore, before most people have a chance to win or lose the money game, a systematic savings program must be formulated and practiced in order to accumulate funds.

No one but the investor himself has the right to formulate his personal objectives. If a person desires to build a fortune from a limited amount of funds, then he should realize that the risks are great. Generally, a younger investor can better afford to make risky investments since, as a rule, he has little to lose and a whole lifetime of gainful employment to recoup his losses. By the same token, an investor nearing retirement should lean heavily toward securing his principal, regardless of how much or how little he has. He cannot afford to take risks because if he loses at this stage of life, the chances are that he will be unable to rebuild his assets.

Aside from this general rule, little can be said about how much risk you should take. That's up to you. However, the one general principle that should be kept in mind is that the greater the return you are promised, the greater the risk. As we saw in Chapter 6, a relatively risk-free investment designed to insure principal has yielded only about 2 percent per year after allowance for inflation. Stocks, which entail additional risks, have earned on average about 6 percent per year after allowance for inflation. Ventures promising an even higher return, such as real estate trusts and options trades, do so only with a corresponding increase in risk. There is nothing inherently wrong with such ventures so long as the investor realizes the gamble involved.

Whatever amount of risk the investor decides to accept, he still has the problem of placing his funds in the right vehicle—stocks, bonds, savings accounts, real estate, education, insurance, gold, pizza parlors, and so on. The choices are virtually limitless, and the correct choice, which will yield the highest return for the risk, depends on economic conditions and particularly on inflation.

SURVIVING INFLATION—POLICIES FOR PRUDENT INVESTORS

As noted in Chapter 5, the nation as a whole does not gain from unexpected inflation. In fact, it probably loses due to serious distortions in prices and wages. Nonetheless, some individuals lose and some gain, depending on how their incomes and assets are affected. Debtors clearly win because they are able to pay off debt with cheaper dollars, while creditors lose for the opposite reason. Owners of real assets, such as well-selected real estate, tend to benefit over an inflationary cycle, since returns often go up more than inflation. On the other hand, owners of fixed-income assets, such as bonds and cash, lose because the purchasing power of fixed-income assets declines and in the case of long-term bonds, the actual dollar value also declines due to higher interest rates.

The average worker's wage tends to rise more rapidly than does inflation, and hence, as a rule, workers do not lose out. Those on long-term contracts, including most union workers, lose in the early phase of inflation but catch up later. The compensation of nonunion workers tends to respond most rapidly to escalating inflation. Individuals on fixed incomes, of course, lose because of declines in purchasing power. To the extent that retired workers have built-in escalators, such as social security payments, this loss in purchasing power is avoided. Workers with low skills or low job mobility tend to gain in the early stages of an inflation, since marginal jobs are more readily available. Unless the tax system is escalated for inflation, all taxpayers lose because they pay a higher percentage of their real income in taxes, while the government gains by receiving an unlevied increase in tax receipts.

Therefore, to the extent that faster monetary growth and faster inflation characterize the future, the name of the game is to avoid categories of assets and incomes that lose during inflation, and to concentrate income and assets in categories that gain from the income redistribution and asset appreciation.

Alternative investments

Even if you are not an expert on inflation detection and investments, there are prudent inflation defenses that everyone can adopt. Prudence dictates diversification of assets, but diversification among assets and income sources that provide long-run inflation protection.

Home ownership. Most of us have the choice of buying a home or renting. For most people, a home represents the largest investment of a lifetime. Although we all look upon a home as a place to live and raise families, we should also recognize that it represents a major investment of savings. We noted in Chapter 6 that residential and farm real estate investments have represented excellent inflation hedges in the past and are likely to continue to do so. Unanticipated inflation tilts the residence choice from renting toward buying. Not only does the private homeowner enjoy the tax benefit of deducting interest payments from taxable income, but a home carefully selected with respect to location, size, and style is likely to appreciate in value more than prices rise. If inflation is an ongoing affair, the sooner one can afford to buy a house the better. Inflation expectations argue for the purchase of as large a house as can be afforded. Financing the house with sizable debt means that the homeowner will also gain by paying off the debt over a lifetime with cheaper dollars. So the homeowner gains from unexpected inflation in at least three ways—tax advantages, appreciating values, and repayment of debt with depreciated dollars.

Education. Investment in education and training is another major expenditure. Educational investment usually offers a good return and also represents an important inflation hedge. The development of job skills helps insure that later income streams will be higher and that income will rise with inflation. Low-skilled jobs tend to be most sensitive to erratic economic policies. Once an effort is made to control inflation, jobs requiring the lowest skills are usually the most vulnerable to layoffs. Hence, an investment in education tends to be a hedge against future loss of income. However, since the investment will be made well in advance of returns, due to inflation, the dollars invested will be more valuable than the dollars returned, and it is therefore necessary that the future income stream grow as inflation continues. The acquisition of educational skills by partial debt financing represents one way of gaining as a debtor.

Insurance. Insurance expenditures may also take a large bite out of income. Life insurance represents a means of providing an instant estate in the event of premature death. During periods of unanticipated inflation, heavy reliance on term insurance is the cheapest way of providing an adequate estate, and it avoids investments in the fixed-value assets represented by most ordinary life insurance policies. Given inflation, fixed dollar payments to be received 20 years in the future are worth much less in terms of purchasing power than are the dollars invested.

Cash on hand and liquid assets. Most people find it prudent to maintain a sizable cushion of assets that can be readily converted into cash to care for unforeseen financial emergencies. To the extent that a friendly bank stands ready to loan on request, the size of liquid reserves can and should be reduced. Placing reserve funds in U.S. savings bonds has represented a very poor investment in recent years. Interest rates on these bonds have usually lagged the inflation rate, and early redemption reduces the realized returns. Furthermore, in recent years the maintenance of liquid funds in financial institutions, such as banks and savings and loans, has not provided adequate inflation protection. Because of federally imposed ceiling rates, financial institutions cannot pay interest rates sufficient to compensate for serious inflation, except for deposits exceeding $100,000. Moving from passbook savings to large negotiable certificates of deposit normally provides a higher rate of return, but the substantial amount required places this alternative outside the reach of most investors. If federal regulations on ceiling rates are abandoned, as is now expected, savings accounts are likely to provide better inflation protection, as financial institutions pay rates that more fully reflect the underlying inflation rate.

Savings accounts may be used when market rates are below the savings rate. As funds accumulate, they should be shifted into such marketable investments as Treasury bills and high-grade commercial paper when the market rates exceed the savings rate. Unfortunately, the investor generally needs at least $10,000 to purchase these instruments. The disadvantage of such short-term investments is that they mature and must be reinvested frequently, but the compensating advantage is that capital loss is avoided as inflation accelerates and interest rates rise. Normally, the interest rate on renewed investments more than keeps up with the inflation rate.

This is not true for a completely risk-free security, such as a Treasury bill. Over time, the returns from these securities have been just sufficient to offset the effects of higher inflation.[1] For high-grade commercial paper, the return after allowing for inflation has been about 2 percent per year. Short-term investments avoid purchasing power and capital losses from inflation and usually provide a positive real rate of return. Furthermore, liquidity

---

[1] Roger G. Ibbotson and Rex A. Sinquefield, "Stocks, Bonds, Bills, and Inflation: Year-by-Year Historical Returns (1926-1974)," *Journal of Business,* vol. 49, no. 1 (1976), p. 42.

is assured, since these securities have a ready market and can be sold at short notice without significant capital variation.

In recent years, money market funds have made it possible for the small investor to acquire diversification and professional management for investment units below $10,000. The funds are typically invested in short-term debt securities, such as Treasury bills, bank certificates of deposit, and commercial paper. These funds do not charge for accepting the investment, but they do charge about 1 percent per year for fees and expenses. This charge further reduces the moderate returns from these investments. However, the investor is rewarded with a safe, secure pool of funds.

Stocks and bonds. After the home has been bought, educational and insurance needs provided for, and adequate liquid reserves acquired, what next? We do not recommend bonds for periods of rising inflation. Higher inflation tends to result in higher interest rates on new bonds. This reduces the market value of existing bonds, which have lower fixed-interest payments than do the new bonds. Even if you hold your bond to maturity, the lower payments and the erosion in the real value of the principal make it an undesirable investment.

Despite the volatility of common stock prices, long-term returns from stocks have exceeded on average the returns from all other general categories of investments that we have been able to verify. However, it is hard to remember this when stock prices are in a sinking phase, and net worth is steadily eroding. The great risk of common stock ownership is that the investor will lose his nerve at just the wrong time, sell out his holdings at or near the low of the market, and fail to repurchase for better markets. Furthermore, the investor should diversify his holdings of stocks in an effort to limit risks. If fewer stocks are held, risks increase and returns can be expected to be even more erratic than those for the entire market.

Minimum fees charged by most investment advisors or trust departments usually make utilization of these services prohibitively expensive unless the investor has $250,000 or more to invest. Brokers provide investment advice, but often follow-up recommendations are not forthcoming, and there is sometimes an irresistible tendency for the broker to encourage excessive transactions costs. Consequently, until a sizable investment fund has been accumulated, the common stock investor must usually depend on mutual fund management.

A mutual fund is an investment company that is organized to pool and manage the funds of different investors. It is designed to provide a means for obtaining a broad diversification of investments. The mutual fund itself owns stocks, bonds, and other securities, while the investors own shares of the fund. Different funds have different objectives, such as growth, income and security, which they are required to state so that the investor can choose a fund with investment objectives similar to his own.

All but a handful of mutual funds are open-end companies. This means that the number of shares in the mutual fund changes with participation. When more money is invested, the fund increases its shares outstanding; when redemptions exceed new investment, the number of shares is decreased. As a rule, the value of a share in the mutual fund reflects the market value of the fund's investments divided by the number of the fund's shares outstanding. Hence, if the mutual fund has a representative portfolio of stocks, the value of its shares will move in line with the stock market.

Now for the bad news. Most open-end mutual funds charge a sizable initial fee of about 8 percent of the amount placed with the fund. Thereafter, an investor typically pays a management fee of about ½ percent per year. Although the management fee is a bargain, provided that the manager has the required talents, the 8 percent fee is fairly steep.

The investor can avoid a sizable initial charge with a "no-load" mutual fund. However, in return for not paying the initial 8 percent sales charge, he will not be able to rely on salesmen. Rather, he must take it upon himself to determine which no-load funds are in line with his own objectives and which will best fulfill his needs.

Finally, there are closed-end investment companies which do not stand ready to refund their shares. Shares in such companies are bought and sold on various exchanges for a price determined in the marketplace. This price may reflect not only the market value of the investments held by a closed-end company, but also such other factors as a limited or extraordinary demand for closed-end companies, faith (or a lack of it) in the funds managers, and so on. It generally takes a greater amount of investigation on the part of the investor to successfully purchase shares in a closed-end company than in an open-end mutual fund.

Either way, the investor should carefully review the objectives, management, and track record of the various investment companies before committing his funds. An excellent source of such information is *Investment Companies, Mutual Funds, and Other Types,* an annual publication of Wiesenberger Services, Inc., which can be found in most libraries and brokerage houses.

Real estate. Real estate tends to provide a good hedge against inflation, since returns on real estate tend to rise more during inflationary periods than does the general price level. Furthermore, real estate provides numerous tax advantages related to deducting interest payments and depreciation allowances. However, various expenses are often associated with owning real estate. Unless the property can be continuously rented at a sufficient return to offset these expenses, the average investment in real estate is likely to prove disappointing. As a rule, special management skills are needed to select and maintain property and to insure a continuous flow of rental income. For the investor who has such skills, real estate can represent a prudent investment during inflationary periods.

Precious metals, gems, art, antiques. The first thing to remember about "precious" items is that they are precious not because of their potential return but because of their value relative to their size. Since, by definition, the prices of real assets rise during an inflationary period, precious items tend to increase in value. Moreover, the evidence that we have been able to accumulate suggests that during inflationary periods the prices of precious items tend to rise more than prices in general. This is probably due to the increased tendency of individuals to use such items as stores of value when prices are rising rapidly.

Several points are in order, however, before you run out and purchase a houseful of precious items for investment purposes. To begin with, such items are not recommended for the prudent investor. They yield no income and often involve significant costs, such as insurance, storage, and verification fees. They cost money just to hold, and therefore, their prices must increase just to keep the investor from losing. During periods of extremely rapid unanticipated inflation, the investor who is able to choose wisely among various precious goods is likely to end up with a high return. However, the goods should usually be sold before inflation is fully anticipated or slows down. The reason for this is that over an extended period of time the prices of precious items, such as gold, silver, and diamonds, do not tend to rise much faster than prices in general. Hence, the prudent investor who makes these items a part of his general investment portfolio is likely to be disappointed with their performance.

Pensions. The worker should recognize that a claim on a pension upon retirement represents a good inflation hedge prior to retirement. Most pension benefit payments are determined by length of service and the average salary received in the latter years of employment. Since salaries usually increase with experience, and current salaries tend to reflect the current rate of inflation, potential pension benefits adjust upward with inflation. However, most private pension plans promise to pay a fixed dollar amount per year, upon retirement and the pensioner therefore is vulnerable to future inflation. Recently, social security payments were indexed or escalated for inflation so that maintenance of the purchasing power they provide is assured so long as this provision is retained. Federal government retirees are at least partially protected by indexed pension benefits, as are retired members of the armed forces. But those on fixed pensions can do little to prevent the erosion of their incomes by inflation. Any hedging must be done long before retirement, when savings should be built up and assets managed wisely so as to establish a cushion against the erosion of a pension's value.

Continuing to work after you retire from your lifelong position represents another means of providing inflation protection. Of course, health problems may eliminate this option. Furthermore, at present social security rules make this option a costly one prior to age 72. Under these rules one is not eligible for full social security payments if his earned income exceeds the maximum postretirement earned income that is allowed. If such postretirement income can be bunched into a limited number of months, full social security payments can be received in all other months. There is currently great pressure for increasing the maximum earnings permitted while full social security benefits are drawn. As the ceiling is raised, postretirement work will become a better inflation hedge for workers qualified to draw social security. Furthermore, it will permit the nation to benefit longer from trained and experienced workers. The nation can ill afford a disincentive system which forces idleness among citizens who prefer to work and want to provide a further inflation hedge for themselves and their families.

Rules for winning as a prudent investor

Where do we end up? How can the prudent investor best protect the value of his assets and still win the money game?

1. Develop a systematic savings plan as early in life as possible, so as to provide for a continuous accumulation of assets. Remember, before winning the money game, you must acquire the assets necessary to play.

2. Be alert to the types of incomes and assets that tend to perform well in an inflationary environment and position yourself so that when inflation redistributes income and wealth you are on the receiving end rather than the giving end.

3. Regardless of prospective developments, don't put all your eggs in one or two baskets. Diversify your assets. No one knows with any precision what the future has in store, and diversification is simply the prudent way of hedging against the unknown.

4. To the extent that unexpected rapid inflation is an economic fact of life, the single best investment you are likely to make is your house. Moreover, in this environment, the more expensive the house and the more attractive the location, the better the investment.

5. Over the long haul a diversified portfolio of common stocks and short-term fixed-income securities is recommended. Short-term securities tend to be a fairly safe hedge against inflation, but can be expected to yield a relatively low return—about 2 percent-3 percent after inflation. A diversified portfolio of common stocks is likely to carry a higher average return—about 6 percent after allowing for inflation and associated costs. The chances for a decline in the value of an investor's assets make stocks a higher-risk alternative. As a general rule, the longer stocks are held, the lower the risk. For a young investor who plans to commit his funds for at least five years, a prudent diversification might include a house, about 60 percent of his remaining assets in a diversified

portfolio of stocks, and about 40 percent in short-term fixed-income securities, although the precise commitment would depend on the amount of risk the individual wishes to incur.

6. Avoid get-rich-quick schemes which offer a potential for high returns. Be especially leery of real estate investments which won't be continuously producing rent, and of purchases of precious metals and stones which may have significant costs associated with holding them.

These rules are not designed to make you rich overnight, but they should provide guidelines for a relatively secure portfolio which yields a comfortable appreciation of approximately 4 percent per year after allowance for inflation.

POLICIES FOR AGGRESSIVE INVESTORS

For better or worse, most of us are greedy. At a rate of 4 percent per year it would take 19 years before an investor would double the real value of his portfolio. For those who want to double the real value of their assets sooner and are willing to incur a greater risk, the opportunities are there. The aggressive investor can switch the bulk of his assets into and out of various investments, depending on the extent to which he is willing to accept risks.

There are several rules for winning which should guide the aggressive investor.

1. Recognize that everyone wants a higher than average return, but that to obtain it you must take greater than average risks.
2. Follow business conditions closely and develop timing principles that will add to long-run returns.
3. Feel confident that you understand the essential factors that cause business activity and inflation to behave as they do.
4. Recognize the effect of the economic environment on the value of particular assets.

Playing the stock market

Unfortunately, there is no precise tool available for always buying stocks low and selling them high. However, certain approaches based on financial and economic analysis often serve to strengthen confidence and hence contribute to better than random results. Since financial markets tend to be relatively efficient, there is no substitute for careful and continuous analysis of financial and economic trends as they unfold. It's a rather safe bet that knowledge well known to the marketplace has already been discounted in the market value of existing assets. It is therefore necessary to approach the timing problem utilizing the best-known tools available.

Perhaps the worst mistake that an aggressive investor can make is to permit prevailing sentiments in the marketplace to overrule his judgment concerning relative risks. It's all too easy in the depths of a serious bear market (when stock prices fall) to become emotionally depressed and dispose of assets near the low in the cycle. Conversely, the buoyant atmosphere characterizing bull markets (when stock prices rise) encourages heavy financial bets at or near the peak. To put it differently, it is mandatory for an aggressive investor to attempt to imagine reasonable scenarios contrary to prevailing opinions. However, it is equally important that his contrary opinions be well-immersed in tested theory and current facts.

It has long been recognized that stock markets have a persistent tendency to move ahead of the business cycle. Bull markets usually emerge before business pickup; bear markets tend to begin before a slowdown in economic activity. In fact, one of the best leading indicators of the business trend is the stock market. Hence, in attempting to get a handle on the probable future trend of stock prices, it's not enough to know the current state of the economy. Attention must be focused on factors likely to influence economic activity and profits in the future. Consequently, government policies likely to influence economic activity with a lag should be the focus of the analysis.

It is the thesis of this book that the primary factor initiating subsequent spending trends, and hence income, employment, profits, and inflation, is the change in monetary policy as measured by the change in the money supply. Sufficient evidence has been presented in previous chapters to enable you to judge whether our theory is a viable one or whether we have been chasing a will-o'-the-wisp.

A declining trend in monetary growth usually precedes or

accompanies bear markets in stocks. Alternatively, rising monetary growth slightly leads or slightly follows initial bull markets. Chart 9-1 relates monetary growth to stock price trends. You will note that prior to the early 1960s declining monetary growth typically preceded bear markets by many months. In recent years the lead has often shortened and has become almost coincident. As market participants became more knowledgeable concerning the impact

Chart 9-1
Money and stock prices

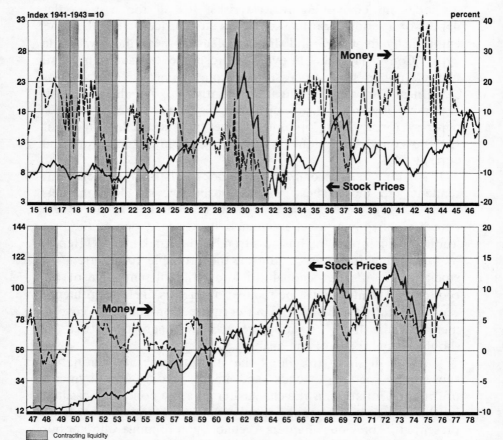

Contracting liquidity

Money, defined as currency plus demand deposits, are 6-month seasonally adjusted annual rates of change plotted at the midpoint of the interval.
Stock prices are Standard & Poor's composite stock price index.

Source: Board of Governors of the Federal Reserve System; National Bureau of Economic Research; Standard & Poor's Corporation

of changing monetary growth on stock prices, this knowledge plus activity in the market drastically shortened the lead of money over stock prices. Nonetheless, forgetting for the moment the practical difficulties of determining at the time the peak and trough of monetary growth trends, it is clear that they are closely related to bear and bull stock markets. Furthermore, it is our view that changes in money are major determinants of the observed fluctuation in stock prices.

As a general rule, an aggressive investor should reduce or eliminate stockholdings whenever he is convinced that monetary policy is tightening, and should increase stock participation whenever he is convinced that a more expansive policy is either under way or about to begin. Although the aggressive investor is unlikely to sell at the peak and buy at the bottom, by following such a rule he will almost certainly avoid being out of stocks during a bull market and fully committed during a sinking market.

Some would say that variations in lags plus the difficulty of correctly determining changing monetary trends, make such a rule operationally useless. Having been actively involved in timing decisions on stock purchases and sales for many years, we are convinced that the results are better than random though far from perfect. Combining a careful analysis of monetary policy with a knowledge of the state of the business cycle and of corporate profits, will, at a minimum, prevent the wrong decision. Such information will serve to strengthen convictions which otherwise might be inadequate. Frequently, careful monetary analysis will not only enable the investor to avoid gross error but will also encourage him to take the correct market action.

The ideal time for holding stocks is during a period of expanding monetary growth, slowing inflation, declining interest rates, and rising corporate profits. Such a period seems most likely to develop in the final stages of a recession and early in the recovery. Monetary authorities will be moving to easier money to fight the recession; the recession will begin to reduce the rate of inflation; interest rates will reflect the decelerating inflation and reduced private activity; and corporate profits will begin to improve following cost-cutting efforts. Conversely, stockholdings should be pared or eliminated during a period in which monetary growth declines, interest rates rise as inflation expectations rise, and growth in profits slows. Such a period usually develops following a speedup in monetary growth and a relatively high utilization of resources. Whether the investor will want to chance stocks during a period of rapid inflation should depend on his evaluation of corporate profitability.

In general, profits do poorly during periods of volatile monetary growth. In the past, high monetary growth accompanied by serious inflation has inevitably induced political efforts to slow the inflation. The transition from serious to moderate inflation has brought less monetary growth and a weak stock market.

Investment strategies and inflation

While profits are a key to stock performance, price developments can be an important factor in determining which type of investment to hold. Historically, periods of falling prices have generally been great for bonds and bad for stocks and real assets. On average (but not always) stocks performed best during periods of price stability and moderate inflation, while real assets did best in periods of rapid inflation. Table 9–1 summarizes the yearly returns to alternative investments under different inflationary conditions and over extended periods of time.

Since it would appear that the only two labels which apply to today's world are "moderate inflation" and "rapid inflation," the prospect for either stable or declining prices in the immediate

Table 9-1
Real returns to assets—returns minus inflation (log linear least squares annual growth rates)

	Housing	Farm- land	Gold	Silver	Commercial paper	Bonds	Stocks
Deflation	1 %	−4 %	n.a.	−8 %	10 %	10 %	−4 %
Price stability	4	3	n.a.	−1	2	5	13
Moderate inflation	4	5	n.a.	0	3	1	9
Rapid inflation	6	9	12 %	7	−5	−8	3
1890-1975	4.8	n.a.	−0.7	−0.9	1.3	1.6	6.8
1912-1975	4.9	3.9	−0.6	0.0	0.6	1.4	7.8
1950-1975	5.0	6.3	1.3	3.3	1.7	−0.8	7.2

Averages for different inflationary periods rounded to nearest percentage point.
n.a.—not available.
Source: See Data Appendix.

future seems extremely remote. Investment strategies would thus appear fairly clear-cut—investments should be concentrated in real assets such as real estate as opposed to financial assets such as bonds. Unfortunately, the investment decision is not that simple. For most of the historical period over which these returns apply, investors had very low expectations for future inflation. As a result, little or no inflationary premium was incorporated into investments. Hence, any inflation which developed was generally unexpected.

Today the situation has changed. Most people expect inflation to continue in the future. During the 10 years ending in 1975 inflation averaged between 5 percent and 6 percent per year. As a result, most investments have incorporated a premium which assumes that future price increases will continue in this range. Since a certain amount of inflation is already expected and factored into various investments, the key to their performance in the future depends upon how inflation differs from what is now anticipated. For example, if inflation actually matches expectations, then there would be little chance of profiting from that development, because most investors already anticipate it. The result would be investment performance similar to that which occurred historically under conditions of price stability. Hence, if future inflation matches current expectations, the real returns to alternative investments are likely to be similar to those shown in Table 9-1 under the heading "price stability."

In order for the performance of investments in the future to match the pattern shown for moderate inflation it will be necessary for inflation to be moderately higher than is currently expected. Similarly, in order to obtain substantial returns to real assets, inflation would have to be substantially higher than most people currently expect. Finally, the pattern of investment performance shown historically under "deflation" or falling prices is likely to occur if inflation rates develop which are lower than current expectations.

The implications of past patterns for investment performance have to be adjusted for current inflationary expectations. If you believe that future inflation will be lower than that which is expected by most people, your best bet might be fixed-income securities, particularly corporate bonds. Whether or not stocks are attractive in such a setting would depend on developing profit trends. If you anticipate inflation to be much higher than that expected by most investors, real assets should be your choice. To the extent that your views about future inflation are in line with those of most other investors, stocks represent the best investment vehicle (providing the outlook for profits is also positive).

Although factors other than inflation can have a strong influence on the returns to various assets, anticipating future inflationary performance can go a long way toward positioning the aggressive investor's portfolio on the winning side of the battle.

What does the future hold?

For the late 1960s and early 1970s we have witnessed oscillating monetary growth with a rising trend. With a lag this policy has also resulted in oscillating inflation rates with a rising trend. If this were to be indicative of our future, the proper investment policy would be to maintain a relatively heavy commitment in real assets including real estate. To the extent that the environment for corporate profits is favorable, stocks would also represent a good investment.

However, although it has become commonplace to argue that what has been will continue, there is reason to believe that the instability which has characterized the past decade will not continue into the future. Many investors and workers suffered serious losses in income and asset values during the past ten years. It is no longer popular to argue that more inflation brings more sustainable employment. The famous trade-off no longer works—if it ever did! Retirees living on fixed pensions have suffered, though social security recipients have been partially protected by escalating payments. There has been growing concern about the adequacy of social security taxes and of the funds for paying social security recipients if the recent course of inflation continues.

Many of the government programs that were designed to solve existing social inequities and economic problems have failed to achieve their stated objectives or have become very costly. In the meantime, taxes have soared and taxpayers have become increasingly resistant to further increases. At present, over 40 percent of national income is being allocated to government spending on the state, local, and federal levels. Furthermore, in the past five years more than half of the increase in national income has been due to increases in government outlays. Sizable and accelerating federal deficits have taken their toll on the savings available to the private sector of the economy. These deficits must be financed either by the creation of new money or by the absorption of savings which would otherwise be available to the private sector. If the new money route is chosen, to the extent that monetary growth accelerates significantly, inflation will inevitably increase, along with all the other problems that have been evident in the late 1960s and early 1970s. On the other hand, financing deficits by absorbing private savings will reduce the savings available for housing and the other forms of capital spending needed for job creation and growth in coming years. During the 1960s and early 1970s, the U.S. economy had allocated a smaller percentage of its total output to investments for the future than had the economies of many other developed countries. Finally, it is becoming more widely recognized that if we are to get inflation under control and provide savings and investments for the future, the growth in government spending must be slowed and the tax system must be changed to encourage savings and investment rather than consumption.

The worldwide inflation that followed accelerated money supply growth, and then the recession that followed tighter money, reminded all of us of the need to pursue a more stable and moderate monetary policy. The adoption of the 1974 Congressional Budget and Impoundment Control Act reflected growing taxpayer concern about rising federal expenditures. Congress is now forced to formulate spending priorities and to set a ceiling on total outlays and deficits. The Joint Monetary Resolution, adopted in 1975, calls for long-term monetary growth commensurate with real growth as well as greater public discussion of monetary policy formulation. Widespread discussion of these issues is a vehicle that has the potential for achieving a less volatile and more moderate monetary policy.

Will all the recent trends toward conservatism in spending and policymaking have an impact on further inflation? We can't be sure, but we dare to hope so. Ultimately the answer depends on the desires of the American voters. If they continue to insist on the quick fix, the easy answer, something for nothing, then our fate will be serious and volatile inflation. If that were our certain future, it would be relatively easy to propose and implement a winning investment policy, namely, avoid loss of purchasing power while extracting some gain from less-sophisticated income recipients and investors. The principles and rules are laid out above, and the only remaining challenge is how to implement them.

But what if recent tendencies toward financial restraint and economic conservatism become effective at the ballot box, and elected and appointed officials begin to avoid the short-run palliative for the longer-run gain. What if we run a budget surplus once in a while? What if government spending stops growing relative to the private sector and shows some tendency to decline? What if the Federal Reserve forsakes volatile and expansive monetary growth in favor of stable, moderate increases in the money supply? Under these conditions the investment problem would be much less concerned with the difficult art of timing and more concerned with designing an investment portfolio to fit particular investor needs. The principal concern of investors would be to select individual issues on the basis of fundamental growth trends rather than to gauge how a particular investment will be influenced by inflation and volatile business conditions. In our judgment, these conditions would lead to greater and more consistent economic growth and to trends in employment far superior to the recent record. But perhaps we are naive to even dream of such a setting. Politicians have long benefited by promising the impossible and then demonstrating the emptiness of their promises.

Whatever lies ahead, the serious investor must closely monitor current and future business trends and the government policies that will influence those trends. The best way to accomplish this is to follow closely what political leaders say and do and to anticipate the influence that their moves will have on basic economic forces. If, as has occurred so often in the past, economic policies develop which include a rapid increase in the money supply as part of the "solution" to the nation's problems, the fallout from such policies will adversely affect many. It is our hope that whatever the future economic policies may be, the principles presented in this book will help increase your chances for victory in the money games that lie ahead.

Data appendix*

I am ill at these numbers.
William Shakespeare, Hamlet

Most of the data used for the tables and charts in this book are readily available from the sources credited in the footnotes. Unfortunately, this was not the case for the data on the returns to various investments. Much of the data collected for this purpose had to be obtained from various original sources. Too often, consistent series were unavailable for the entire time period covered. Where overlapping data were available, we spliced and transformed the data into what we believe is a fairly consistent and useful series for the time interval covered. As a general rule, the earlier the time period, the less reliable the data become.

In addition to the difficulties of obtaining consistent series, there is the problem of determining the total return to a particular asset over a given time period. For an asset that does not earn any

*The authors are indebted to many individuals for their aid and advice in assembling and presenting the data for returns to investments. We are particularly indebted to Eldon Kreider for his technical advice on calculating holding period returns; to Maureen Doherty for her aid in obtaining the series for financial assets; and to Nanci Rogers for her contribution toward obtaining the data on real assets.

227

income, such as interest, dividends, or rent, the total return is simply the change in the price of the asset. However, for most of the popular assets, the income associated with holding them is a key ingredient in calculating the total return. While the precise procedure for calculating total returns to the various income-earning assets is different for each asset, it is helpful to begin by presenting the general procedure used to calculate those returns over a given period of time. Once this procedure has been described, we will proceed to discuss the data for each asset with respect to adjustments, reliability, and the specific method used to obtain rates of return.

GENERAL PROCEDURES FOR OBTAINING RATES OF RETURN

For many assets, the total return during the period that the asset is held involves two parts: (1) the change in the price of the asset from the beginning to the end of the period; (2) the income earned from the asset during the period. This relationship can be expressed as follows:

FORMULA FOR TOTAL RETURN TO AN ASSET

Let:

P_t = price of asset at time t

$Y_{t-1, t}$ = income from asset between time $t-1$ and t

$R_{t-1, t}$ = dollar change in value between time $t-1$ and t

By definition:

$$R_{t-1, t} = P_t - P_{t-1} + Y_{t-1, t}$$

The percentage return to the asset during the period $t-1$ to t is given by r_t:

$$r_t = \frac{R_{t-1, t}}{P_{t-1}} = \frac{P_t - P_{t-1} + Y_{t-1, t}}{P_{t-1}}$$

Transforming the equation:

$$1 + r_t = \frac{P_t}{P_{t-1}} + \frac{Y_{t-1, t}}{P_{t-1}}$$

$$(1) \qquad 1 + r_t = \frac{P_t}{P_{t-1}} + i_{t-1,\,t}$$

where $i_{t-1,\,t}$ = the income return during the period $t-1$ to t as a percentage of the price of the asset at time $t-1$.

In order to present compound returns to the asset over an extended period of time, an index was developed, using the following formula:

$$(2) \qquad S_t = S_{t-1}\,(1 + r_t)$$

where S_t is the accumulated value to the asset at time t.

There are several ways of determining an average return to an asset over time. The most fundamental procedure would be to obtain an arithmetic mean or average of the returns where the formula for such an average is expressed as:

$$\frac{1}{n} \sum_{t=1}^{n} (1 + r_t)$$

An arithmetic mean, however, is not an accurate measure for our purposes since it does not allow for the impact of compounding returns or interest earned on interest. In effect, the arithmetic mean calculates the average return to a fixed dollar investment. Since for our purposes the amount of the investment is constantly changing as price and income are added to the initial amount, it is appropriate to use what is known as a geometric mean. The geometric mean for a series of returns is given by the formula:

$$\left[\prod_{t=1}^{n} (1 + r_t) \right]^{1/n}$$

where Π is the symbol for multiplication of $(1 + r_1)$, $(1 + r_2)$, ... $(1 + r_n)$. For determining the geometric mean for a series of returns between time j and time k, the formula is:

$$\left[\prod_{t=j+1}^{k} (1 + r_t) \right]^{1/(k-j)}$$

Using our index for determining the geometric mean for a series of returns between time j and time k, the formula is:

$$[S_k/S_j]^{1/(k-j)}$$

The geometric mean determined in this manner is compounded at discrete intervals. In terms of the annual data used in our analysis, this formula yields a geometric mean which is compounded annually. The indexes in terms of S_t for each of the assets are presented at the end of this chapter, where we have arbitrarily set S_0 the initial value of S_t equal to 1. The reader can apply the above formula to determine the average annual compound return to an asset for any particular time period.

While more appropriate for our purposes than the arithmetic mean, the geometric mean is totally dependent on the values for the beginning and ending periods. If either of these values happens to be extremely high or low relative to the trend, the geometric mean is likely to give an unstable and somewhat misleading view of the expected returns for the period as a whole. A statistical procedure for obtaining a compound return which incorporates all of the values rather than just those of the starting and ending periods, is known as a log linear least squares growth rate. This procedure involves regressing the natural logarithm of S_t on a time variable to obtain a continuously compounded growth rate. This growth rate can then be transformed into a simple compound rate with the formula:

$$e^b - 1$$

where b represents the slope coefficient from the regression and e is the base of natural logarithms. When we found it desirable to use log linear growth rates, we have so indicated.

THE DATA

Financial assets

Data for returns to financial assets were revalued annually at the end of the year. The end of the year was chosen to accommodate information on dividends to stocks which is only available on a calendar year basis for earlier periods.

Commercial paper

The asset chosen for an investment in short-term fixed-income securities was four-to-six month commercial paper. This asset represents an IOU of a corporation for which the principal is due sometime within four to six months. This particular asset was chosen because of the existence of a consistent series of interest rates over an extended historical period and because some element of risk is attached to holding it. Although the series is referred to as prime-quality commercial paper, if the corporate borrower were to go bankrupt during the four to six months before maturity, the holder could lose his entire investment. In order to obtain a consistent series over the entire period covered, we had to splice series together. The early data through 1935 consisted of commercial paper rates in New York City from Macaulay (see bibliography), and the subsequent data consisted of four-to-six month prime commercial paper rates as reported by the Federal Reserve.

In order to consider an investment in commercial paper on a basis comparable to an investment in stocks or bonds, we should assume that in each case the investor has diversified his holdings of corporate debt among top-rated companies. In this sense, the possible failure of a company would impact only a small portion of the investor's holdings. Since companies generally do not go from a top-quality rating to bankruptcy overnight, we might also assume that in our portfolio assets are sold immediately (even at a slight loss) if the company's standing becomes questionable. The procedure for calculating the returns to commercial paper was fairly straightforward. Since the paper is redeemed at face value every six months, the returns depend entirely on the interest rates existing when the paper was bought. We considered the commercial paper rates in December and in June as representing the income earned to commercial paper. These rates had to be divided in half and compounded, since the returns would only apply to a six-month period. The annual return was then substituted into formula (2) presented above to generate an index of returns to commercial paper.

Bonds

In order to obtain data on a return to a long-term fixed-income security or bond, we attempted to choose a series which depicted the highest grade of corporate bonds available. The data prior to 1900 consisted of yields on the highest-quality railroad bonds (Macaulay); from 1900 to 1949 the yields were for high-quality 30-year bonds (Durand-Homer); from 1950 to 1975 the yields were for the Standard and Poor's AAA composite index. As far as we could determine, the Macaulay and Durand-Homer yields for high-grade corporate bonds were the most reliable historical series. These series appeared to be consistent with each other and with the S&P index mentioned above. However, in order to avoid discontinuities the Durand-Homer yields were lowered by .03 percentage points and the Macaulay yields were raised by .084 percentage points.

In calculating the returns to corporate bonds over a given period, we needed to incorporate both the interest or coupon yield attached to the bond and the change in the market value or price of the bond which resulted from a change in market interest rates. We assumed that the data on bond yields were representative of coupon yields for the respective dates. References in Macaulay and our own spot checks revealed that this assumption was reasonable. Our next step was to approximate the market value of a bond portfolio at the end (December) of each successive year. To do this, we utilized a slight variation of the formula mentioned above:

$$1 + r_t = \frac{P_t}{\text{Par}} + i_{t-1,\,t}$$

For the first year the bond was held, the interest income was given by the coupon rate at the start of the year; hence $i_{t-1,\,t}$ was actually i_{t-1}, or the new issue rate of bonds in December of the previous year. Par represented the price paid for the bond the previous year, which was always assumed to be equal to 100. P_t represented the current price or market value of the bond which was purchased the previous year and was calculated as (1) the present value of the sum of the principal of the bond that would have been paid at maturity (discounted at the current market rate of interest):

$$\frac{\text{Par}}{(1 + i_t)^m}$$

and (2) the discounted present value of the bonds coupon summed over the life of the bond:

$$\sum_{j=1}^{m} \frac{\text{Par} \cdot i_{t-1}}{(1 + i_t)^j}$$

where m represented the number of years remaining to maturity. Hence, by definition:

$$P_t = \frac{\text{Par}}{(1 + i_t)^m} + \sum_{j=1}^{m} \frac{\text{Par} \cdot i_{t-1}}{(1 + i_t)^j}$$

The procedure used for determining the holding period return to a bond attempted to revalue the bond (or bond portfolio) each year at its market value. Although we believe this procedure to be the best for our purposes, it is not ideal in that it does not allow for the changes in the maturity distribution of a bond portfolio. As a bond approaches maturity, its price or market value tends to be governed less by changes in interest rates and more by its redemption date. Since a diversified bond portfolio would be likely to include some bonds approaching maturity, the returns on such a portfolio would differ from those calculated from our index. Technically, our series on returns to bonds assumed a bond portfolio with a fixed maturity of 30 years from 1871 to 1949 and 20 years thereafter. Our switch to 20 years in the most recent period reflected the tendency toward shorter maturity schedules. The change in maturity assumption had little impact on the holding period returns.

Stocks

The data on returns to stocks after 1926 were based on the Standard and Poor's composite index of stock prices and dividends per share. For earlier years, the Cowles Commission series was the original source for the data. The Cowles Commission series is an extension of the Standard and Poor's series, the same method of construction being used, and as far as possible, the same companies. Once again, a slightly varied form of formula (1) was used:

$$1 + r_t = \frac{P_t + D_{t-1, t}}{P_{t-1}}$$

where $D_{t-1, t}$ represented the dividends per share paid to holders of the stock during the year t.

Housing

As far as we can determine, there are no reliable data on the average price of a new house prior to 1963, when the U.S. Department of Commerce began to collect such data. Consequently, in order to approximate a series on the average price of a new house, a construction cost index has been used as a substitute. Previous studies have used this procedure on the assumption that the movement of such an index reasonably reflects changes in new-house prices. Our series is the result of two existing indexes which are spliced together. From 1890 to 1914, the residential housekeeping construction cost index compiled by Leo Grebler[1] has been used, and thereafter the Boeckh index of residential construction cost.[2] Once the index was constructed it was placed on a 1967 = 1 basis and multiplied by $24,600 (the average price of a house in 1967). This produced a historical series which was designed to approximate the price of a house from 1890 to 1975.

This series was then compared with any historical data we could find on the prices of houses. Owing to the scarcity of information on historical housing prices, we considered all the available information in an attempt to verify the accuracy of our price index. We

---

[1] Leo Grebler, David M. Blank, and Louis Winnick, *Capital Formation in Residential Real Estate: Trends and Prospects* (Princeton, N.J.: Princeton University Press, 1956), p. 342.

[2] U.S. Department of Commerce, Bureau of the Census, *Historical Statistics of the United States: Colonial Times to 1957* (Washington, D.C.: U.S. Government Printing Office, 1960), p. 385. Plus updates.

discovered that data were available only when a specific study had been undertaken, leading to scattered information pertaining only to limited time periods and specific housing groups, as dictated by the unique purpose of the individual study. While none of the data are terribly consistent, in our judgment the comparisons are close enough to suggest that our series has captured the general trend in housing prices over time.

The data from 1929 to 1975 on the income return from housing, or rental income, were obtained from U.S. Department of Commerce estimates of rental income to persons from nonfarm owner-occupied housing units. The Commerce Department data include, among other expenses, charges for depreciation and mortgage interest. We decided not to allow mortgage interest as an expense, and hence added it to the rental income data. This adjustment, which serves to raise the rental income figures, was made so that the returns to all assets can be considered on a similar cash-purchased basis.

Once we had rental income figures in the desired form, the next step was to obtain the net rate of return to residential real estate by dividing the rental income figures by the total value of residential real estate. Data are available from 1929 to 1975 for the net value of nonfarm owner-occupied housekeeping residential structures.[3] Net stocks measured in this way represent the depreciated value of the capital stock. These figures, however, do not include the value of the land associated with the housing units. Since our data on the prices of houses and rental income either explicitly or implicitly include lot values, we needed to add the corresponding value of land to the stated value of the net housing stock. This was accomplished by assuming that in each year land value could be estimated as a specified percentage of the value of the residential housing stock. The specific percentages we used are based on several benchmark estimates of the U.S. Department of Commerce, Bureau of Economic Analysis. These estimated land values together with the value of the net housing stock were considered as the total net value of residential real estate, by

---

[3] John C. Musgrave, "New Estimates of Residential Capital in the United States, 1925-73," *Survey of Current Business*, vol. 54, no. 10 (1974), pp. 32-38. Update—U.S. Department of Commerce.

which rental income is divided. This procedure gave us a series on the net rate of return to owner-occupied nonfarm houses from 1929 to 1975.

Since no data are available on rental income prior to 1929, we assumed that the average rate of return for the 1929–75 period, 3.35 percent could be applied to the earlier period from 1890 to 1928. Since we have no real basis for making this assumption, the returns for these earlier years should be viewed as highly tentative. We also assumed that the rental return figures could be applied to our series on the price of a new house. We do not believe that this assumption introduces any major problems. Once the data were collected, the now familiar formula (1) was used to determine the returns to housing.

Farmland

Determining a consistent series for the total returns to farmland is a complicated task because the available information is inconsistent over time. Generally, total returns to farmland were calculated in the same manner as total returns to housing. The rental income from farmland was divided by the total value of farmland and farm service buildings, yielding the rate of return. The average price per acre of farmland and the rate of return were then used with formula (1) to obtain the total returns to farmland.

The Economic Research Service of the U.S. Department of Agriculture (USDA) has compiled an index on the average value per acre of farm real estate in the 48 contiguous states from 1912 through 1975. This series, based on a 1967 = 1 scale was multiplied by $165.75 (the average price per acre in 1967) to yield a series on the average price per acre of farmland from 1912 to 1975.

A historical series for the rental return, or rental income, from farmland has been calculated by the USDA, but in recent years changes to allow for improvement in the series have resulted in significant inconsistencies for the series over time. Moreover, since 1960 the USDA has stopped calculating net income to agriculture, from which rental income is figured, but instead has been calculating a new series on the net income from farm production. For our purposes, the original series is more useful.

Because of these problems, we have recalculated the entire series for rental income from farm real estate in a consistent manner, using data on specific series made available by the USDA Economic Research Service.

General procedure. Rental income to farm real estate was figured as the total net income from agriculture minus four specific imputations. These are: imputed returns to labor needed in farm production, imputed returns to non-real estate capital, imputed returns to operator's management, and an allowance for farm mortgage interest. These imputations were subtracted in order to yield a series that would reflect income from farmland and farm service buildings only rather than include other non-real estate assets. This method was used over the entire time period.

Since the base measure of net income from agriculture is not available from 1960 to 1975, we calculated this measure ourselves for each of those 16 years, using various other USDA series as follows:

> total net income of farm operators plus government payments
> + total wages paid to hired farm labor
> + interest on farm real estate mortgage debt
> + interest on non-real estate debt
> + net rent to nonoperator landlords
> − imputed interest charge on farm dwellings
> = net income from agriculture

This creates a series consistent with the USDA net income from agriculture series for 1912 through 1959, and the same four imputations were subtracted from this series to yield a continuous series on rental income from farm real estate over the entire period.

The figures on rental income from farm real estate were then divided by the total value of farm real estate, including both farmland and farm service buildings, for each year to create a series on the rate of return to farmland. As with housing, the assumption was made that the rate of return to all farmland could be applied to the average value per acre of farmland.

APPENDIX BIBLIOGRAPHY

Cowles, Alfred, 3d, and Associates. *Common Stock Indexes, 1871-1937.* Indiana: Principia Press, Inc., 1939.

Grebler, Leo; Blank, David M.; and Winnick, Louis. *Capital Formation in Residential Real Estate: Trends and Prospects.* Princeton, N.J.: Princeton University Press, 1956.

Homer, Sidney. *A History of Interest Rates.* New Brunswick, N.J.: Rutgers University Press, 1963.

Macaulay, Frederick R. *Some Theoretical Problems Suggested by the Movements of Interest Rates, Bond Yields, and Stock Prices in the United States since 1856.* New York: National Bureau of Economic Research, 1938.

Musgrave, John C. "New Estimates of Residential Capital in the United States, 1925-73." *Survey of Current Business,* vol. 54, no. 10 (1974), pp. 32-38.

Yearbook of the American Bureau of Metal Statistics, 53d annual issue for the year 1973. York, Pa.: Maple Press Co., 1974.

Table A-1
Total returns to financial assets (end of period, index 1871 = 1.0)

Date	Commercial Paper	Bonds	Stocks	Consumer price index
1871	1.00000	1.00000	1.00000	1.00000
1872	1.08119	1.07600	1.12853	1.00000
1873	1.17866	1.13900	1.05440	0.973000
1874	1.27079	1.30800	1.15925	0.919000
1875	1.33869	1.46300	1.18554	0.878000
1876	1.41578	1.57000	1.05044	0.865000
1877	1.48698	1.65700	1.00521	0.838000
1878	1.55789	1.77400	1.12037	0.797000
1879	1.63125	1.96000	1.66478	0.797000
1880	1.71799	2.22100	2.05995	0.811000
1881	1.80050	2.30800	2.22781	0.811000
1882	1.90430	2.39900	2.27660	0.797000
1883	2.01419	2.51000	2.20782	0.770000
1884	2.12908	2.63400	1.91516	0.757000
1885	2.22105	2.89300	2.40245	0.757000
1886	2.31474	3.06300	2.69832	0.757000
1887	2.44498	3.13700	2.63234	0.757000
1888	2.57184	3.34800	2.67891	0.757000
1889	2.68689	3.50300	2.87691	0.757000
1890	2.83792	3.48600	2.60132	0.757000
1891	3.02283	3.65300	3.18697	0.757000
1892	3.14150	3.82000	3.37409	0.757000
1893	3.36459	3.97300	2.85084	0.730000
1894	3.47601	4.28400	2.90947	0.689000
1895	3.57226	4.47700	3.04821	0.676000
1896	3.73481	4.64400	3.10252	0.676000
1897	3.86382	4.99200	3.62265	0.676000
1898	3.99355	5.23400	4.44649	0.676000
1899	4.12115	5.34500	4.89798	0.676000
1900	4.32037	5.59300	5.81496	0.676000
1901	4.51011	5.74200	6.98532	0.689000
1902	4.72411	5.79100	7.34659	0.716000
1903	4.98942	5.81900	6.29222	0.730000
1904	5.22806	6.09000	8.19538	0.730000
1905	5.44006	6.29200	9.79372	0.743000
1906	5.74505	6.27600	10.4913	0.770000
1907	6.08573	6.13300	7.44324	0.770000
1908	6.43908	6.69900	10.6701	0.757000
1909	6.66968	6.96400	12.6791	0.770000
1910	7.00836	7.11600	11.6911	0.784000
1911	7.30361	7.35300	12.3592	0.797000
1912	7.62177	7.55000	13.3574	0.807000
1913	8.08123	7.53100	12.0977	0.814000
1914	8.47154	7.87300	11.6789	0.822000
1915	8.81377	8.39300	15.7092	0.838000
1916	9.11193	8.79000	17.1278	0.935000
1917	9.52232	8.07600	13.0336	1.10800
1918	10.0718	8.72200	16.1765	1.33500
1919	10.6510	8.61000	19.3277	1.53200
1920	11.3874	8.63900	15.8121	1.56800
1921	12.2331	9.80500	17.9993	1.40000

240

Table A-1 (continued)

Date	Commercial Paper	Bonds	Stocks	Consumer price index
1922	12.7991	10.8700	22.8144	1.36500
1923	13.4162	10.9270	23.5899	1.40000
1924	14.0164	11.6820	29.4343	1.39700
1925	14.5419	12.3010	37.8143	1.45100
1926	15.1487	13.1340	41.7428	1.43000
1927	15.8009	14.3320	57.0288	1.40000
1928	16.4948	14.1910	81.3775	1.38600
1929	17.4518	14.5920	74.9275	1.38900
1930	18.1958	15.7520	57.0077	1.30500
1931	18.6507	15.3000	33.2236	1.18100
1932	19.2881	16.8500	30.2367	1.05900
1933	19.5980	17.9750	46.2547	1.06500
1934	19.8102	20.4470	45.5677	1.08600
1935	19.9590	22.4620	66.6728	1.11900
1936	20.1090	24.8930	88.8640	1.13200
1937	20.2853	25.1340	58.7082	1.16800
1938	20.4764	27.1090	76.3484	1.13500
1939	20.5985	28.3610	75.7705	1.13000
1940	20.7140	29.7100	68.2480	1.14100
1941	20.8281	30.6030	60.6362	1.25100
1942	20.9553	31.3260	72.2890	1.36800
1943	21.1001	32.3300	90.8607	1.41100
1944	21.2523	33.2890	108.379	1.44100
1945	21.4120	34.2700	147.062	1.47300
1946	21.5729	34.9880	135.626	1.74100
1947	21.7892	34.0400	143.072	1.89700
1948	22.0734	34.0590	150.833	1.94900
1949	22.4190	37.6350	177.626	1.91400
1950	22.7160	38.1930	231.889	2.02400
1951	23.1759	37.0400	286.084	2.14300
1952	23.7132	38.3210	336.753	2.16200
1953	24.3169	38.8410	332.824	2.17600
1954	25.7823	41.2680	503.328	2.16500
1955	25.1941	40.7620	659.167	2.17300
1956	26.0029	38.4410	701.633	2.23500
1957	26.9765	39.8490	628.117	2.30300
1958	27.7021	39.8110	894.662	2.34300
1959	28.7027	38.9250	1000.15	2.37800
1960	29.9631	41.8380	1002.99	2.41400
1961	30.8901	43.3930	1269.84	2.43000
1962	31.8927	46.5850	1157.67	2.45900
1963	32.9652	47.6210	1418.19	2.50000
1964	34.2903	49.6300	1649.39	2.53000
1965	35.7718	49.6980	1851.80	2.57800
1966	37.6120	47.7770	1666.88	2.66500
1967	39.6410	46.5000	2062.38	2.74600
1968	42.0163	47.7430	2286.00	2.87600
1969	45.0948	44.8890	2095.83	3.05100
1970	49.0209	49.4290	2169.36	3.21900
1971	51.7995	54.2270	2475.64	3.32700

Table A-1 (concluded)

Date	Commercial Paper	Bonds	Stocks	Consumer price index
1972	54.2574	57.8440	2939.05	3.44100
1973	57.9625	59.6420	2512.82	3.74300
1974	63.9146	58.6210	1858.79	4.20000
1975	68.7177	63.6370	2544.99	4.49500

Source: U.S. Department of Labor, Bureau of Labor Statistics; U.S. Department of Commerce, Bureau of the Census; Board of Governors of the Federal Reserve System; National Bureau of Economic Research; Cowles Commission for Research in Economics; Standard and Poor's Corporation; Sidney Homer, *A History of Interest Rates;* Harris Trust and Savings Bank.

Table A-2
Total returns to real assets (annual averages)

Date	Consumer price index (1860 = 1.0)	Gold (1860 = 1.0)	Silver (1860 = 1.0)	Housing (1890 = 1.0)	Farmland (1912 = 1.0)
1860	1.00000	1.00000	1.00000		
1861	1.00000	1.00000	0.98518		
1862	1.11111	1.00000	1.00000		
1863	1.37037	1.00000	0.99629		
1864	1.77778	1.00000	0.99629		
1865	1.74074	1.00000	0.99037		
1866	1.62963	1.00000	0.99185		
1867	1.59259	1.00000	0.98518		
1868	1.51852	1.00000	0.98222		
1869	1.48148	1.00000	0.98148		
1870	1.40741	1.00000	0.98370		
1871	1.37037	1.00000	0.98148		
1872	1.37037	1.00000	0.97925		
1873	1.37037	1.00000	0.96074		
1874	1.29630	1.00000	0.94666		
1875	1.22222	1.00000	0.91851		
1876	1.18519	1.00000	0.85925		
1877	1.18519	1.00000	0.88888		
1878	1.11111	1.00000	0.85185		
1879	1.07407	1.00000	0.82963		
1880	1.11111	1.00000	0.85185		
1881	1.11111	1.00000	0.83703		
1882	1.11111	1.00000	0.84444		
1883	1.07407	1.00000	0.82222		
1884	1.03704	1.00000	0.82444		
1885	1.03704	1.00000	0.78888		
1886	1.03704	1.00000	0.73703		
1887	1.03704	1.00000	0.72444		
1888	1.03704	1.00000	0.69629		
1889	1.03704	1.00000	0.69333		

Table A-2 (continued)

Date	Consumer price index (1860 = 1.0)	Gold (1860 = 1.0)	Silver (1860 = 1.0)	Housing (1890 = 1.0)	Farmland (1912 = 1.0)
1890	1.03704	1.00000	0.77481	1.00000	
1891	1.03704	1.00000	0.73185	0.99922	
1892	1.03704	1.00000	0.72296	1.00273	
1893	1.03704	1.00000	0.57925	1.03350	
1894	0.96296	1.00000	0.46666	1.03029	
1895	0.92592	1.00000	0.48355	1.04977	
1896	0.92592	1.00000	0.49674	1.09115	
1897	0.92592	1.00000	0.44288	1.10521	
1898	0.92592	1.00000	0.43155	1.19205	
1899	0.92592	1.00000	0.44133	1.32120	
1900	0.92592	1.00000	0.45429	1.43994	
1901	0.92592	1.00000	0.43666	1.46985	
1902	0.96296	1.00000	0.38637	1.57213	
1903	1.00000	1.00000	0.39681	1.68352	
1904	1.00000	1.00000	0.42385	1.71969	
1905	1.00000	1.00000	0.44705	1.86094	
1906	1.03704	1.00000	0.49474	2.11344	
1907	1.07407	1.00000	0.48390	2.28251	
1908	1.03704	1.00000	0.39158	2.28512	
1909	1.03704	1.00000	0.38149	2.45232	
1910	1.07407	1.00000	0.39619	2.62323	
1911	1.07407	1.00000	0.39484	2.67543	
1912	1.11111	1.00000	0.45063	2.83352	1.00000
1913	1.10000	1.00000	0.44289	2.82503	1.05277
1914	1.11481	1.00000	0.40600	2.93654	1.11502
1915	1.12593	1.00000	0.36803	3.12533	1.13844
1916	1.21111	1.00000	0.48593	3.43569	1.21552
1917	1.42222	1.00000	0.60308	4.15091	1.42303
1918	1.67037	1.00000	0.71683	5.11695	1.67286
1919	1.91852	1.00000	0.82312	6.14305	1.91559
1920	2.22222	1.00000	0.74740	8.18450	2.30567
1921	1.98519	1.00000	0.46410	6.78977	2.07729
1922	1.85926	1.00000	0.50020	6.45702	1.78041
1923	1.89259	1.00000	0.48054	7.48084	1.70580
1924	1.89630	1.00000	0.49467	7.62122	1.61611
1925	1.94444	1.00000	0.51159	7.79517	1.58098
1926	1.96296	1.00000	0.46005	8.14039	1.57466
1927	1.92593	1.00000	0.41755	8.29142	1.51580
1928	1.90000	1.00000	0.43093	8.60512	1.46020
1929	1.90000	1.00000	0.39254	9.43599	1.45728
1930	1.85185	1.00000	0.28262	9.75570	1.35419
1931	1.68889	1.00000	0.21259	9.37587	1.21252
1932	1.51481	1.00000	0.20660	8.34369	0.97608
1933	1.43704	1.00000	0.25723	8.66910	0.76915
1934	1.48519	1.69328	0.37017	9.71684	0.82121
1935	1.52222	1.69328	0.47609	9.77644	0.92354
1936	1.53704	1.69328	0.33397	10.4287	0.94939
1937	1.59259	1.69328	0.33246	11.9921	1.05325
1938	1.56296	1.69328	0.32018	12.7241	1.07326
1939	1.54074	1.69328	0.28949	13.3646	1.09795

243

Table A-2 (concluded)

Date	Consumer price index (1860 = 1.0)	Gold (1860 = 1.0)	Silver (1860 = 1.0)	Housing (1890 = 1.0)	Farmland (1912 = 1.0)
1940	1.55556	1.69328	0.25757	14.1966	1.13089
1941	1.63333	1.69328	0.25765	15.7713	1.21005
1942	1.80741	1.69328	0.28394	17.1736	1.48454
1943	1.91852	1.69328	0.33148	18.5159	1.78039
1944	1.95185	1.69328	0.33148	20.7590	2.10720
1945	1.99630	1.69328	0.38465	22.9674	2.46081
1946	2.16667	1.69328	0.59371	25.8336	2.93532
1947	2.47778	1.69328	0.53200	31.8314	3.54991
1948	2.67037	1.69328	0.55082	36.2325	4.21877
1949	2.64444	1.69328	0.53281	36.2338	4.61252
1950	2.67037	1.69328	0.54940	39.0618	4.75202
1951	2.88148	1.69328	0.66198	43.0358	5.78178
1952	2.94444	1.69328	0.62919	45.3569	6.66664
1953	2.96667	1.69328	0.63102	47.5688	6.94691
1954	2.98148	1:69328	0.63148	48.8115	6.97683
1955	2.97037	1.69328	0.65999	51.9262	7.35919
1956	3.01481	1.69328	0.67281	55.9773	7.76672
1957	3.12222	1.69328	0.67274	58.9028	8.34598
1958	3.20741	1.69328	0.65958	61.4540	9.09366
1959	3.23333	1.69328	0.67557	65.6396	9.95711
1960	3.28519	1.69328	0.67685	69.1140	10.4435
1961	3.31852	1.69328	0.68480	71.8833	10.8726
1962	3.35556	1.69328	0.80385	75.9517	11.8250
1963	3.39630	1.69328	0.94749	80.5674	12.7972
1964	3.44074	1.69328	0.95777	86.1010	13.8871
1965	3.50000	1.69328	0.95777	92.3716	15.1326
1966	3.6000	1.69328	0.95777	100.199	17.0843
1967	3.70370	1.69328	1.14791	110.450	18.8295
1968	3.85926	1.89937	1.58859	122.919	20.6311
1969	4.06667	2.04112	1.32642	137.824	22.4416
1970	4.30741	1.76052	1.31172	150.222	23.8402
1971	4.49259	1.97436	1.14492	168.559	25.4805
1972	4.64074	2.81858	1.24781	191.276	28.8096
1973	4.92963	4.71698	1.89449	215.426	36.1757
1974	5.47037	7.70489	3.48739	240.067	47.5344
1975	5.97037	7.79003	3.27298	263.802	56.5192

Source: U.S. Department of Commerce, Bureau of the Census; U.S. Department of Commerce, Bureau of Economic Analysis; U.S. Department of Agriculture, Economic Research Service; National Bureau of Economic Analysis; American Bureau of Metal Statistics; Harris Trust and Savings Bank.

Table A-3
Data for real assets (annual averages)

Date	Average price per troy ounce of gold ($)	Average price per troy ounce of silver ($)	Average price of a house ($)	Average rate of return on housing ($)	Average price per acre of farmland ($)	Rate of return on farmland ($)
1860	20.6700	135.000				
1861	20.6700	133.000				
1862	20.6700	135.000				
1863	20.6700	134.500				
1864	20.6700	134.500				
1865	20.6700	133.700				
1866	20.6700	133.900				
1867	20.6700	133.000				
1868	20.6700	132.600				
1869	20.6700	132.500				
1870	20.6700	132.800				
1871	20.6700	132.500				
1872	20.6700	132.200				
1873	20.6700	129.700				
1874	20.6700	127.800				
1875	20.6700	124.000				
1876	20.6700	116.000				
1877	20.6700	120.000				
1878	20.6700	115.000				
1879	20.6700	112.000				
1880	20.6700	115.000				
1881	20.6700	113.000				
1882	20.6700	114.000				
1883	20.6700	111.000				
1884	20.6700	111.300				
1885	20.6700	106.500				
1886	20.6700	99.5000				
1887	20.6700	97.8000				
1888	20.6700	94.0000				
1889	20.6700	93.6000				
1890	20.6700	104.600	2804.30	3.35		
1891	20.6700	98.8000	2711.30	3.35		
1892	20.6700	97.6000	2632.61	3.35		
1893	20.6700	78.2000	2625.46	3.35		
1894	20.6700	63.0000	2532.46	3.35		
1895	20.6700	65.2800	2496.69	3.35		
1896	20.6700	67.0600	2511.00	3.35		
1897	20.6700	59.7900	2460.92	3.35		
1898	20.6700	58.2600	2568.23	3.35		
1899	20.6700	59.5800	2754.23	3.35		
1900	20.6700	61.3300	2904.46	3.35		
1901	20.6700	58.9500	2868.69	3.35		
1902	20.6700	52.1600	2968.84	3.35		
1903	20.6700	53.5700	3076.15	3.35		
1904	20.6700	57.2210	3040.38	3.35		
1905	20.6700	60.3520	3183.46	3.35		
1906	20.6700	66.7910	3498.22	3.35		

Table A-3 (continued)

Date	Average price per troy ounce of gold ($)	Average price per troy ounce of silver ($)	Average price of a house ($)	Average rate of return on housing ($)	Average price per acre of farmland ($)	Rate of return on farmland ($)
1907	20.6700	65.3270	3655.61	3.35		
1908	20.6700	52.8640	3541.15	3.35		
1909	20.6700	51.5020	3677.07	3.35		
1910	20.6700	53.4860	3805.84	3.35		
1911	20.6700	53.3040	3755.76	3.35		
1912	20.6700	60.8350	3848.76	3.35	36.4650	2.7
1913	20.6700	59.7910	3712.84	3.35	38.1225	0.7
1914	20.6700	54.8110	3734.30	3.35	39.7800	1.5
1915	20.6700	49.6840	3845.55	3.35	39.7800	2.1
1916	20.6700	65.6010	4090.40	3.35	41.4375	2.5
1917	20.6700	81.4170	4781.73	3.35	44.7525	8.4
1918	20.6700	96.7720	5703.51	3.35	49.7250	5.8
1919	20.6700	111.122	6625.29	3.35	54.6975	4.1
1920	20.6700	100.900	8540.87	3.35	66.3000	-0.7
1921	20.6700	62.6540	6855.74	3.35	61.3275	-2.6
1922	20.6700	67.5280	6308.43	3.35	53.0400	-0.9
1923	20.6700	64.8730	7071.78	3.35	51.3825	-1.1
1924	20.6700	66.7810	6970.96	3.35	49.7250	-2.1
1925	20.6700	69.0650	6898.95	3.35	48.0675	1.2
1926	20.6700	62.1070	6970.96	3.35	48.0675	-0.4
1927	20.6700	56.3700	6870.14	3.35	46.4100	-0.3
1928	20.6700	58.1760	6898.95	3.35	44.7525	-0.1
1929	20.6700	52.9930	7201.41	5.05	44.7525	-0.2
1930	20.6700	38.1540	7014.17	5.06	43.0950	-3.5
1931	20.6700	28.7000	6466.86	5.32	39.7800	-3.0
1932	20.6700	27.8920	5473.07	5.15	33.1500	-3.4
1933	20.6700	34.7270	5473.07	3.90	26.5200	-1.5
1934	35.0000	49.9730	5948.36	3.13	28.1775	0.5
1935	35.0000	64.2730	5804.33	3.11	29.8350	6.2
1936	35.0000	45.0870	6005.97	3.09	29.8350	2.8
1937	35.0000	44.8830	6711.71	2.90	31.4925	5.1
1938	35.0000	43.2250	6913.35	3.01	31.4925	1.9
1939	35.0000	39.0820	7042.98	3.10	31.4925	2.3
1940	35.0000	34.7730	7273.42	2.86	31.4925	3.0
1941	35.0000	34.7830	7863.94	2.75	31.4925	7.0
1942	35.0000	38.3330	8296.02	3.22	34.8075	11.0
1943	35.0000	44.7500	8670.49	3.16	38.1225	9.5
1944	35.0000	44.7500	9419.44	3.20	43.0950	4.7
1945	35.0000	51.9280	10096.4	3.22	48.0675	4.7
1946	35.0000	80.1510	11090.2	2.40	53.0400	8.1
1947	35.0000	71.8200	13423.4	1.80	59.6700	7.5
1948	35.0000	74.3610	15007.7	1.81	64.6425	9.7
1949	35.0000	71.9300	14705.3	2.06	67.9575	4.0
1950	35.0000	74.1690	15511.8	2.20	66.3000	5.6
1951	35.0000	89.3680	16707.3	2.29	76.2450	5.8
1952	35.0000	84.9410	17153.8	2.65	84.5325	4.0
1953	35.0000	85.1880	17456.2	3.06	86.1900	2.2
1954	35.0000	85.2500	17326.6	3.38	84.5325	2.4

246

Table A-3 (concluded)

Date	Average price per troy ounce of gold ($)	Average price per troy ounce of silver ($)	Average price of a house ($)	Average rate of return on housing ($)	Average price per acre of farmland ($)	Rate of return on farmland ($)
1955	35.0000	89.0990	17845.1	3.29	87.8475	1.5
1956	35.0000	90.8300	18637.2	3.22	91.1625	1.7
1957	35.0000	90.8200	18982.9	3.31	96.1350	1.9
1958	35.0000	89.0440	19155.7	3.39	101.108	3.6
1959	35.0000	91.2020	19789.5	3.39	109.395	1.2
1960	35.0000	91.3750	20120.7	3.56	112.710	1.8
1961	35.0000	92.4490	20178.3	3.71	114.367	2.6
1962	35.0000	108.521	20524.0	3.88	120.998	2.8
1963	35.0000	127.912	20956.1	3.89	127.628	2.6
1964	35.0000	129.300	21561.0	3.87	135.915	1.9
1965	35.0000	129.300	22252.3	3.95	142.545	3.9
1966	35.0000	129.300	23202.9	4.03	154.148	4.4
1967	35.0000	154.968	24600.0	3.97	165.750	2.5
1968	39.2600	214.460	26400.4	3.70	177.353	2.4
1969	42.1900	179.067	28589.6	3.54	187.298	3.0
1970	36.3900	177.082	30116.3	3.47	193.928	2.6
1971	40.8100	154.564	32665.6	3.45	202.215	2.5
1972	58.2600	168.455	35863.0	3.36	218.790	4.5
1973	97.5000	255.756	39161.2	3.14	248.625	10.5
1974	159.260	470.798	42312.0	3.14	309.953	5.4
1975	161.020	441.852	45141.0	3.00	354.705	3.9

Source: U.S. Department of Commerce, Bureau of the Census; U.S. Department of Commerce, Bureau of Economic Analysis; U.S. Department of Agriculture, Economic Research Service; National Bureau of Economic Research; American Bureau of Metal Statistics; Harris Trust and Savings Bank.

Index